THE IDEOLOGICAL ORIGINS OF BLACK NATIONALISM

THE
IDEOLOGICAL
ORIGINS
OF
BLACK
NATIONALISM

BY
STERLING STUCKEY

BEACON PRESS
BOSTON

Copyright © 1972 by Sterling Stuckey
Library of Congress catalog card number: 72–75547
International Standard Book Number: 0–8070–5428–3
Beacon Press books are published under the auspices of
the Unitarian Universalist Association
Published simultaneously in Canada by Saunders of Toronto, Ltd.
All rights reserved
Printed in the United States of America

CONTENTS

INTRODUCTION

The precise details of certain experiences that bear directly on black nationalism will remain forever enshrouded in obscurity— the degree to which Africans during the seventeenth and eighteenth centuries continued to think positively of their ancestral home; the extent to which they preferred living apart from white people; the length of time the majority of them remained essentially African in America; and the exact nature of Pan-African acculturation, the process by which differences between Africans from various parts of Africa, the West Indies, and North America were virtually destroyed on the anvil of American slavery.[1] But we *do* know something of the broad contours of these developments, and that is more than sufficient to suggest that many of the ingredients of black nationalism, together with the conditions necessary for their perpetuation, were very much in evidence by the time the forces of slavery were becoming, as the third decade of the nineteenth century opened, more entrenched than ever.

[1] The most brilliant clues to more precise answers to these questions can be found in the books of Du Bois and in the essays of Paul Robeson. Both men, but Robeson especially, derive their sense of the Afro-American's "nationality" every bit as much from an internal as from an external exploration of his condition in America, demonstrating that despite the tremendous blows taken by the African in America the essential ingredients of a black nationalism have been, though largely unrecognized, present all along. The author wants to suggest at this point that the originators of the ideology that we refer to as black nationalism emphasized the need for black people to rely primarily on themselves in vital areas of life—economic, political, religious, and intellectual—in order to effect their liberation. As formulated by Afro-American ideologists of the 1830's—and later by "Sidney" in the 1840's—this attitude probably owed more to African traditions of group hegemony (which persisted in some forms during slavery) than to

1

The effort to consolidate and deepen the slave system, a move-ment which made great strides in the three decades before the outbreak of the Civil War, suggests that the desire for autonomy among a significant number of blacks, surely as old as the 1600's, may well have crystallized into ideology some years before the crucial decade of the 1850's, some time before the violent—but edifying—clash of arms. The documents in this volume support that hypothesis, for they indicate that black nationalist ideology, contrary to the view advanced in certain quarters, developed at least two decades before Martin Delany became nationally known for his advocacy of black hegemony. It is appropriate that some of the forces which made possible that flowering of black nationalist thought at least be tentatively proposed in this introductory essay.

---

any models from European thought or experience. The tendency, for ex-ample, for the earliest ideological nationalists to leap beyond the limits of Afro-America to embrace the totality of African humanity indicates their almost elemental, instinctual recoil from the constraints of a narrow na-tionalism—a development made possible by the strange detribalizing pro-cess which enabled black people for the first time in their history to think of the oneness of African peoples and to perceive practically the whole of the African continent as a single entity.

I have deliberately avoided the various categories of black nationalism which have been coined in our time—cultural nationalism, revolutionary nationalism, religious nationalism, and so on. I have done so with respect to revolutionary nationalism because in ante-bellum America almost any form of advocacy of black control was revolutionary. While I attribute very great importance to the cultural dimension, I avoid the term cultural na-tionalism precisely because the nationalists included in this volume stopped short of an ideology of cultural nationalism (which in fact did not come in America until the emergence of W. E. B. Du Bois at the turn of the century). Had a nationalist of ante-bellum America realized the enormous importance of black culture, had he been cognizant of its radical opposition to the culture of the larger society, that awareness, articulated into theory, would have been as revolutionary a development as calling for a massive slave uprising. In a word, the greatest effort should be made to permit the men who speak to us through these documents to define, in their own way, what they meant by what we now call black nationalism. For evidence of the historical lineaments of black nationalism, see W. E. B. Du Bois, *Dusk of Dawn* (New York: Harcourt, Brace & Company, 1940), and Sterling Stuckey, "The Cultural Philosophy of Paul Robeson," *Freedomways,* Vol. 11, No. 1, 1971.

I

There is some evidence that the abortive but important American Revolution and the Haitian Revolt not only contributed to an intensification of the desire among many "free" and slave blacks for liberation but awakened in some the desire for unity in their ranks and control over their own destinies, for *independence* from an oppressive, racist society. Surely such impulses were, in varying degrees, presupposed in the actions of Paul Cuffee the emigrationist, Richard Allen the Church Father, and in the activities of the Africans involved in the founding of mutual aid and benefit organizations which sprang into being, interestingly, at the time America was in the process of becoming a nation.

The parallel between the growth of the American nation and the development of Afro-American infrastructures is not meant to be drawn too sharply. But considering the position of oppressed blacks and the ambiguity of the major documents used by white settlers to rationalize rebellion and to begin their nation, it is small wonder that a certain tension, with creative potential for the promotion of nationalist sentiments, was set up in the minds of some blacks. It was obvious to black leaders that their people were not meaningfully included in the new nation, particularly since the great majority of them were still slaves. Despite the fact that the Declaration of Independence (and the Constitution) in some ways helped to promote the countervailing value of freedom, the freedom at issue was freedom for whites. Therein, but certainly not exclusively, lay the seedground for black nationalist organizations and sentiment. And it was precisely in such ironic soil that an ideology of black nationalism would eventually take root.

What was implicit, uncertain for the founders of the African organizations during the period from roughly the seventeen eighties to the second decade of the nineteenth century had by 1813 become pronounced and sure for certain slaves on an island off the coast of South Carolina, men who sang of *independence* and freedom and referred to themselves as Africans. Considering the fact that South Carolina continued to receive imports of slaves, many directly from Africa, after the abolition of the slave trade in 1808, and bearing in mind the relative isolation of the islands off the coast of Charleston, the slaves who sang their Hymn of Freedom must surely have been in many ways much more African than the great majority of blacks in other parts of the country. As their song makes clear, they were at least as nationalistic as the men who made the American "Revolution." Moreover, their spirits had not been broken and their concern for their women and children was apparently undiminished by the slave experience:

> Look to Heaven with manly trust
> And swear by Him that's always just
> That no white foe with impious hand
> (Repeat)
> Shall slave your wives and daughters more
> or rob them of their virtue dear.
> Be armed with valor firm and true,
> Their hopes are fixed on Heaven and you
> That truth and justice will prevail
> And every scheme of bondage fail.

The African consciousness of the slaves was captured in a portion of another stanza of the song:

> Hail! all hail! ye Afric clan
> Hail! ye oppressed, ye Afric band,
> Who toil and sweat in slavery bound

And then the nationalistic, the revolutionary burden of the hymn, the desire for control over their destiny:

> And when your health and strength are gone
> Are left to hunger and to mourn.
> Let *Independence* be your aim,
> Ever mindful what 'tis worth.
> Pledge your bodies for the prize
> Pile them even to the skies! [2] (italics added)

A few years later, the nationalist or separatist thrust of the Hymn of Freedom was expressed in a broader, more concrete way in the city of Charleston when "free" and slave black

[2] Quoted in John Hammond Moore, "A Hymn of Freedom—South Carolina, 1813," *The Journal of Negro History*, January 1965, Vol. L, No. 1, pp. 52–53.

Methodists broke from the white Methodist church and established a branch of the African Methodist Episcopal Church. Denmark Vesey, the leader of the slave conspiracy at Charleston in 1822, had been a participant in the separatist church movement. His conspiracy, on a number of levels, contained elements of black nationalism: He compared the slaves to the Israelites, which suggests that he perceived them as a separate people under white American oppression; he used the Haitian Revolution, the supreme ante-bellum example of black nationalism, to encourage people of color to resist oppression; and his co-conspirators in a real sense reflected the Pan-African composition of his movement, for Africans from at least three different tribes were active in his plot. Easily the most colorful and influential of this last group was Gullah Jack, an Angolan said to have been a conjurer.[3]

In spite of impressive evidence of black nationalism among enslaved blacks, the slave South did not offer as many opportunities as the North for slave or "free" blacks to frame their thoughts into statements calling for a transformation of values and the creation of institutions designed to enable black people to move from oppression and dependency to liberation and autonomy. But if there were blacks who, by virtue of their relative isolation from white American values, were potential black nationalists, they were the southern slaves. This was so in part because the new infusions of Africans from Africa and the West Indies (where they greatly outnumbered their white owners) not only led to a more significant African presence in America but reinforced the Africanness of slaves born in this country. Overall, the southern slave, ever forming the creative, radiating center of the black ethos in America, through his music and dance, through his folktales and religion, projected much that was African into an essentially European environment.[4]

[3] See John O. Killens, ed., *The Trial Record of Denmark Vesey* (Boston: Beacon Press, 1970), and Robert S. Starobin, *Denmark Vesey* (Englewood Cliffs, N.J.: Prentice-Hall, Inc., 1970).

[4] For a discussion of African influences on Afro-American art during slavery, see Sterling Stuckey, "Through the Prism of Folklore: The Black Ethos in Slavery," *The Massachusetts Review*, Vol. IX, No. 3, Summer 1968.

In the North, the fact that almost all blacks, as late as the second decade of the nineteenth century, referred to themselves as either "Africans" or "free Africans" demonstrates that they marked themselves off—and were marked off by force of circumstances—from the larger society. They considered themselves Africans (though most apparently had lost a great deal of their Africanness) even as they made distinctions in the degree of "civilization" between themselves and their people in the ancestral home. There is little evidence that, for blacks generally, being American was considered desirable, even if attainable, until well into the nineteenth century.[5]

What, then, was the sense of reality out of which the ideology of black nationalism was fashioned? A consciousness of a shared experience of oppression at the hands of white people, an awareness and approval of the persistence of group traits and preferences in spite of a violently anti-African larger society, a recognition of bonds and obligations between Africans everywhere, an irreducible conviction that Africans in America must take responsibility for liberating themselves—these were among the pivotal components of the world view of the black men who finally framed the ideology.

Why did the working out of black nationalist theory take place in the North? Perhaps because the narrow limits of freedom there, broader than in the South, afforded black men more time in which to theorize on the condition of their people. No doubt because as the nineteenth century opened people of color had already established something of an intellectual tradition in that section of the country.[6] As America approached

[5] This very point is in dire need of investigation, though there are already important leads which indicate that black people were quite "African" in their music, folktales, and religion during most of the slave era. The writer, currently attempting to reconstruct the history of the names controversy among blacks, has already found much to support the view that the majority of blacks did not begin to think of themselves as Americans until the post–Civil War period. For a brilliant discussion of the presence of Africa in America during slavery, see W. E. B. Du Bois, ed., *The Negro Church* (Atlanta, 1903), especially chapters 1–4.

[6] The early Afro-American intellectual tradition is presented in Dorothy Porter, *Early Negro Writing* (Boston: Beacon Press, 1971). Not since

the fourth decade of the new century with sectional differences about to explode into bitter hostilities, all that remained was for the nationalist perspective on the condition of black people to be fashioned into theory. With a deep dedication to African peoples at the center of their consciousness, with the contradictions between American practice and preachment starkly evident in the post "Revolutionary" period, two black men, Robert Alexander Young and David Walker, speculated on the status of African peoples in a way which broke beyond the shackles which America sought to impose on the African mind.[7] They created black nationalist ideology.

II

Robert Alexander Young, using his own funds, published his *Ethiopian Manifesto* in February of 1829. Brief as that document is, it contains essential elements of black nationalism. Young's statement reflected his deep concern over the place occupied by African peoples throughout the world. There is in Young's *Ethiopian Manifesto,* as there is in David Walker's *Appeal,* something of the primordial, the suggestion of profound beginnings, intimations of the coming sovereignty of certain ideas. But there is also clearcut evidence of the confusion of other, only half articulate beliefs. Just when one thinks it possible to get at certain ideas stripped of their strange hues and accents, failure inevitably ensues, for both the *Ethiopian Manifesto* and Walker's *Appeal,* published months apart, like all first births, remain in some ways enveloped in a special aura of mystery.

Aptheker published his *A Documentary Hi tory of the Negro People in the United States* have we had a documentary of the quality of the Porter volume.

[7] I am deeply indebted to Mr. Russell Maylone, Curator of special collections at Northwestern University, for securing Young's *Ethiopian Manifesto.* Failing to find the pamphlet at a number of outstanding collections of Negro materials, I turned to Mr. Maylone, who not only located the library at which *The Ethiopian Manifesto* could be found but had a copy Xeroxed and forwarded to Northwestern *within four days.* That rare document can be found at the main section of the New York Public Library.

What is clear, on a reading of Young, is that he was religious to the point of being oracular, in a way strikingly suggestive of Nat Turner. Not only does he envision the coming of a black messiah—an incontestable expression of black nationalism—but there are references to signs and seasons which remind one of the slave preacher of Southampton County, Virginia.[8] There is also about Young's personality something of the studied, willed quality which calls Turner to mind.

The *Ethiopian Manifesto* contains one of the earliest extant calls for the reassembling of the African race, one of the first formulations of the imperative need for Africans, severely oppressed and locked in degradation, *to become a people* (Martin Delany would later refer to them as a broken people), *"a nation in themselves"* (italics added). Moreover, though he somewhat overstated his case in arguing that his thought was not influenced by other men—not borrowed "either from the sense of white men or of black"—there are not a few concepts put forth by Young which were indeed indigenous to African or Ethiopian peoples in America, especially the allusion to a God of the Ethiopians, a conceptualization with far-reaching cultural as well as political and religious implications. From a reading of the text, it is evident that Young seems to make practically no distinction between African peoples throughout the world. For him all people of African ancestry were Africans irrespective of their place of birth. Pan-Negroism (or Pan-Africanism) was a first principle of his brand of nationalism.[9]

III

David Walker presented a great many more of the ideas which would later become associated with black nationalism. Indeed, it is likely that his *Appeal to the Colored Citizens of the World*

[8] Within the American context, Young's messiah would be considered black, even though his father, according to Young, was a white man and his mother black.

[9] For a first-class discussion of early Pan-Negroism, see Hollis Lynch, "Pan-Negro Nationalism in the New World Before 1862," in Okon E. Uya, ed., *Black Brotherhood* (Lexington, Mass.: Heath, 1971).

contains the most all-embracing black nationalist formulation to appear in America during the nineteenth century. Indeed, there is scarcely an important aspect of Afro-American nationalist thought in the twentieth century which is not prefigured in that document. While it is true that there is a certain diffuseness about Walker's formulation of the place of Africans in the world, there is nonetheless a comprehensiveness of approach, a penetration of insight and a daring of conception regarding the need for African peoples to rule themselves which mark his *Appeal* as unmistakably nationalist in ideology.

Published in September of 1829, the *Appeal* went through three printings, with the second and third editions appearing in less than a year. Two decades following the initial appearance of that document, Henry Highland Garnet republished it together with his *Address To The Slaves,* which indicates the esteem in which Garnet held Walker. It is altogether likely that Garnet was influenced considerably by the nationalism of Walker, and that other of his contemporaries found Walker's thoughts on the need for black autonomy of some interest. We do not have concrete proof on this matter, but the *Appeal* itself is the best argument for the essential soundness of that speculation.

But there is a more important question to pose: How does one account for the failure of so many scholars to credit the *Appeal* with being, in its own right, one of the most important black nationalist statements of the nineteenth century? Perhaps the main reason for this has been the emphasis devoted to Walker's cry for people of color to rise up and destroy their oppressors, an attention which serves to obscure the nationalist dimensions of the *Appeal*. It is also likely that a tendency on the part of scholars to interpret the past in the burning light of current concerns contributed to their failure to focus on the nationalist concepts that pervade the *Appeal*.[10] Considering

[10] A notable exception to this general rule is Herbert Aptheker. Aptheker in 1956 published "Consciousness of Negro Nationality to 1900," in *Toward Negro Freedom* (New York, 1956). He correctly noted that a "passionate sense of nationality pervades the entire body of David Walker's famous Appeal . . . to the Coloured Citizens of the World," p. 106.

the fever pitch to which integrationist sentiment was brought in this country following World War II, it is small wonder that Walker has not been considered a major nationalist. Related to the neglect of the nationalist dimension in Walker is simply the unwarranted assumption referred to at the outset: the belief that major black nationalist ideologists did not exist before the advent of Martin Delany.[11]

David Walker's *call for the establishment of a black nation* (he had recognized the need for the creation of black infrastructures in an earlier piece in *Freedom's Journal*) is surely one of the first such formulations on record. In another reference to the need for black hegemony, he could not have been more explicit: "Our sufferings will come to an *end*, in spite of all the Americans this side of *eternity*. Then we will want all the learning and talents among ourselves, and perhaps more, *to govern ourselves*" (last italics added). Walker's heavy emphasis on the need for people of color to transcend an ignorance born of oppression is still another aspect of black nationalism, as would be demonstrated by a long line of subsequent nationalists. Many of them would display a profound regard for knowledge, and most would posit that, in Walker's words, "learning originated" with their ancient ancestors, the Ethiopians and the Egyptians. It is not being advanced that this view was peculiar to nationalists—rather, it is being argued that for nationalists knowledge has been held in especially high esteem.

David Walker's intense interest in history, especially the history of African peoples, is another feature of his thought that has been echoed for over a century in the thought of other nationalists. In addition to espousing the view that his ancestors in Ethiopia and Egypt had been responsible for the beginnings of civilization, he said, in one of the most important observations ever made on the role of the black historian, that "the Lord shall raise up coloured historians in succeeding generations, to present the crimes of this nation to the then gazing world." In each vital area, Walker stressed the importance of African peoples

[11] Harold Cruse, perhaps more than anyone else, has promoted this misconception. See Cruse's *The Crisis of the Negro Intellectual* (New York: Morrow, 1967), p. 5.

shouldering the responsibility for their liberation, though he did not discount—and here again is a cardinal tenet of nineteenth century black nationalism—assistance from whites. Thus, whatever the degree and quality of support from whites in countering, for example, the racism of Thomas Jefferson, Walker thought it unthinkable that people of color should not take the lead in their own defense. He explained it this way:

> For let no one of us suppose that the refutations which have been written by our white friends are enough—they are *whites* —we are *blacks*. We, and the world wish to see the charges of Mr. Jefferson refuted by the blacks *themselves* . . . for we must remember that what the whites have written . . . is other men's labours, and did not emanate from the blacks.

Walker's nationalism illustrates almost perfectly a black nationalist tendency to exaggerate the degree of acquiescence to oppression by the masses of black people. Where else among black people can one find such gloomy and devastating, such stereotypical portraits of black humanity as among nationalists? One sees this dimension of nationalism expressed in some considerable measure in most of the documents in this collection, especially in the *Appeal,* Garnet's *Address To The Slaves,* and in Delany's "Political Destiny." (Perhaps such a view of African peoples reached its grim consummation in the writings of Alexander Crummell, especially in the years following the Civil War—that is, to be sure, before the arrival of Elijah Muhammad in the twentieth century.)

If David Walker in his *Appeal* brooded over the degradation of his people, if he excoriated them for their apathy and cowardice—and in this respect the same can be said of Garnet in his *Address To The Slaves*—there was no greater believer than he in the inherent worth, the redeeming power, of black humanity. Though he thought God on the Africans' side, he urged them to make a determined effort of their own to overthrow their oppressors. Hence his almost desperate call for an end to disunity in their ranks. That theme, the presence of disunity and the need for unity, so deeply grounded in the *Appeal,* is a distinguishing feature of the literature of black nationalism.

A very original and significant dimension of Walker's black nationalism, and perhaps his greatest contribution to black nationalist and Pan-African theory, is expressed in those sections of the *Appeal* in which he focused on Africans around the world, on their attributes, the nature of their oppression, the ties between them, and *the imperative need for universal African revolt.* An advocate of the view that people of African descent everywhere were Africans, Walker insisted that the happiness and glory of all "coloured people under Heaven, shall never be fully consummated, but with the *entire emancipation of your enslaved brethren all over the world.*"

Walker's attitude toward his people in the diaspora, the great scattering of Africans throughout much of the Americas as a result of centuries of slave trading and slavery, was in one crucial respect not peculiar to him: a very significant number of "free" and very likely a far greater number of enslaved blacks considered themselves and Africans elsewhere in the Americas members of one African family. What is different with Walker is not his conception that Africans everywhere are one but his great emphasis on the need for unity between black peoples throughout the world.

An especially notable feature of the African, one which would play a decisive role in history, was Walker's belief, which mounted to the level of mythology, that the African was endowed with physical strength and fighting power clearly superior to that of the white man. The desired Pan-African revolt could be more easily achieved, he was certain, if the black man but knew his power. Other black nationalists, in varying degrees, affirmed this view with such consistency that the hypothesis is especially associated with their ideology. Henry Highland Garnet, Alexander Crummell, and Martin Delany are but a few who subscribed to some variant of the Walker thesis. In short, nationalists tended to give greater emphasis to the matter of black strength, possibly because they have generally had greater faith in the potential and power of their people than those leaders and theorists who wanted to see people of color absorbed into American life.

Among the many characteristics of Walker's *Appeal* which

anticipate twentieth century nationalists, especially Nation of Islam partisans, are the following: a conception of the white man as the devil—which immediately brings Elijah Muhammad to mind, even though Walker, unlike Elijah, made certain exceptions; an attitude toward white women—"I would not give a pinch of snuff to be married to any white person I ever saw in all the days of my life"—which is also close to that of contemporary nationalists; and a concern about his possible fate for having written the *Appeal*—the possibility of being assassinated—which is similar to Malcolm X's remarks while writing his autobiography. These and other considerations simply serve to impress upon one the seeming timelessness of certain nationalist concerns among black people. But they do not constitute the burden of Walker's message, which was the unity of fate, the oneness of destiny, the Pan-African future of black people. To pave the way for the freedom of the African, he considered his life of little consequence. In 1830, a year following the publication of the *Appeal*, he was found dead, possibly the victim of poisoning.

IV

The next important black nationalist theorist to appear after Young and Walker, was the Reverend Lewis Woodson of Pittsburgh, a man who, according to historian Floyd Miller, used the pseudonym Augustine. Woodson contributed significantly to the further development of black nationalist ideology, especially between 1837 and 1841. Moreover, according to Miller, it was from Woodson that Martin Delany received much of his training in the ideology of black nationalism.[12] Woodson pursued his quest for black liberation on a number of fronts and, like his nationalist contemporaries, will prove to be an elusive target indeed for those seeking to attach a simplistic definition to his variety of black nationalism.

[12] See Floyd Miller, "The Father of Black Nationalism: Another Contender," *Civil War History*, December 1971, pp. 310–319. Miller has done some of the most important detective work in the field of Afro-American history. His discovery of numerous sections of Delany's *Blake* was a major achievement (Boston: Beacon Press, 1970).

In his seven letters on "Moral Work For Colored Men," six of which appear in this volume, Woodson devoted major attention to the means by which the moral elevation of his people might be achieved. Though his picture of black humanity is not as cheerlessly, as bleakly drafted as those drawn by Young, Walker, and Garnet, his prescription for the rehabilitation of his people is no less devoid of appreciation for the creative dimension of Afro-American culture. Like Walker and Garnet, who reflected at length on the characteristics of the masses of blacks, Woodson seemed unmindful of slave songs, folktales, religion, and dance. In a word, he seemed to be unaware of the distinctive black ethos or life style in slavery.

Still, Woodson's observations on the character development of his people are frequently brilliant. This quality is very much in evidence in his references to the need for people of color to lead themselves. "So long as we admit of others taking the lead in our moral improvement and elevation," he wrote, "we never can expect it to be according to our wish or desire." Though acutely aware of the perils of dependency, and though convinced that his people would move to liberate themselves, he affirmed a representative black nationalist position in refusing to deny aid from friends or allies, "to whom I cling with most unyielding tenacity, but as showing the proper and lawful use of them."

Deeply concerned over *disunity* within the ranks of his people—the perennial concern of black nationalists—Woodson's views on this question are especially arresting but not very original, considering the preoccupation of Young and Walker with this issue. His call for a General Convention of representative black leaders, his recognition of the need for enduring institutions—these concerns, principally owing to the clarity and fullness with which he puts them forth, appear to be important contributions to the ideology of black nationalism. "Without a national institution of some description," he observed in one letter to *The Colored American,* "our affairs can never attain any degree of consistence or permanence. There can be no *head* or *centre* around which we may rally. Our *numbers, means* and *capacity,* will remain useless, for want of something to combine and concentrate them." It could well be, however, that Woodson's most distinctive contribution to the development of nationalist ideology (see letters seven through nine) was his exhortation to his people to move to the countryside, to form separate settlements—a partial prescription for their ills also recommended by Garnet, who shared his views in this regard.

V

As effective an ideologist of black nationalism as Woodson was, he was not the equal of a young nationalist who was responsible for one of the most sophisticated statements of black nationalism, framed in four letters, ever made. Appearing in the pages of *The Colored American* in 1841, these remarks, in response to William Whipper's attacks on those who were making "complexional distinctions" (see Appendix II), were signed by a person who referred to himself simply as Sidney, and they were all written in February and March of 1841. In trying to discover who Sidney was, the writer searched for a black man with that last name, settling, in the first instance, on Thomas S. Sidney, a former classmate of Henry Highland Garnet and Alexander Crummell at the African School in New York. Such a choice seemed natural enough, especially since Thomas Sidney was, as the decade of the 1840's opened, gaining a reputation as a very brilliant and radical young intellectual. And since the author of the letters possessed a fresh, aggressive, and incontestable intelligence, it seemed reasonable to conclude that Thomas S. Sidney was their author. But when it was discovered that Thomas S. Sidney died in 1840, *before* the appearance of the four letters included in this volume, the editor was confronted with a real conundrum.

Recalling that Sidney had referred to his presence at the Albany Convention in 1840 (See Appendix I), the roster of leading participants published in *The Colored American* was reviewed, but, alas, no one named Sidney was listed. Perhaps a Sidney was among those less influential participants whose names were not published; if so, then what would have been the point of withholding the first name? The search for Sidney appeared to lead into a cul de sac. While it was clear that the letters were written by someone at the convention who preferred to disguise his identity, it seemed no less certain that a major intellectual at the convention, indeed of Afro-America, was the author of the letters. Two pivotal figures at the Albany meetings seemed to be likely choices, Alexander Crummell and Henry H. Garnet, both of whom had known Thomas Sidney for more than a decade. Had one written the letters and, as a tribute to his recently departed friend, signed the name Sidney? While that is a possibility, a somewhat remote and peculiar one at that, more evidence was obviously needed.

An examination of the letters, it was thought, might reveal additional clues, and it did except that the evidence adduced from a close reading of the material suggests, once again, that either Garnet or Crummell might have written the letters. Sidney's relatively sparse references to religion and his style of writing suggest that perhaps Garnet rather than Crummell was using the pseudonym. References to the contending forces of black autonomy and those propelled by a "cosmopoliting spirit," a contest also discussed in the section of this essay in which Garnet is considered, are also very similar to Garnet's assessment of the black condition for what appears to have been roughly the same period. While a fairly esoteric reference to a battle waged by Presbyterians in Sidney's first letter shifts one's attention to Garnet, who was a Presbyterian divine of impressive learning, certain passages in another letter, while they express sentiments to which Garnet subscribed, are so close to the language and spirit of Alexander Crummell's Albany Convention Report (See Appendix I) that it is possible to conclude that Crummell and Sidney were one. But why would either man have elected to disguise his identity behind a pseudonym? The answer cannot be supplied at this time. On the other hand, the author may well have been someone other than Garnet or Crummell, but that seems rather unlikely. Since some additional evidence undoubtedly is hidden in this volume, let the reader join in the search.

What *is* certain is that the man who offered the unusually perceptive remarks on black nationalism was mainly concerned with revealing the historical and philosophical bases for people of color coming together to solve their problems. His approach was preeminently from the inside. Sidney believed that people of African ancestry must rely on their own energies, their own perceptions, their own father's example in order to sunder their bonds.

VI

Neither Woodson nor Sidney exercised the black nationalist influence of Henry Highland Garnet. Indeed, perhaps no other figure in ante-bellum America was as influential as Garnet in advancing black nationalist ideas and projects. Born into a family of rebellious black slaves, and said to have been of royal African lineage, this man who delighted in his African heritage was, following his *Address To The Slaves* in 1843, second only to Frederick Douglass among black leaders of ante-bellum America.

Garnet's *Address To The Slaves*, failing to win approval at the Buffalo Convention of 1843, was not published until 1848. At that time, he personally published the *Address* together with Walker's *Appeal*. The *Address*, which stirred a major controversy within the Negro Convention movement, and aroused the ire of some influential white Abolitionists, must be considered nationalistic on a number of grounds. For one thing, the literature of black rebellion contains few documents in which the collective oppression, the common history of blacks is as vividly, as passionately recorded. For another, their dreadful subjection, as described by Garnet, had led to the development of a certain servile mentality which only rebellion, he implied, could undo— a view reiterated by nationalists during subsequent periods.

In Garnet's case, his questioning of the manhood of the enslaved had telescoped Walker's more extended treatment of that subject. Garnet's expression of pride in Africa, his commitment to keep the faith with the millions of ancestors who perished in the slave trade and slavery, and his profound grasp of the relationship between the suffering and misery of his people and the wealth of America contributed to his belief that there was nothing at all wrong with the slaves' rising up to overthrow American slavery. But he also made it clear beyond doubt that *all* black people must be prepared to support the movement of the slaves to break their bonds, that there must be unity among the oppressed.

Following the Buffalo Convention, Garnet gave expression to another vital feature of nationalism: the right of the oppressed to think and act for themselves. Unable to win approval for his *Address* at the Buffalo Convention, he later had to defend the document against white critics. The assault against him came from Maria Weston Chapman, editor pro tem of *The Liberator,* who upbraided him for not having sought the advice of certain friends before embarking on such a violent strategy of liberation, one very much at odds with the Garrisonian preference for moral suasion as an instrument of social change. Garnet returned a classic line: "I can think on the subject of human rights without 'counsel,' either from the men of the West, or the women of the East." The real basis, therefore, of the split of interest between Garnet and the Garrisonians over his *Address* was, in his view, the presumption on the part of whites that they could think *for* black people.

While living in New York, Garnet had very early exposure to Africans from the West Indies and from the continent of Africa. This doubtless helped to make his interest in Africans everywhere (an attitude set forth in the Boston speech of 1859) a natural development for him. In his Boston speech, and in numerous statements before that one, it is evident that he felt a strong sense of solidarity with Africa's transplanted children. Having visited at least two West Indian islands—Cuba in the 1840's and Jamaica in the following decade—he was of a generation of outstanding blacks who had a considerable degree of contact with their West Indian brothers *on West Indian soil.* In sum, his remarks in Boston on the West Indies, "Hayti is *ours,* Jamaica is *ours,* and Cuba will soon be *ours*" (italics added), had evolved out of the very fabric of his own life: a tradition of respect in his family for the African heritage, early contact with Afro-West Indians and Africans in the U.S., and visits to the islands had impressed upon him the essential concord of interests of African peoples. These factors, together with Garnet's realization that Pan-Negro co-

operation was necessary to effect the final liberation of peoples
of African descent, had been central to his thought well before
the decade of the 1850's.

For the student of Afro-American history one aspect of the
Boston statement by Garnet should be, together with sections
of the letters of "Sidney" and Woodson, of very great interest:
these documents highlight a vital portion of American history
which is virtually unknown: black people in the North as early
as the 1830's and 40's and perhaps as late as the 1850's, went
through periods during which forces of integration and black
nationalism (though these terms were not used until much later),
grappled on a major scale for authority within black communities. Judging especially from the remarks of Garnet and
"Sidney," there is reason to believe that "cosmopoliting" forces
were very strong on occasions, sometimes nearly carrying the
day before being rolled back a distance by the forces of black
autonomy. Not infrequently this battle between contending
world views was played out under cover of arguments over what
people of color should call themselves.

The nationalist and integrationist movements of ante-bellum
America foreshadow the present not only with respect to the
struggle over names sometimes being a surface manifestation
of fundamental ideological differences, but also in the realm
of the arts. Then, as now, Afro-Americans debated whether they
should be concerned primarily about themselves or about
universals. "Sidney's" references to the "cosmopoliting spirit" of
certain Afro-Americans, to their emphasis on universals—and
Garnet's remarks on the same subject—read as if they were
framed in the 1970's, just as William Whipper's attacks on all-
black organizations appear to be of equally recent vintage. In
any event, for roughly two decades, Garnet was in the thick of
struggles between cosmopolites and advocates of black
hegemony, warning the former group that they were mistaken
in trying to escape their color, that they would one day realize
they had erred.

It is worth noting, with regard to Garnet's activities on behalf
of the African Civilization Society, that he drew the fire of many
of the most distinguished leaders of people of color not mainly

because he was an advocate of black people's having control over their institutions—rather, he was attacked before, during, and following the Boston speech because his selective emigrationist activities were thought by some to be intimately tied to the American Colonization Society, a charge so damaging that few men would care even to debate the matter publicly.

But Garnet had long been defending his views on emigration. In 1849, he had aroused the ire of no less an assailant than Frederick Douglass, whose reflections on Garnet's interest in emigration initiated what became an especially bitter and protracted exchange between the two men. Their feud over emigration was no doubt fueled by an earlier passage of arms following Garnet's call for a slave rebellion in his *Address To The Slaves,* an exhortation which Douglass had steadfastly opposed.

For years a staunch opponent of emigration, Garnet had not joined Alexander Crummell in raising objections to the antiemigration resolution which was introduced at the Albany Convention of 1840. In the same year, in a brilliantly crafted statement before the American Anti-Slavery Society, Garnet had put forth the view that he would always oppose emigration. But roughly a decade later, he and Crummell were in essential agreement regarding the need for selective emigration of people of color to West Africa, a position more consonant with Garnet's nationalist stance and his early exposure to and interest in African peoples.

Just as Garnet came under severe criticism from certain quarters following his Buffalo call to violence, and just as his commitment to involvement in the politics of the Liberty Party had met with a chilly reception in white and black anti-slavery circles, so too did his attitude toward emigration to Africa arouse widespread opposition. The reader will note that the seriousness of the attacks against Garnet is reflected no less in J. Sella Martin's introduction of Garnet than in the tone of Garnet's rejoinder to his critics. As in his advocacy of other causes once unpopular but later more widely accepted by black leaders, Garnet saw still another of his lonely causes, emigration, achieve very substantial endorsement from black leaders, especially as the decade of the 1860's opened with such great interest in emigration to Haiti.

Garnet was a serious advocate of black people's possessing the land, of their founding towns and settlements for the purpose of controlling their lives.[13] Morever, he encouraged his people to patronize other blacks with services to offer. And like David Walker, "Sidney," Woodson, and Delany, he saw no contradiction between people of color struggling to achieve control of their destinies while seeking the franchise, while attempting to remove the proscriptions imposed on them by the "free institutions" of the northern states. On the contrary, such measures, far from being reformist in slaveholding America, complemented efforts to help people of color achieve the desired autonomy.[14]

The fact that Alexander Crummell, a life-long nationalist, was called upon to chair the committee at the Albany Convention which drafted "certain instructions or recommendations to the people on petitioning" for the franchise in New York State is an illustration of the important role which he and other nationalists of ante-bellum America played in fighting for the ballot. As the Albany minutes reveal, there was no small admiration among distinguished blacks for America's "free institutions," even though there was intense hatred of slavery and oppression. While Garnet and Crummell at times praised American institutions, both men on other occasions could and did subject those institutions, which were warped by slavery and racism, to withering assault.

VII

"The Political Destiny of the Colored Race on the American Continent" was Martin Delany's most trenchant statement on

[13] For a discussion of Garnet's views on black people founding towns and villages, see Henry H. Garnet, *A Memorial Discourse*; with an introduction by James McCune Smith (Philadelphia, 1865), p. 39.

[14] The Afro-American quest for the ballot during the slave era was a radical—no mere reformist—move. To seek the ballot in most northern states was, at times, to risk one's life, for to agitate or organize for the ballot in a country like the United States was sufficient to enrage the great bulk of white Americans. Like the slave who relied on day-to-day resistance to oppose his bondage, those blacks who fought for the ballot were rejecting the country's attempt to assign them to a permanent place of degradation.

black nationalism, and must be considered one of the seminal political documents in American history. Drafted in 1854 for the emigration conference in Cleveland, the statement was his report to the delegates at that conference. The severity of conditions confronting Afro-Americans in the North during the decade of the 1850's doubtless contributed significantly to his tone of hard opposition to the oppressors of blacks and of profound skepticism regarding the future of his people in the United States. The fugitive slave law of 1850, practically giving any white person license to turn over a black to slaveholders, was a somber and accurate index of black-white relations in the decade.

The very harshness of the times caused Delany, at least until the Civil War and Reconstruction years, to give up on American political processes. He had earlier, true to nationalist form, attended meetings of the convention movement, seeking through less radical means than emigration to better the lot of people of color. He would later renew these concerns, though under quite different circumstances. In an important sense, then, his attitude over the long haul toward the possibility of freedom's being won in America is not necessarily reflected in the "Political Destiny of the Colored Race." As with Garnet, Woodson, and Alexander Crummell, Delany was more an emigrationist at certain times than at others—a perfectly sane attitude, especially when one considers the tremendous odds against any black leader, no matter how profound his program. It was not exceptional for a nationalist leader to try first one and then another strategy for breaching the walls of captivity.

Before the emergence of Delany into national prominence, no recognized *ideologist* of black nationalism had placed as much emphasis as he on the need for black people to have land to set aside for purposes of establishing their own nation outside the boundaries of America. David Walker, in fact, had steadfastly opposed even limited emigration to Liberia, so convinced was he that the Liberian experiment was but another instrument of the slave overlord's domination of millions of blacks in the South. While it is true that Woodson eventually expressed interest in emigration, he was not very influential in national

Afro-American circles, and so had little impact, save through Delany, on his people. Alexander Crummell, later a giant in Afro-American life and a believer in selective emigration (recall, he opposed the anti-emigration resolution at the Albany Convention), was out of the country throughout the decade of the 1850's, which meant that his growing prestige as a thinker could scarcely yield practical results from thousands of miles away in Liberia. And while it is true that Garnet as early as 1849 had come out for limited emigration, he continued to believe that his people would secure their freedom in America.

Delany's emigration philosophy was predicated on a disaffection with American life that appeared to be much greater than that of other ante-bellum emigrationists, though the gap between them had closed considerably by the beginning of the decade of the 1860's. It was precisely this disaffection which led Delany to emphasize the importance of a territorial base away from white America. His almost total absence of faith in the possibility of the black man's winning freedom in America grew out of his belief that the whole history of white people had been toward crushing "the colored races wherever found." More than that, the government of the United States, he remarked in "The Political Destiny," was the enemy of black people. There is reason to believe that Delany, certainly during the slave era, suffered somewhat less from the attraction-repulsion attitude toward America that was characteristic of so many black leaders of his time and later. Not surprisingly, he extended his grim view of the government and nation to whites generally, though he made it clear that all whites were not antagonists of his people. But those who favored the liberation of blacks, he was quick to add, were not running the country.

When Delany joined Garnet's African Civilization Society, he proceeded to lead a movement to purge that organization of its white officers, a position consonant with the precepts, if not the actions, of every important black nationalist of the period. Garnet, who headed the Society, had permitted whites to play important roles in the organization, a decision for which he paid dearly, especially in light of the charge that his white associates were agents of the American Colonization Society.

Delany had said often enough that he cared little or nothing for the opinions of white men. His move against white officers of the African Civilization Society squared perfectly with that sentiment.

In "The Political Destiny of the Colored Race," Delany put forth the view that his people should emigrate to the West Indies and to Central and South America. Though he later emigrated to Canada, he was by no means certain that people of African ancestry were safe there since he thought the Anglo-Saxon wanted to dominate all people of color within reach. In any case, his knowledge of Latin America was, as the document reveals, not very accurate. Not only did he not understand, for example, the state of Brazilian race relations, but his information regarding the number of black people in Latin America was far from accurate.[15]

Nevertheless, Delany's observations on people of color generally mark him as one of the most original political thinkers of his day. This is all the more evident when his extremely advanced position vis-à-vis the American Indian is taken into account. In fact, he was way ahead of his black contemporaries in this latter respect. In both "The Political Destiny of the Colored Race" and *Blake: The Huts of America,* his novel, he displayed a respect for and a sense of solidarity with Indians that were altogether remarkable. His attitude toward Indians was an aspect of his overall views on the racial factor in human history. In "The Political Destiny" he foresaw a racial cleavage of apocalyptic scope:

> It would be duplicity longer to disguise the fact that the great issue, sooner or later, upon which must be disputed the world's destiny will be a question of black and white, and every individual will be called upon for his identity with one or the other.

"The problem of the twentieth century," Du Bois would later remark in *The Souls of Black Folk,* "is the problem of the color line. . . ."

Delany made explicit what most nationalists of his time had merely implied. He argued that just as other peoples had special

[15] Hollis Lynch, "Pan-Negro Nationalism," p. 52.

traits, so too did the Afro-American. Moreover, he emphasized
the desirability of people of color cultivating their esthetic and
spiritual qualities. He referred to the need for black people to
develop and build upon their special gifts so that they might not
only further nationalist goals but "instruct the world" as well.
Unfortunately, apart from an occasional remark about slave
singing, there is little evidence that Delany had any real understanding of the art or religion of the masses of black people. Thus
he too missed a singular opportunity to add to political and
economic nationalism a form of nationalism which awaited
theoretical articulation and propagation, an artistic and cultural
nationalism more deeply grounded in the African heritage than
other expressions of nationalism. By carefully rearranging the
peculiarly African in light of American exigencies, and by build-
ing from such a cultural base, the ante-bellum nationalist might
have helped break the cycle of contests between assimilationists
and nationalists and thereby elevated the struggle of his people
to a higher and less confused plane.

While the tradition of black pride extends about as far back
as written records left by blacks; while at times attacks on
blackness elicited graceful but forceful returns from men such
as Benjamin Banneker in the late eighteenth—and angry and
aggressive rejoinders from men like David Walker in the
early nineteenth—century; while Garnet was quietly proud of
his Africanness and insisted that those among his people who
tried to flee their blackness were making a terrible mistake;
while these and other expressions of black pride were shared
by not inconsiderable numbers of black people from time to
time in the slave era, it remained for Martin Delany to provide
a fuller dimension to blackness by giving it more attention than
his contemporaries. This he did to the extent of becoming, in a
somewhat measured way, a celebrant of blackness.[16] But as

[16] One can detect Delany's unmistakable satisfaction with blackness in
two recently published, superbly researched, volumes on him. For exhaus-
tive treatments of Delany, see Dorothy Sterling, *The Making of an Afro-
American: Martin Robison Delany, 1812–1885* (Garden City: Doubleday,
1971); and Victor Ullman, *Martin R. Delany: The Beginnings of Black
Nationalism* (Boston: Beacon Press, 1971).

"The Political Destiny" makes eminently clear, if Delany was proud of blackness and other characteristics of his people, he could with equal zeal subject certain of their traits, as he conceived them, to ruthless criticism. Perhaps it is not unfair to say that black nationalists, more than any other group of Afro-American ideologists, have been able to combine in terrible and uneasy tension the most devastating criticisms of, and the most sublime faith in, their people. This tendency is especially evident in Walker and Garnet. But it is no less fair to note that, in the main, nationalists were perhaps more consistently critical of the masses of blacks than other ideologists.

Delany almost rivaled Walker and Garnet in describing the degradation of black people. In "The Political Destiny" he said, rather mildly for him, that they were suffering from a great disease, political in nature, one requiring "a healing balm to a sorely diseased body—a wrecked but not entirely shattered system." He proposed a remedy, emigration, and provided a vision of a better day for those fortunate enough to leave these shores and to settle in more congenial surroundings "where our political enclosure and national edifice can be reared, established, walled, and proudly defended on this great elementary principle of original identity."

As one ponders the seminal theoretical works by black men of the slave era, it becomes evident that with few exceptions the terms "black nationalists" and "integrationists," when thought of as mutually exclusive, are not simply inadequate as means of understanding the individuals being labeled but prevent us from understanding major ideologies and movements. For instance, the view advanced by Harold Cruse that Martin Delany was the prototype black nationalist and Frederick Douglass the prototype integrationist is not merely a rank oversimplification but a barometer of the extent to which he lacks familiarity with the sources.[17] Not only can one trace black nationalism and

[17] Anyone who has studied the Negro Convention Movement should know that the leaders of that movement cannot be easily cataloged, tucked away in discreet niches. Thus those who indulge in the scholarly pastime of denouncing Douglass as an integrationist betray the paucity of their

integrationism back to previous originators more than a decade before either Douglass or Delany rose to prominence, but it is in error to contend that there was not something of the *integrationist* in Delany and much of the *nationalist* in the young Douglass; that the ideologies and programs of these men did not overlap.

As their writings indicate, most of the nationalists in this volume usually refused to allow themselves to be tied to a single methodological approach. It was not unusual for them, Walker and Garnet being cases in point, to pursue multiple paths to the ultimate goal, which was not necessarily the establishment of a black nation. As important and vital as that objective was to them, as deeply committed to black autonomy as they were, the final goal was, the documents make evident, *the freedom of their people.*

If that freedom could have been effected without ridding the land of white people, nationalists, as rational men, would not have been displeased. On the other hand, if freedom could come to their people only through the elimination of whites, then ante-bellum nationalists would no doubt have favored acting on that reality.[18] The fact of the matter is that major nationalist theoreticians have generally been exceedingly humanistic. One readily perceives this quality in the documents included here.

---

grasp of the history of his period—and signal a certain sloppiness regarding their treatment of more recent history? A cursory reading of William Whipper's letters in Appendix II makes it quite clear that he was no mean advocate of a colorblind America. If any ante-bellum black was the prototype "integrationist," it was William Whipper, certainly not Frederick Douglass. For a pathfinding treatment of the Negro Convention Movement, see Howard H. Bell, *The Negro Convention Movement,* Ph.D. dissertation, Northwestern University, 1953.

[18] Theodore Draper has remarked, sweepingly enough, that black nationalists, following a "fantasy," want to get rid of white people. Only by drawing upon nationalist literature of the twentieth century, and even then while ignoring representative nationalist writings, can he provide a defense for this intemperate assertion. Surely the nationalist position over the long haul has been anything but what Draper, not bothering to honor or to seek to understand the sources, would have us believe. See Theodore Draper, *The Rediscovery of Black Nationalism* (New York: Viking, 1969), especially Chapter XI.

(Note in particular the deep sense of humanism which under-girds the report that Crummell drafted for the Albany Convention.) In fact, a strong tendency to reach beyond themselves toward union with mankind has been a marked characteristic of most nationalist theoreticians from David Walker to Paul Robeson.[19] The nationalists' concern for their fellow man should be kept in mind in order to avoid doing violence to the meaning of historic black nationalism.

Finally, from the appearance of the *Ethiopian Manifesto* and *The Appeal To The Colored Citizens Of The World* in 1829 to the 1860's there were no monolithic conceptions of black nationalism projected by major nationalist figures. Where are the ante-bellum—or for that matter later nineteenth century—nationalists who did not, on a reading of the turbulent times, try first one formula and then another, or whose works *and actions* did not suggest more than one possible solution to the problem of African oppression in America? Almost all were willing to settle for a place in American life, provided their people, as black people, had significant control over their destinies. But there has also been the clearly expressed willingness of some nationalists even to transcend color, provided white Americans were no longer obsessed with America's remaining a white country. It was when such options were thought unavailable

[19] In a statement as notable for violence against history as for impressive perversity, Ossie Davis, a self-styled man of "honor and repute," attacked Robeson for, among other things, not being "a strict constructionist" who takes his blackness "pure and unalloyed." Wildly, Davis claimed that Marcus Garvey and Monroe Trotter were believers in pure blackness—whatever that is—and in so doing revealed his ignorance of both men. Unable to name other names, he reduced himself to: "Always there were some blacks who preferred to go it alone, today perhaps more so than ever." An examination of the record will reveal that, on the contrary, it is virtually impossible to find a black leader of any substance who believed in and acted on the Davis attribution and for a good enough reason: the holocaust of the American experience has been more than sufficient to impress upon black leaders the importance of not foreclosing any opportunity to mitigate the plight of their people. For a remarkable melding of easy cruelty and hard opportunism, see Ossie Davis' two-part article that, strangely enough, is called "To Paul Robeson," in *Freedomways*, First and Second Quarters, 1971.

that the nationalist was more likely to favor a separate black nation either adjacent to the U.S. or elsewhere in the world, usually in Africa.

When nationalists advocated the total removal of their people from America—and few indeed have been those who have thought this strategy either realistic or desirable—it should not be said that even they, considering centuries of merciless oppression of Afro-Americans, were less realistic than believers in the American Dream. Moreover, the record seems to suggest rather the opposite: that those people of color (and their white allies) who believed in the absorptive powers of America were vastly more deluded than those blacks who decided to depend mainly on their own people, their own energies in a hostile land.

STERLING STUCKEY

1

ETHIOPIAN MANIFESTO,

ISSUED IN DEFENCE
OF THE

BLACK MAN'S RIGHTS

IN THE SCALE OF

UNIVERSAL FREEDOM

New York
Printed for the Author
1829

Southern District of New-York, s s.

BE IT REMEMBERED, That on the 18th day of February, A.D. 1829, in the 53d year of the Independence of the United States of America, Robert Alexander Young, of the said district, hath deposited in this office the title of a book the right whereof he claims as author, in the words following, to wit:

"The Ethiopian Manifesto, issued in defence of the Black Man's Rights, in the scale of Universal Freedom."

In conformity to the Act of Congress of the United States, entitled "An Act for the Encouragement of Learning, by securing the copies of Maps, Charts, and Books, to the author and proprietors of such copies, during the time therein mentioned." And also to an Act, entitled "An Act supplementary to an act, entitled an act for the encouragement of learning, by securing

the copies of Maps, Charts, and Books, to the authors and proprietors of such copies, during the times therein mentioned, and
extending the benefits thereof to the arts of designing, engrav-
ing, and etching historical and other prints."

FRED I. BETTS,
Clerk of the Southern District of New-York.

ETHIOPIAN MANIFESTO

By the Omnipotent will of God, we, Rednaxela, sage, and asserter to the Ethiopian of his rights, do hereby declare, and make known, as follows:—

Ethiopians! the power of Divinity having within us, as man, implanted a sense of the due and prerogatives belonging to you, a people, of whom we were of your race, in part born, as a mirror we trust, to reflect to you from a review of ourselves, the dread condition in which you do at this day stand. We do, therefore, to the accomplishment of our purpose, issue this but a brief of our grand manifesto, herefrom requiring the attention towards us of every native, or those proceeding in descent from the Ethiopian or African people; a regard to your welfare being the great and inspiring motive which leads us to this our undertaking. We do therefore strictly enjoin your attention to these the dictates from our sense of justice, held forth and produced to your notice, but with the most pure intention.

Ethiopians! open your minds to reason; let therein weigh the effects of truth, wisdom, and justice (and a regard to your individual as general good), and the spirit of these our words we know full well, cannot but produce the effect for which they are by us herefrom intended.—Know, then, in your present state or standing, in your sphere of government in any nation within which you reside, we hold and contend you enjoy but few of your rights of government within them. We here speak of the whole of the Ethiopian people, as we admit not even those in their state of native simplicity, to be in an enjoyment of their rights, as bestowed to them of the great bequest of God to man.

The impositions practised to their state, not being known to them from the heavy and darksome clouds of ignorance which so woefully obscures their reason, we do, therefore, for the re-

covering of them, as well as establishing to you your rights,
proclaim, that duty—imperious duty, exacts the convocation of
ourselves in a body politic; that we do, for the promotion and
welfare of our order, establish to ourselves a people framed
unto the likeness of that order, which from our mind's eye we
do evidently discern governs the universal creation. Beholding
but one sole power, supremacy, or head, we do of that head,
but hope and look forward for succour in the accomplishment
of the great design which he hath, in his wisdom, promoted us
to its undertaking.

We find we possess in ourselves an understanding; of this we
are taught to know the ends of right and wrong, that depression
should come upon us or any of our race of the wrongs inflicted
on us of men. We know in ourselves we possess a right to see
ourselves justified therefrom, of the right of God; knowing, but
of his power hath he decreed to man, that either in himself he
stands, or by himself he falls. Fallen, sadly, sadly low indeed,
hath become our race, when we behold it reduced but to an
enslaved state, to raise it from its degenerate sphere, and instill
into it the rights of men, are the ends intended of these our
words; here we are met in ourselves, we constitute but one,
aided, as we trust, by the effulgent light of wisdom to a discernment of the path which shall lead us to the collecting together
of a people, rendered disobedient to the great dictates of nature,
by the barbarity that hath been practised upon them from generation to generation of the will of their more cruel fellow-men.
Am I, because I am a descendant of a mixed race of men, whose
shade hath stamped them with the hue of black, to deem myself
less eligible to the attainment of the great gift allotted of God
to man, than are any other of whatsoever cast you please,
deemed from being white as being more exalted than the black?

These words, which carry to the view of others the dictates
of my mind. I borrow not from the sense of white men or of
black: learn, my brother and fellow-Ethiopian, it is but the
invigorating power of Deity instills them to my discernment.
Of him do I know I derive my right; of him was I on the conception of a mother's womb created free; who then in the shape
of man shall dare to rob me of my birthright as bestowed to

me in my existence from God? No, I am in myself a man, and as a man will live, or as a man will die; for as I was born free of the will allotted me of the freedom of God, so do I claim and purport to establish an alike universal freedom to every son and daughter descending from the black; though however mixed in grades of colour through an intercourse of white with black; still as I am in myself, but a mixture of like, I call to witness, if the power of my mind hath not a right to claim an allegiance with all descendants of a race, for the justification of whose rights reason hath established within me the ends for their obtainment? God, an almighty, sole, and governing God, can alone direct me to the ends I have, but of his will to fulfill, be they here to the view of the universal world from him established; for as I do in myself stand upright, and claim in myself, as outwardly from myself, all my rights and prerogatives as pertaining to me in my birthright of man, so do I equally claim to the untutored black of every denomination, be he in bondage or free, an alike right; and do hereby publicly protest against the infringement of his rights, as is at this day practised by the fiendish cast of men who dare, contrary to the knowledge of justice, as hath been implanted of God in the soul of man, to hold him in bondage, adducing from his servitude a gorgeous maintenance. Accursed and damned be he in mind, soul and body, who dare after this my protest, to claim the slightest alleged right to hold a man, as regards manly visage, shape, and bearing, equal in all points, though ignorant and untaught with himself, and in intrinsic worth to the view of Deity; by far in his sacred presence, must he appear the better man, the calm submission to his fate, pointing him to the view of justice at the throne of God, as being more worthy of the rights of man, than the wretch who would claim from him his rights as a man.

I pause. Custom here points to me her accursed practises, if founded in error, as base injustice; shall they stand? nay, aught they to be allowed or sanctioned, for so to do by the cognizance of the just, the wise, the great, the good, and sound men of discretion of this world? I speak for no man, understanding but in myself my rights, that from myself shall be made known to a people, rights, which I, of the divine will of God, to them establish. Man—white man—black man—or, more properly, ye monsters incarnate, in human shape, who claim the horrid right to hold nature's untutored son, the Ethiopian, in bondage, to you I do herefrom speak. Mark me, and regard well these my words; be assured, they convey the voice of reason, dictated to you through a prophetic sense of truth. The time is at hand when many signs shall appear to you, to denote that Almighty God regards the affairs of afflicted men:—for know, the cries of bitter servitude, from those unhappy sons of men, whom ye have so long unjustly oppressed with the goading shafts of an accursed slavery, hath ascended to Deity. Your God, the great and mighty God, hath seen your degradation of your fellow brother, and mortal man; he hath long looked down with mercy on your suffering slave; his cries have called for a vindication of his rights, and know ye they have been heard of the Majesty of Heaven, whose dignity have you not offended by deeming a mortal man, in your own likeness, as but worthy of being your slave, degraded to your brute? The voice of intuitive justice speaks aloud to you, and bids you to release your slave; otherwise stings, eternal stings, of an outraged and goading conscience will, ere long, hold all them in subjection who pay not due attention to this, its admonition. Beware! know thyselves to be but mortal men, doomed to the good or evil, as your works shall merit from you. Pride ye not yourselves in the greatness of your worldly standing, since all things are but moth when contrasted with the invisible spirit, which in yourself maintains within you your course of action. That within you will, to the presence of your God, be at all times your sole accuser. Weigh well these my words in the balance of your conscientious reason, and abide the judgment thereof to your own standing, for we tell you of a surety, the decree hath already passed the judgment seat of an undeviating God, wherein he hath said, "surely hath the cries of the black, a most persecuted people, ascended to my throne and craved my mercy; now, behold! I will stretch forth mine hand and gather them to the palm, that they become unto me a people, and I unto them their God." Hearken, therefore, oh! slaveholder, thou task inflicter against the rights of men, the day is at hand, nay the hour draweth nigh, when

poverty shall appear to thee a blessing, if it but restore to thy
fellow-man his rights; all worldly riches shall be known to thee
then but as a curse, and in thine heart's desire to obtain contentment, when sad reverses come upon thee, then shalt thou
linger for a renewal of days, that in thine end thou might not
curse the spirit which called thee forth to life. Take warning,
again we say, for of a surety from this, God will give you signs
to know, in his decrees he regards the fallen state of the sons
of men. Think not that wisdom descries not from here your
vanity. We behold it, thou vain bloated upstart worldling of a
slaveholder, laugh in derision of thy earthly taught and worldly
sneer; but know, on thee we pronounce our judgment, and as
fitting thee, point out to thy notice this our sign. Of the degraded of this earth, shall be exalted, one who shall draw from
thee, as though gifted of power divine, all attachment and regard of thy slave towards thee. Death shall he prefer to a
continuance of his race:—being doomed to thy vile servitude,
no cohabitation shall be known between the sexes, while suffering under thy slavery; but should ungovernable passion
attain over the untaught mind an ascendancy, abortion shall
destroy the birth. We command it, the voice of imperative justice, though however harsh, must be obeyed. Ah! doth your
expanding judgment, base slaveholder, not from here descry
that the shackles which have been by you so undeservingly
forged upon a wretched Ethiopian's frame, are about to be
forever from him unlinked. Say ye, this can never be accomplished? If so, must indeed the power and decrees of Infinity
become subservient to the will of depraved man. But learn,
slaveholder, thine will rests not in thine hand: God decrees to
thy slave his rights as man. This we issue forth as the spirit
of the black man or Ethiopian's rights, established from the
Ethiopian's Rock, the foundation of his civil and religious rights,
which hereafter will be exemplified in the order of its course.
Ethiopians, throughout the world in general, receive this as but
a lesson presented to you from an instructive Book, in which
many, many therein are contained, to the vindication of its
purpose. As came John the Baptist, of old, to spread abroad
the forthcoming of his master, so alike are intended these our

words, to denote to the black African or Ethiopian people, that
God has prepared for them a leader, who awaits but for his
season to proclaim to them his birthright. How shall you know
this man? By indubitable signs which cannot be controverted
by the power of mortal, his marks being stamped in open visage,
as equally so upon his frame, which constitutes him to have
been particularly regarded in the infinite work of God to man.

Know ye, then, if a white man ever appeared on earth, bearing in himself the semblance of his former race, the man we
proclaim ordained of God, to call together the black people
as a nation in themselves. We say, in him will be seen, in appearance, a white man, although having been born of a black
woman, his mother. The proof is strong, and in Grenada's
Island, Grand Anta Estate, there, some time ago, did dwell his
mother—his father then owner of the said estate. The church
books of St. Georgestown, the capital of Grenada, can truly
prove his birth. As another instance wherein providence decreed he should appear peculiar in his make, the two middle
toes on each of his feet were, in his conception, webbed and
bearded. Now, after the custom of the ancient order of men,
with long and flowing hair, by like appearances may he be
known; none other man, but the one bearing the alike marks,
and proving his identity from the island on which he was born,
can be the man of whom we speak. To him, thou poor black
Ethiopian or African slave, do thou, from henceforth, place a
firm reliance thereon, as trusting in him to prove thy liberator
from the infernal state of bondage, under which you have been
so long and so unjustly laboring. To thee he pledges himself,
in life to death, not to desert thee, his trust being in the power
of the Almighty, who giveth not the race to the swift nor the
battle to the strong, but decrees to all men the justice he establishes. As such, we draw from him the conception of your
rights, and to its obtainment we issue this to you, our first pledge
of faith, binding ourselves herefrom to render to you, at all times,
such services as shall tend most to your advantage in effecting
a speedy deliverance from your mortal and most deadly foe,
the monster of a slaveholder. We would most particularly direct
you to such government of yourselves as should be responsible

but to God, your maker, for the duty exacted of you to your fellow-men; but, under goading situations, where power and might is but the construction of law, it then behooves the depressed and vilely injured to bear his burthen with the firmness of his manhood:—So at this time, we particularly recommend to you, degraded sons of Africa, to submit with fortitude to your present state of suffering, relying in yourselves, from the justice of a God, that the time is at hand, when, with but the power of words and the divine will of our God, the vile shackles of slavery shall be broken asunder from you, and no man known who shall dare to own or proclaim you as his bondsman. We say it, and assert it as though by an oracle given and delivered to you from on high. God, in his holy keeping, direct thee, thou poor untaught and degraded African slave, to a full conception of these the words we have written for your express benefit. Our care and regard of you will be that of a fostering parent toward a beloved offspring. The hatred of your oppressor we fear not, nor do we his power, or any vile machinations that may be resorted to by incendiaries towards us. We hold ourself, with the aid of our God therewith, at all times ready to encounter, trusting but in God, our Creator, and not in ourselves, for a deliverance from all worldly evil.

Peace and Liberty to the Ethiopian first, as also all other grades of men, is the invocation we offer to the throne of our God.

REDNAXELA

DATED FROM THE

ETHIOPIAN'S ROCK,

IN THE

THIRTY-SEVENTH YEAR

FROM ITS

FOUNDATION,

THIS THIRTEENTH DAY OF FEBRUARY, A.D.

1829

2

WALKER'S

APPEAL,

IN FOUR ARTICLES;

TOGETHER WITH

A PREAMBLE,

TO THE

COLOURED CITIZENS OF THE WORLD,

BUT IN PARTICULAR, AND VERY EXPRESSLY, TO THOSE OF

THE UNITED STATES OF AMERICA,

WRITTEN IN BOSTON, STATE OF MASSACHUSETTS,
SEPTEMBER 28, 1829.

THIRD AND LAST EDITION

WITH ADDITIONAL NOTES, CORRECTIONS, &C.

BOSTON:
REVISED AND PUBLISHED BY DAVID WALKER.

1830.

It will be recollected, that I, in the first edition of my "Appeal," [1] promised to demonstrate in the course of which, viz. in the course of my Appeal, to the satisfaction of the most incredulous mind, that we Coloured People of these United States, are, the most wretched, degraded and abject set of beings that ever lived since the world began, down to the present day, and, that, the white Christians of America, who hold us in slavery (or, more properly speaking, pretenders to Christianity), treat us more cruel and barbarous than any Heathen nation did any people whom it had subjected, or reduced to the same condition, that the Americans (who are, notwithstanding, looking for the Millennial day) have us. All I ask is, for a candid and careful perusal of this the third and last edition of my Appeal, where the world may see that we, the Blacks or Coloured People, are treated more cruel by the white Christians of America, than devils themselves ever treated a set of men, women and children on this earth.

It is expected that all coloured men, women and children,[2] of every nation, language and tongue under heaven, will try to procure a copy of this Appeal and read it, or get some one to read it to them, for it is designed more particularly for them. Let them remember, that though our cruel oppressors and murderers, may (if possible) treat us more cruel, as Pharaoh did the children of Israel, yet the God of the Etheopeans, has been pleased to hear our moans in consequence of oppression; and the day of our redemption from abject wretchedness draweth near, when we shall be enabled, in the most extended sense of the word, to stretch forth our hands to the LORD Our GOD, but there must be a willingness on our part, for GOD to do these things for us, for we may be assured that he will not take us by the hairs of our head against our will and desire, and drag us from our very, mean, low and abject condition.

[1] See my Preamble in first edition, first page. See also 2nd edition, Article 1, page 9.

[2] Who are not deceitful, abject, and servile to resist the cruelties and murders inflicted upon us by the white slave holders, our enemies by nature.

APPEAL, &c.

My dearly beloved Brethren and Fellow Citizens.

HAVING travelled over a considerable portion of these United States, and having, in the course of my travels, taken the most accurate observations of things as they exist—the result of my observations has warranted the full and unshaken conviction, that we (coloured people of these United States), are the most degraded, wretched, and abject set of beings that ever lived since the world began; and I pray God that none like us ever may live again until time shall be no more. They tell us of the Israelites in Egypt, the Helots in Sparta, and of the Roman Slaves, which last were made up from almost every nation under heaven, whose sufferings under those ancient and heathen nations, were, in comparison with ours, under this enlightened and Christian nation, no more than a cypher—or, in other words, those nations of antiquity, had but little more among them than the name and form of slavery; while wretchedness and endless miseries were reserved, apparently in a phial, to be poured out upon our fathers, ourselves and our children, by *Christian* Americans!

These positions I shall endeavour, by the help of the Lord, to demonstrate in the course of this APPEAL, to the satisfaction of the most incredulous mind—and may God Almighty, who is the Father of our Lord Jesus Christ, open your hearts to understand and believe the truth.

The *causes,* my brethren, which produce our wretchedness and miseries, are so very numerous and aggravating, that I believe the pen only of a Josephus or a Plutarch, can well enumerate and explain them. Upon subjects, then, of such incomprehensible magnitude, so impenetrable, and so notorious, I shall be obliged to omit a large class of, and content myself with giving you an exposition of a few of those, which do indeed rage to such an alarming pitch, that they cannot but be a perpetual source of terror and dismay to every reflecting mind.

I am fully aware, in making this appeal to my much afflicted and suffering brethren, that I shall not only be assailed by those whose greatest earthly desires are, to keep us in abject ignorance and wretchedness, and who are of the firm conviction that Heaven has designed us and our children to be slaves and *beasts of burden* to them and their children. I say, I do not only expect to be held up to the public as an ignorant, impudent and restless disturber of the public peace, by such avaricious creatures, as well as a mover of insubordination—and perhaps put in prison or to death, for giving a superficial exposition of our miseries, and exposing tyrants. But I am persuaded, that many of my brethren, particularly those who are ignorantly in league with slave-holders or tyrants, who acquire their daily bread by the blood and sweat of their more ignorant brethren—and not a few of those too, who are too ignorant to see an inch beyond their noses, will rise up and call me cursed—Yea, the jealous ones among us will perhaps use more abject subtlety, by affirming that this work is not worth perusing, that we are well situated, and there is no use in trying to better our condition, for we cannot. I will ask one question here.—Can our condition be any worse?—Can it be more mean and abject? If there are any changes, will they not be for the better, though they may appear for the worst at first? Can they get us any lower? Where can they get us? They are afraid to treat us worse, for they know well, the day they do it they are gone. But against all accusations which may or can be preferred against me, I appeal to Heaven for my motive in writing—who knows that my object is, if possible, to awaken in the breasts of my afflicted, degraded and slumbering brethren, a spirit of inquiry and investigation respecting our miseries and wretchedness in this REPUBLICAN LAND OF LIBERTY!!!!!!

The sources from which our miseries are derived, and on which I shall comment, I shall not combine in one, but shall put them under distinct heads and expose them in their turn; in doing which, keeping truth on my side, and not departing from the strictest rules of morality, I shall endeavour to penetrate, search out, and lay them open for your inspection. If you cannot or will not profit by them, I shall have done *my* duty to you, my country and my God.

And as the inhuman system of *slavery,* is the *source* from which most of our miseries proceed, I shall begin with that *curse to nations,* which has spread terror and devastation through so many nations of antiquity, and which is raging to such a pitch at the present day in Spain and in Portugal. It had one tug in England, in France, and in the United States of America; yet the inhabitants thereof, do not learn wisdom, and erase it entirely from their dwellings and from all with whom they have to do. The fact is, the labour of slaves comes too cheap to the avaricious usurpers, and is (as they think) of such great utility to the country where it exists, that those who are actuated by sordid avarice only, overlook the evils, which will as sure as the Lord lives, follow after the good. In fact, they are so happy to keep in ignorance and degradation, and to receive the homage and the labour of the slaves, they forget that God rules in the armies of heaven and among the inhabitants of the earth, having his ears continually open to the cries, tears and groans of his oppressed people; and being a just and holy Being will at one day appear fully in behalf of the oppressed, and arrest the progress of the avaricious oppressors; for although the destruction of the oppressors God may not effect by the oppressed, yet the Lord our God will bring other destructions upon them— for not unfrequently will he cause them to rise up one against another, to be split and divided, and to oppress each other, and sometimes to open hostilities with sword in hand.

Some may ask, what is the matter with this united and happy people?—Some say it is the cause of political usurpers, tyrants, oppressors, &c. But has not the Lord an oppressed and suffering people among them? Does the Lord condescend to hear their cries and see their tears in consequence of oppression? Will he let the oppressors rest comfortably and happy always? Will he not cause the very children of the oppressors to rise up against them, and ofttimes put them to death? "God works in many ways his wonders to perform."

I will not here speak of the destructions which the Lord brought upon Egypt, in consequence of the oppression and consequent groans of the oppressed—of the hundreds and thousands of Egyptians whom God hurled into the Red Sea for afflicting his people in their land—of the Lord's suffering people in Sparta or Lacedemon, the land of the truly famous Lycurgus—nor have I time to comment upon the cause which produced the fierceness with which Sylla usurped the title, and absolutely acted as dictator of the Roman people—the conspiracy of Cataline—the conspiracy against, and murder of Caesar in the Senate house—the spirit with which Marc Antony made himself master of the commonwealth—his associating Octavius and Lipidus with himself in power—their dividing the provinces of Rome among themselves—their attack and defeat, on the plains of Phillippi, of the last defenders of their liberty (Brutus and Cassius)—the tyranny of Tiberius, and from him to the final overthrow of Constantinople by the Turkish Sultan, Mahomed II. A.D. 1453.

I say, I shall not take up time to speak of the *causes* which produced so much wretchedness and massacre among those heathen nations, for I am aware that you know too well, that God is just, as well as merciful!—I shall call your attention a few moments to that *Christian* nation, the Spaniards—while I shall leave almost unnoticed, that avaricious and cruel people, the Portuguese, among whom all true hearted Christians and lovers of Jesus Christ, must evidently see the judgments of God displayed. To show the judgments of God upon the Spaniards, I shall occupy but a little time, leaving a plenty of room for the candid and unprejudiced to reflect.

All persons who are acquainted with history, and particularly the Bible, who are not blinded by the God of this world, and are not actuated solely by avarice—who are able to lay aside prejudice long enough to view candidly and impartially, things as they were, are, and probably will be—who are willing to admit that God made man to serve Him *alone,* and that man should have no other Lord or Lords but Himself—that God Almighty is the *sole proprietor* or *master* of the WHOLE human family, and will not on any consideration admit of a colleague, being unwilling to divide his glory with another—and who can dispense with prejudice long enough to admit that we are *men,* notwithstanding our *improminent noses* and *woolly heads,* and believe that we feel for our fathers, mothers, wives and children, as well as the whites do for theirs.—I say, all who are permitted to see and believe these things, can easily recognize the judgments of God among the Spaniards. Though others may lay the cause of the fierceness with which they cut each other's throats, to some other circumstances, yet they who believe that God is a God of justice, will believe that SLAVERY *is the principal cause.*

While the Spaniards are running about upon the field of battle cutting each other's throats, has not the Lord an afflicted and suffering people in the midst of them, whose cries and groans in consequence of oppression are continually pouring into the ears of the God of justice? Would they not cease to cut each other's throats, if they could? But how can they? The very support which they draw from government to aid them in perpetrating such enormities, does it not arise in a great degree from the wretched victims of oppression among them? And yet they are calling for PEACE!—PEACE!! Will any peace be given unto them? Their destruction may indeed be procrastinated awhile, but can it continue long, while they are oppressing the Lord's people? Has He not the hearts of all men in His hand? Will he suffer one part of his creatures to go on oppressing another like brutes always, with impunity? And yet, those avaricious wretches are calling for PEACE!!!! I declare, it does appear to me, as though some nations think God is asleep, or that he made the Africans for nothing else but to dig their mines and work their farms, or they cannot believe history, sacred or profane.

I ask every man who has a heart, and is blessed with the privilege of believing—Is not God a God of justice to *all* his creatures? Do you say he is? Then if he gives peace and tranquillity to tyrants, and permits them to keep our fathers, our mothers, ourselves and our children in eternal ignorance and wretchedness, to support them and their families, would he be to us a God of *justice?* I ask, O ye *Christians*!!! who hold us and our children in the most abject ignorance and degradation, that ever a people were afflicted with since the world began—I say, if God gives you peace and tranquillity, and suffers you thus to go on afflicting us, and our children, who have never given you the least provocation—would he be to us *a God of justice?* If you will allow that we are MEN, who feel for each other, does not the blood of our fathers and of us their children, cry aloud to the Lord of Sabaoth against you, for the cruelties and murders with which you have, and do continue to afflict us. But it is time for me to close my remarks on the suburbs, just to enter more fully into the interior of this system of cruelty and oppression.

ARTICLE I.

OUR WRETCHEDNESS IN CONSEQUENCE OF SLAVERY

MY BELOVED BRETHREN:—The Indians of North and of South America—the Greeks—the Irish, subjected under the king of Great Britain—the Jews, that ancient people of the Lord—the inhabitants of the islands of the sea—in fine, all the inhabitants of the earth (except however, the sons of Africa), are called *men,* and of course are, and ought to be free. But we (coloured people), and our children are *brutes*!! and of course are, and *ought to be* SLAVES to the American people and their children forever!! to dig their mines and work their farms; and thus go on enriching them, from one generation to another with our *blood* and our *tears!!!!*

I promised in a preceding page to demonstrate to the satisfaction of the most incredulous, that we (coloured people of these United States of America), are the *most wretched, degraded* and *abject* set of beings that *ever lived* since the world began, and that the white Americans having reduced us to the wretched state of *slavery,* treat us in that condition *more cruel* (they being an enlightened and Christian people), than any heathen nation did any people whom it had reduced to our condition. These affirmations are so well confirmed in the minds of all unprejudiced men, who have taken the trouble to read histories, that they need no elucidation from me. But to put them beyond all doubt, I refer you in the first place to the children of Jacob, or of Israel in Egypt, under Pharaoh and his people. Some of my brethren do not know who Pharaoh and the Egyptians were—I know it to be a fact, that some of them take the Egyptians to have been a gang of *devils,* not knowing any better, and that they (Egyptians) having got possession of the Lord's people, treated them *nearly* as cruel as *Christian Americans* do us, at the present day. For the information of such, I would only mention that the Egyptians, were Africans or coloured people, such as we are—some of them yellow and others dark—a mixture of Ethiopians and the natives of Egypt— about the same as you see the coloured people of the United States at the present day.—I say, I call your attention then, to the children of Jacob, while I point out particularly to you his son Joseph, among the rest, in Egypt.

"And Pharaoh, said unto Joseph, thou shalt be over my house, and according unto thy word shall all my people be ruled: only in the throne will I be greater than thou." [1]

"And Pharaoh said unto Joseph, see, I have set thee over all the land of Egypt." [2]

"And Pharaoh said unto Joseph, I am Pharaoh, and without thee shall no man lift up his hand or foot in all the land of Egypt." [3]

Now I appeal to heaven and to earth, and particularly to the American people themselves, who cease not to declare that our condition is not *hard,* and that we are comparatively satisfied to rest in wretchedness and misery, under them and their children. Not, indeed, to show me a coloured President, a Governor, a Legislator, a Senator, a Mayor, or an Attorney at the Bar.— But to show me a man of colour, who holds the low office of a Constable, or one who sits in a Juror Box, even on a case of one of his wretched brethren, throughout this great Republic!!— But let us pass Joseph the son of Israel a little farther in review, as he existed with that heathen nation.

"And Pharaoh called Joseph's name Zaphnathpaaneah; and he gave him to wife Asenath the daughter of Potipherah priest of On. And Joseph went out over all the land of Egypt." [4]

[1] See Genesis, chap. xli.
[2] xli. 44.
[3] xli. 44.
[4] xli. 45.

Compare the above, with the American institutions. Do they not institute laws to prohibit us from marrying among the whites? I would wish, candidly, however, before the Lord, to be understood, that I would not give a *pinch of snuff* to be married to any white person I ever saw in all the days of my life. And I do say it, that the black man, or man of colour, who will leave his own colour (provided he can get one, who is good for any thing) and marry a white woman, to be a double slave to her, just because she is *white*, ought to be treated by her as he surely will be, viz.: as a NIGER!!!! It is not, indeed, what I care about inter-marriages with the whites, which induced me to pass this subject in review; for the Lord knows, that there is a day coming when they will be glad enough to get into the company of the blacks, notwithstanding, we are, in this generation, levelled by them, almost on a level with the brute creation: and some of us they treat even worse than they do the brutes that perish. I only made this extract to show how much lower we are held, and how much more cruel we are treated by the Americans, than were the children of Jacob, by the Egyptians.—We will notice the sufferings of Israel some further, under *heathen Pharaoh*, compared with ours under the *enlightened Christians of America*.

"And Pharaoh spake unto Joseph, saying, thy father and thy brethren are come unto thee:"

"The land of Egypt is before thee: in the best of the land make thy father and brethren to dwell; in the land of Goshen let them dwell: and if thou knowest any men of activity among them, then make them rulers over my cattle." [5]

I ask those people who treat us so *well*, Oh! I ask them, where is the most barren spot of land which they have given unto us? Israel had the most fertile land in all Egypt. Need I mention the very notorious fact, that I have known a poor man of colour, who laboured night and day, to acquire a little money, and having acquired it, he vested it in a small piece of land, and got him a house erected thereon, and having paid for the whole, he moved his family into it, where he was suffered to remain but nine

[5] Genesis, chap. xlvii, 5, 6.

months, when he was cheated out of his property by a white man, and driven out of door! And is not this the case generally? Can a man of colour buy a piece of land and keep it peaceably? Will not some white man try to get it from him, even if it is in a *mud hole?* I need not comment any farther on a subject, which all, both black and white, will readily admit. But I must, really, observe that in this very city, when a man of colour dies, if he owned any real estate it most generally falls into the hands of some white person. The wife and children of the deceased may weep and lament if they please, but the estate will be kept snug enough by its white possessor.

But to prove farther that the condition of the Israelites was better under the Egyptians than ours is under the whites. I call upon the professing Christians, I call upon the philanthropist, I call upon the very tyrant himself, to show me a page of history, either sacred or profane, on which a verse can be found, which maintains, that the Egyptians heaped the *insupportable insult* upon the children of Israel, by telling them that they were not of the *human family.* Can the whites deny this charge? Have they not, after having reduced us to the deplorable condition of slaves under their feet, held us up as descending originally from the tribes of *Monkeys* or *Orang-Outangs?* O! my God! I appeal to every man of feeling—is not this insupportable? Is it not heaping the most gross insult upon our miseries, because they have got us under their feet and we cannot help ourselves? Oh! pity us we pray thee, Lord Jesus, Master.—Has Mr. Jefferson declared to the world, that we are inferior to the whites, both in the endowments of our bodies and of minds? It is indeed surprising, that a man of such great learning, combined with such excellent natural parts, should speak so of a set of men in chains. I do not know what to compare it to, unless, like putting one wild deer in an iron cage, where it will be secured, and hold another by the side of the same, then let it go, and expect the one in the cage to run as fast as the one at liberty. So far, my brethren, were the Egyptians from heaping these insults upon their slaves, that Pharaoh's daughter took Moses, a son of Israel for her own, as will appear by the following.

"And Pharaoh's daughter said unto her, [Moses' mother] take

this child away, and nurse it for me, and I will pay thee thy wages. And the woman took the child [Moses] and nursed it.

"And the child grew, and she brought him unto Pharaoh's daughter and he became her son. And she called his name Moses: and she said because I drew him out of the water." [6]

In all probability, Moses would have become Prince Regent to the throne, and no doubt, in process of time but he would have been seated on the throne of Egypt. But he had rather suffer shame, with the people of God, than to enjoy pleasures with that wicked people for a season. O! that the coloured people were long since of Moses' excellent disposition, instead of courting favour with, and telling news and lies to our *natural enemies,* against each other—aiding them to keep their hellish chains of slavery upon us. Would we not long before this time, have been respectable men, instead of such wretched victims of oppression as we are? Would they be able to drag our mothers, our fathers, our wives, our children and ourselves, around the world in chains and hand-cuffs as they do, to dig up gold and silver for them and theirs? This question, my brethren, I leave for you to digest; and may God Almighty force it home to your hearts. Remember that unless you are united, keeping your tongues within your teeth, you will be afraid to trust your secrets to each other, and thus perpetuate our miseries under the *Christians!!!!!* Addition. —Remember, also to lay humble at the feet of our Lord and Master Jesus Christ, with prayers and fastings. Let our enemies go on with their butcheries, and at once fill up their cup. Never make an attempt to gain our freedom or *natural right,* from under our cruel oppressors and murderers, until you see your way clear[7]—when that hour arrives and you move, be not afraid or dismayed; for be you assured that Jesus Christ the King of

[6] See Exodus, chap. ii. 9, 10.

[7] It is not to be understood here, that I mean for us to wait until God shall take us by the hair of our heads and drag us out of abject wretchedness and slavery, nor do I mean to convey the idea for us to wait until our enemies shall make preparations, and call us to seize those preparations, take it away from them, and put every thing before us to death, in order to gain our freedom which God has given us. For you must remember that we are men as well as they. God has been pleased to give us two eyes, two

heaven and of earth who is the God of justice and of armies, will surely go before you. And those enemies who have for hundreds of years stolen our *rights,* and kept us ignorant of Him and His divine worship, he will remove. Millions of whom, are this day, so ignorant and avaricious, that they cannot conceive how God can have an attribute of justice, and show mercy to us because it pleased Him to make us black—which colour, Mr. Jefferson calls unfortunate!!!!!! As though we are not as thankful to our God, for having made us as it pleased himself, as they (the whites) are for having made them white. They think because they hold us in their infernal chains of slavery, that we wish to be white, or of their color—but they are dreadfully deceived—we wish to be just as it pleased our Creator to have made us, and no avaricious and unmerciful wretches, have any business to make slaves of, or hold us in slavery. How would they like for us to make slaves of, and hold them in cruel slavery, and murder them as they do us?—But is Mr. Jefferson's assertions true? viz. "that it is unfortunate for us that our Creator has been pleased to make us *black.*" We will not take his say so, for the fact. The world will have an opportunity to see whether it is unfortunate for us, that our Creator *has made us* darker than the *whites.*

Fear not the number and education of our *enemies,* against whom we shall have to contend for our lawful right; guaranteed to us by our Maker; for why should we be afraid, when God is, and will continue (if we continue humble), to be on our side?

The man who would not fight under our Lord and Master Jesus Christ, in the glorious and heavenly cause of freedom and of God—to be delivered from the most wretched, abject and servile slavery, that ever a people was afflicted with since the foundation of the world, to the present day—ought to be kept with all of his children or family, in slavery, or in chains, to be butchered by his *cruel enemies.*

I saw a paragraph, a few years since, in a South Carolina

hands, two feet, and some sense in our heads as well as they. They have no more right to hold us in slavery than we have to hold them, we have just as much right, in the sight of God, to hold them and their children in slavery and wretchedness, as they have to hold us, and no more.

paper, which, speaking of the barbarity of the Turks, it said: "The Turks are the most barbarous people in the world—they treat the Greeks more like *brutes* than human beings." And in the same paper was an advertisement, which said: "Eight well built Virginia and Maryland *Negro fellows* and four *wenches* will positively be *sold* this day, *to the highest bidder!*" And what astonished me still more was, to see in this same *humane* paper!! the cuts of three men, with clubs and budgets on their backs, and an advertisement offering a considerable sum of money for their apprehension and delivery. I declare, it is really so amusing to hear the Southerners and Westerners of this country talk about *barbarity,* that it is positively, enough to make a man *smile.*

The sufferings of the Helots among the Spartans, were some-what severe, it is true, but to say that theirs were as severe as ours among the Americans, I do most strenuously deny—for in-stance, can any man show me an article on a page of ancient history which specifies, that, the Spartans chained, and hand-cuffed the Helots, and dragged them from their wives and children, children from their parents, mothers from their suckling babes, wives from their husbands, driving them from one end of the country to the other? Notice the Spartans were heathens, who lived long before our Divine Master made his appearance in the flesh.

Can Christian Americans deny these barbarous cruelties? Have you not, Americans, having subjected us under you, added to these miseries, by insulting us in telling us to our face, because we are helpless, that we are not of the human family? I ask you, O! Americans, I ask you, in the name of the Lord, can you deny these charges? Some perhaps may deny, by saying, that they never thought or said that we were not men. But do not actions speak louder than *words?*—have they not made provisions for the Greeks, and Irish? Nations who have never done the least thing for them, while *we,* who have enriched their country with our blood and tears—have dug up gold and silver for them and their children, from generation to generation, and are in more miseries than any other people under heaven, are not seen, but by com-paratively, a handful of the American people? There are indeed, more ways to kill a dog, besides choking it to death with butter.

Further—The Spartans or Lacedemonians, had some frivolous pretext, for enslaving the Helots, for they (Helots) while being free inhabitants of Sparta, stirred up an intestine commotion, and were, by the Spartans subdued, and made prisoners of war. Consequently they and their children were condemned to perpetual slavery.[8]

I have been for years troubling the pages of historians, to find out what our fathers have done to the *white Christians of America,* to merit such condign punishment as they have inflicted on them, and do continue to inflict on us their children. But I must aver, that my researches have hitherto been to no effect. I have therefore, come to the immoveable conclusion, that they (Americans) have, and do continue to punish us for nothing else, but for enriching them and their country. For I cannot conceive of any thing else. Nor will I ever believe otherwise, until the Lord shall convince me.

The world knows, that slavery as it existed among the Romans (which was the primary cause of their destruction) was, comparatively speaking, no more than a *cypher,* when compared with ours under the Americans. Indeed I should not have noticed the Roman slaves, had not the very learned and penetrating Mr. Jefferson said, "when a master was murdered, all his slaves in the same house, or within hearing, were condemned to death." [9] —Here let me ask Mr. Jefferson (but he is gone to answer at the bar of God, for the deeds done in his body while living), I therefore ask the whole American people, had I not rather die, or be put to death, than to be a slave to any tyrant, who takes not only my own, but my wife and children's lives by the inches? Yea, would I meet death with avidity far! far!! in preference to such *servile submission* to the murderous hands of tyrants. Mr. Jefferson's very severe remarks on us have been so extensively argued upon by men whose attainments in literature, I shall never be able to reach, that I would not have meddled with it, were it not to solicit each of my brethren, who has the spirit of a man, to buy a copy of Mr. Jefferson's "Notes on Virginia," and

[8] See Dr. Goldsmith's History of Greece—page 9. See also, Plutarch's Lives. The Helots subdued by Agis, king of *Sparta.*

[9] See his Notes on Virginia, page 210.

put it in the hand of his son. For let no one of us suppose that the refutations which have been written by our white friends are enough—they are *whites*—we are *blacks*.

We, and the world wish to see the charges of Mr. Jefferson refuted by the black *themselves*, according to their chance; for we must remember that what the whites have written respecting this subject, is other men's labours, and did not emanate from the blacks. I know well, that there are some talents and learning among the coloured people of this country, which we have not a chance to develop, in consequence of oppression; but our oppression ought not to hinder us from acquiring all we can. For we will have a chance to develop them by and by. God will not suffer us, always to be oppressed. Our sufferings will come to an *end,* in spite of all the Americans this side of *eternity.* Then we will want all the learning and talents among ourselves, and perhaps more, to govern ourselves.—"Every dog must have its day," the American's is coming to an end.

But let us review Mr. Jefferson's remarks respecting us some further. Comparing our miserable fathers, with the learned philosophers of Greece, he says: "Yet notwithstanding these and other discouraging circumstances among the Romans, their slaves were often their rarest artists. They excelled too, in science, insomuch as to be usually employed as tutors to their master's children; Epictetus, Terence and Phaedrus, were slaves,— but they were of the race of whites. It is not their *condition* then, but *nature,* which has produced the distinction." [10] See this, my brethren!! Do you believe that this assertion is swallowed by millions of the whites? Do you know that Mr. Jefferson was one of as great characters as ever lived among the whites? See his writings for the world, and public labours for the United States of America. Do you believe that the assertions of such a man, will pass away into oblivion unobserved by this people and the world? If you do you are much mistaken—See how the American people treat us—have we souls in our bodies? Are we men who have any spirits at all? I know that there are many *swell-bellied* fellows among us, whose greatest object is to fill their stomachs. Such I do not mean—I am after those who know and feel, that

[10] See his Notes on Virginia, page 211.

we are MEN, as well as other people; to them, I say, that unless we try to refute Mr. Jefferson's arguments respecting us, we will only establish them.

But the slaves among the Romans. Every body who has read history, knows, that as soon as a slave among the Romans obtained his freedom, he could rise to the greatest eminence in the State, and there was no law instituted to hinder a slave from buying his freedom. Have not the Americans instituted laws to hinder us from obtaining our freedom? Do any deny this charge? Read the laws of Virginia, North Carolina, &c. Further: have not the Americans instituted laws to prohibit a man of colour from obtaining and holding any office whatever, under the government of the United States of America? Now, Mr. Jefferson tells us, that our condition is not so hard, as the slaves were under the Romans!!!!!!

It is time for me to bring this article to a close. But before I close it, I must observe to my brethren that at the close of the first Revolution in this country, with Great Britain, there were but thirteen States in the Union; now there are twenty-four, most of which are slave-holding States, and the whites are dragging us around in chains and in handcuffs, to their new States and Territories to work their mines and farms, to enrich them and their children—and millions of them believing firmly that we being a little darker than they, were made by our Creator to be an inheritance to them and their children for ever—the same as a parcel of *brutes*.

Are we MEN!!—I ask you, O my brethren! are we *MEN?* Did our Creator make us to be slaves to dust and ashes like ourselves? Are they not dying worms as well as we? Have they not to make their appearance before the tribunal of Heaven, to answer for the deeds done in the body, as well as we? Have we any other Master but Jesus Christ alone? Is he not their Master as well as ours?—What right then, have we to obey and call any other Master, but Himself? How we could be so *submissive* to a gang of men, whom we cannot tell whether they are *as good* as ourselves or not, I never could conceive. However, this is shut up with the Lord, and we cannot precisely tell—but I declare, we judge men by their works.

The whites have always been an unjust, jealous, unmerciful,

avaricious and blood-thirsty set of beings, always seeking after power and authority.—We view them all over the confederacy of Greece, where they were first known to be any thing (in consequence of education), we see them there, cutting each other's throats—trying to subject each other to wretchedness and misery —to effect which, they used all kinds of deceitful, unfair, and unmerciful means. We view them next in Rome, where the spirit of tyranny and deceit raged still higher. We view them in Gaul, Spain, and in Britain.—In fine, we view them all over Europe, together with what were scattered about in Asia and Africa, as heathens, and we see them acting more like devils than accountable men. But some may ask, did not the blacks of Africa, and the mulattoes of Asia, go on in the same way as did the whites of Europe. I answer, no—they never were half so avaricious, deceitful and unmerciful as the whites, according to their knowledge.

But we will leave the whites or Europeans as heathens, and take a view of them as Christians, in which capacity we see them as cruel, if not more so than ever. In fact, take them as a body, they are ten times more cruel, avaricious and unmerciful than ever they were; for while they were heathens, they were bad enough it is true, but it is positively a fact that they were not quite so audacious as to go and take vessel loads of men, women and children, and in cold blood, and through devilishness, throw them into the sea, and murder them in all kind of ways. While they were heathens, they were too ignorant for such barbarity. But being Christians, enlightened and sensible, they are completely prepared for such hellish cruelties.

Now suppose God were to give them more sense, what would they do? If it were possible, would they not *dethrone* Jehovah and seat themselves upon his throne? I therefore, in the name and fear of the Lord God of Heaven and of earth, divested of prejudice either on the side of my colour or that of the whites, advance my suspicion of them, whether they are *as good by nature* as we are or not. Their actions, since they were known as a people, have been the reverse, I do indeed suspect them, but this, as I before observed, is shut up with the Lord, we cannot exactly tell, it will be proved in succeeding generations. —The whites have had the essence of the gospel as it was preached by my master and his apostles—the Ethiopians have not, who are to have it in its meridian splendor—the Lord will give it to them to their satisfaction. I hope and pray my God, that they will make good use of it, that it may be well with them.[11]

Article II.

OUR WRETCHEDNESS IN CONSEQUENCE OF IGNORANCE

Ignorance, my brethren, is a mist, low down into the very dark and almost impenetrable abyss in which, our fathers for many centuries have been plunged. The Christians, and enlightened of Europe, and some of Asia, seeing the ignorance and consequent degradation of our fathers, instead of trying to enlighten them, by teaching them that religion and light with which God had blessed them, they have plunged them into wretchedness ten thousand times more intolerable, than if they had left them entirely to the Lord, and to add to their miseries, deep down into which they have plunged them tell them, that they are an *inferior* and *distinct race* of beings, which they will be glad enough to recall and swallow by and by. Fortune and misfortune, two inseparable companions, lay rolled up in the wheel of events, which have from the creation of the world, and will continue to take place among men until God shall dash worlds together.

[11] It is my solemn belief, that if ever the world becomes Christianized, (which must certainly take place before long) it will be through the means, under God of the *Blacks*, who are now held in wretchedness, and degradation, by the white *Christians* of the world, who before they learn to do justice to us before our Maker—and be reconciled to us, and reconcile us to them, and by that means have clear consciences before God and man.— Send out Missionaries to convert the Heathens, many of whom after they cease to worship gods, which neither see nor hear, become ten times more the children of Hell, than ever they were, why what is the reason? Why the reason is obvious, they must learn to do justice at home, before they go into distant lands, to display their charity, Christianity, and benevolence; when they learn to do justice, God will accept their offering (no man may think that I am against Missionaries for I am not, my object is to see justice done at home, before we go to convert the heathens).

When we take a retrospective view of the arts and sciences—
the wise legislators—the Pyramids, and other magnificent build-
ings—the turning of the channel of the river Nile, by the sons
of Africa or of Ham, among whom learning originated, and was
carried thence into Greece, where it was improved upon and
refined. Thence among the Romans, and all over the then enlightened parts of the world, and it has been enlightening the
dark and benighted minds of men from then, down to this day.
I say, when I view retrospectively, the renown of that once
mighty people, the children of our great progenitor I am indeed
cheered. Yea further, when I view that mighty son of Africa,
HANNIBAL, one of the greatest generals of antiquity, who
defeated and cut off so many thousands of the white Romans
or murderers, and who carried his victorious arms, to the very
gate of Rome, and I give it as my candid opinion, that had
Carthage been well united and had given him good support,
he would have carried that cruel and barbarous city by storm.
But they were dis-united, as the coloured people are now, in
the United States of America, the reason our natural enemies
are enabled to keep their feet on our throats.

Beloved brethren—here let me tell you, and believe it, that
the Lord our God, as true as he sits on his throne in heaven, and
as true as our Saviour died to redeem the world, will give
you a Hannibal, and when the Lord shall have raised him
up, and given him to you for your possession, O my suffering
brethren! remember the divisions and consequent sufferings
of *Carthage* and of *Hayti*. Read the history particularly of
Hayti, and see how they were butchered by the whites, and
do you take warning. The person whom God shall give you,
give him your support and let him go his length, and behold in
him the salvation of your God. God will indeed, deliver you
through him from your deplorable and wretched condition under the Christians of America. I charge you this day before my
God to lay no obstacle in his way, but let him go.

The whites want slaves, and want us for their slaves, but
some of them will curse the day they ever saw us. As true as
the sun ever shone in its meridian splendor, my colour will root
some of them out of the very face of the earth. They shall have

enough of making slaves of, and butchering, and murdering us in the manner which they have. No doubt some may say that I write with a bad spirit, and that I being a black, wish these things to occur. Whether I write with a bad or a good spirit, I say if these things do not occur in their proper time, it is because of the world in which we live does not exist, and we are deceived with regard to its existence.—It is immaterial however to me, who believe, or who refuse—though I should like to see the whites repent peradventure God may have mercy on them, some however, have gone so far that their cup must be filled.

But what need have I to refer to antiquity, when Hayti, the glory of the blacks and terror of tyrants, is enough to convince the most avaricious and stupid of wretches—which is at this time, and I am sorry to say it, plagued with that scourge of nations, the Catholic religion; but I hope and pray God that she may yet rid herself of it, and adopt in its stead the Protestant faith; also, I hope that she may keep peace within her borders and be united, keeping a strict look out for tyrants, for if they get the least chance to injure her, they will avail themselves of it, as true as the Lord lives in heaven. But one thing which gives me joy is, that they are men who would be cut off to a man, before they would yield to the combined forces of the whole world—in fact, if the whole world was combined against them, it could not do any thing with them, unless the Lord delivers them up.

Ignorance and treachery one against the other—a grovelling servile and abject submission to the lash of tyrants, we see plainly, my brethren, are not the natural elements of the blacks, as the Americans try to make us believe; but these are misfortunes which God has suffered our fathers to be enveloped in for many ages, no doubt in consequence of their disobedience to their maker, and which do, indeed, reign at this time among us, almost to the destruction of all other principles: for I must truly say, that ignorance, the mother of treachery and deceit, gnaws into our very vitals. Ignorance, as it now exists among us, produces a state of things, Oh my Lord! too horrible to present to the world. Any man who is curious to see the full force of ignorance developed among the coloured people of the United States of America, has only to go into the southern and western states of this confederacy, where, if he is not a tyrant, but has the feelings of a human being, who can feel for a fellow creature, he may see enough to make his very heart bleed! He may see there, a son take his mother, who bore almost the pains of death to give him birth, and by the command of a tyrant, strip her as naked as she came into the world, and apply the cow-hide to her, until she falls a victim to death in the road! He may see a husband take his dear wife, not unfrequently in a pregnant state, and perhaps far advanced, and beat her for an unmerciful wretch, until his infant falls a lifeless lump at her feet!

Can the Americans escape God Almighty? If they do, can he be to us a God of Justice? God is just, and I know it—for he has convinced me to my satisfaction—I cannot doubt him. My observer may see fathers beating their sons, mothers their daughters, and children their parents, all to pacify the passions of unrelenting tyrants. He may also, see them telling news and lies, making mischief one upon another. These are some of the productions of ignorance, which he will see practised among my dear brethren, who are held in unjust slavery and wretchedness, by avaricious and unmerciful tyrants, to whom, and their hellish deeds, I would suffer my life to be taken before I would submit. And when my curious observer comes to take notice of those who are said to be free (which assertion I deny), and who are making some frivolous pretensions to common sense, he will see that branch of ignorance among the slaves assuming a more cunning and deceitful course of procedure.—He may see some of my brethren in league with tyrants, selling their own brethren into *hell upon earth,* not dissimilar to the exhibitions in Africa, but in a more secret, servile and abject manner. Oh Heaven! I am full!!! I can hardly move my pen!!! and as I expect some will try to put me to death, to strike terror into others, and to obliterate from their minds the notion of freedom, so as to keep my brethren the more secure in wretchedness, where they will be permitted to stay but a short time (whether tyrants believe it or not)—I shall give the world a development of facts, which are already witnessed in the courts of heaven. My observer may see some of those ignorant and treacherous creatures (coloured people) sneaking about in the large cities, endeavouring to find out all strange coloured people, where they work and where they reside, asking them questions, and trying to ascertain whether they are runaways or not, telling them, at the same time, that they always have been, are, and always will be, friends to their brethren; and, perhaps, that they themselves are absconders, and a thousand such treacherous lies to get the better information of the more ignorant!!! There have been and are at this day in Boston, New-York, Philadelphia, and Baltimore, coloured men, who are in league with tyrants, and who receive a great portion of their daily bread, of the moneys which they acquire from the blood and tears of their more miserable brethren, whom they scandalously delivered into the hands of our *natural enemies!!!!!!*

To show the force of degraded ignorance and deceit among us some farther, I will give here an extract from a paragraph, which may be found in the Columbian Centinel of this city, for September 9, 1829, on the first page of which, the curious may find an article, headed

AFFRAY AND MURDER

Portsmouth, (Ohio) Aug. 22, 1829

A most shocking outrage was committed in Kentucky, about eight miles from this place, on 14th inst. A negro driver, by the name of Gordon, who had purchased in Maryland about sixty negroes, was taking them, assisted by an associate named Allen, and the wagoner who conveyed the baggage, to the Mississippi. The men were handcuffed and chained together, in the usual manner for driving those poor wretches, while the women and children were suffered to proceed without incumbrance. It appears that, by means of a file the negroes, unobserved, had succeeded in separating the iron which bound their hands, in such a way as to be able to throw them off at any moment. About 8 o'clock in the morning, while proceeding on the state road leading from Greenup to Vanceburg, two of them dropped their shackles and commenced a fight, when the wagoner (Petit) rushed in with his whip to compel them to desist. At this moment, every negro was found to be perfectly at liberty; and one of them seizing a club, gave Petit a violent blow on the head, and laid him dead at his feet; and Allen, who came to his assistance, met a similar fate, from the contents of a pistol fired by another of the gang. Gordon was then attacked, seized and held by one of the negroes, whilst another fired twice at him with a pistol, the ball of which each time grazed his head, but not proving effectual, he was beaten with clubs, and left for dead. They then commenced pillaging the wagon, and with an axe split open the trunk of Gordon, and rifled it of the money, about $2,400. Sixteen of the negroes then took to the woods; Gordon, in the mean time, not being materially injured, was enabled, by the assistance of one of the women, to mount his horse and flee; pursued, however, by one of the gang on another horse, with a drawn pistol; fortunately he escaped with his life barely, arriving at a plantation, as the negro came in sight; who then turned about and retreated.

The neighbourhood was immediately rallied, and a hot pursuit given—which, we understand, has resulted in the capture of the whole gang and the recovery of the greatest part of the money. Seven of the negro men and one woman, it is said were engaged in the murders, and will be brought to trial at the next court in Greenupsburg.

Here, my brethren, I want you to notice particularly in the above article, the *ignorant* and *deceitful actions* of this coloured woman. I beg you to view it candidly, as for ETERNITY!!!! Here a *notorious wretch,* with two other confederates had SIXTY of them in a gang, driving them like *brutes*—the men all in chains and hand-cuffs, and by the help of God they got their chains and hand-cuffs thrown off, and caught two of the wretches and put them to death, and beat the other until they thought he was dead, and left him for dead; however, he deceived them, and rising from the ground, this *servile woman* helped him upon his horse, and he made his escape.

Brethren, what do you think of this? Was it the natural *fine feelings* of this woman, to save such a wretch alive? I know that the blacks, take them half enlightened and ignorant, are more humane and merciful than the most enlightened and refined European that can be found in all the earth. Let no one say that I assert this because I am prejudiced on the side of my colour, and against the whites or Europeans. For what I write, I do it candidly, for my God and the good of both parties: Natural observations have taught me these things; there is a solemn awe in the hearts of the blacks, as it respects *murdering* men:[12] whereas the whites (though they are great cowards), where they have the advantage, or think that there are any prospects of getting it, they murder all before them, in order to subject men to wretchedness and degradation under them. This is the natural result of pride and avarice. But I declare, the actions of this black woman are really insupportable. For my own part, I cannot think it was any thing but servile deceit, combined with the most gross ignorance: for we must remember that *humanity, kindness* and the *fear of the Lord,* does not consist in protecting *devils.*

Here is a set of wretches, who had SIXTY of them in a gang, driving them around the country like *brutes,* to dig up gold and silver for them (which they will get enough of yet). Should the lives of such creatures be spared? Are God and Mammon in league? What has the Lord to do with a gang of desperate wretches, who go *sneaking about the country like robbers—* light upon his people wherever they can get a chance, binding them with chains and hand-cuffs, beat and murder them as they would *rattle-snakes?* Are they not the Lord's enemies? Ought they not to be destroyed? Any person who will save such wretches from destruction, is fighting against the Lord, and will receive his just recompense. The black men acted like *block-heads.* Why did they not make sure of the wretch? He would have made sure of them, if he could. It is just the way with black men—eight white men can frighten fifty of them; whereas, if you can only get courage into the blacks, I do declare it, that

[12] Which is the reason the whites take the advantage of us.

one good black man can put to death six white men; and I give it as a fact, let twelve black men get well armed for battle, and they will kill and put to flight fifty whites.—The reason is, the blacks, once you get them started, they glory in death. The whites have had us under them for more than three centuries, murdering, and treating us like brutes; and, as Mr. Jefferson wisely said, they have never *found us out*—they do not know, indeed, that there is an unconquerable disposition in the breasts of the blacks, which, when it is fully awakened and put in motion, will be subdued, only with the destruction of the animal existence. Get the blacks started, and if you do not have a gang of tigers and lions to deal with, I am a deceiver of the blacks and of the whites.

How sixty of them could let that wretch escape unkilled, I cannot conceive—they will have to suffer as much for the two whom, they secured, as if they had put one hundred to death: If you commence, make sure work—do not trifle, for they will not trifle with you—they want us for their slaves, and think nothing of murdering us in order to subject us to that wretched condition—therefore, if there is an *attempt* made by us, kill or be killed. Now, I ask you, had you not rather be killed than to be a slave to a tyrant, who takes the life of your mother, wife, and dear little children? Look upon your mother, wife and children, and answer God Almighty! and believe this, that it is no more harm for you to kill a man, who is trying to kill you, than it is for you to take a drink of water when thirsty; in fact, the man who will stand still and let another murder him, is worse than an infidel, and, if he has common sense, ought not to be pitied.

The actions of this deceitful and ignorant coloured woman, in saving the life of a desperate wretch, whose avaricious and cruel object was to drive her, and her companions in miseries, through the country like cattle, to make his fortune on their carcasses, are but too much like that of thousands of our brethren in these states: if any thing is whispered by one, which has any allusion to the melioration of their dreadful condition, they run and tell tyrants, that they may be enabled to keep them the longer in wretchedness and miseries. Oh! coloured people of these United States, I ask you, in the name of that God who made us, have we, in consequence of oppression, nearly lost the spirit of man, and, in no very trifling degree, adopted that of brutes? Do you answer, no?—I ask you, then, what set of men can you point me to, in all the world, who are so abjectly employed by their oppressors, as we are by our *natural enemies?*

How can, Oh! how can those enemies but say that we and our children are not of the HUMAN FAMILY, but were made by our Creator to be an inheritance to them and theirs for ever? How can the slave-holders but say that they can bribe the best coloured person in the country, to sell his brethren for a trifling sum of money, and take that atrocity to confirm them in their avaricious opinion, that we were made to be slaves to them and their children? How could Mr. Jefferson but say,[13] "I advance it therefore as a suspicion only, that the blacks, whether originally a distinct race, or made distinct by time and circumstances, are *inferior* to the whites in the endowments both of body and mind?" "It," says he, "is not against experience to suppose, that different species of the same genus, or varieties of the same species, may possess different qualifications." [Here, my brethren, listen to him.] "Will not a lover of natural history, then, one who views the gradations in all the races of *animals* with the eye of philosophy, excuse an effort to keep those in the department of MAN as *distinct* as nature has formed them?"— I hope you will try to find out the meaning of this verse—its widest sense and all its bearings: whether you do or not, remember the whites do. This very verse, brethren, having emanated from Mr. Jefferson, a much greater philosopher the world never afforded, has in truth injured us more, and has been as great a barrier to our emancipation as any thing that has ever been advanced against us. I hope you will not let it pass unnoticed. He goes on further, and says: "This *unfortunate* difference of colour, and *perhaps of faculty,* is a powerful obstacle to the emancipation of these people. Many of their advocates, while they wish to vindicate the liberty of human nature, are anxious also to preserve its *dignity* and *beauty.* Some of these, embarrassed by

[13] See his Notes on Virginia, page 213.

the question, 'What further is to be done with them?' join themselves in opposition with those who are actuated by sordid
avarice only."

Now I ask you candidly, my suffering brethren in time, who
are candidates for the eternal worlds, how could Mr. Jefferson
but have given the world these remarks respecting us, when
we are so submissive to them, and so much servile deceit pre-
vail among ourselves—when we so *meanly* submit to their murderous lashes, to which neither the Indians nor any other people under Heaven would submit? No, they would die to a man,
before they would suffer such things from men who are no
better than themselves, and *perhaps not so good.* Yes, how can
our friends but be embarrassed, as Mr. Jefferson says, by the
question, "What further is to be done with these people?" For
while they are working for our emancipation, we are, by our
treachery, wickedness and deceit, working against ourselves and
our children—helping ours, and the enemies of God, to keep us
and our dear little children in their infernal chains of slavery!!!
Indeed, our friends cannot but relapse and join themselves
"with those who are actuated by *sordid avarice* only!!!"

For my own part, I am glad Mr. Jefferson has advanced his
positions for your sake; for you will either have to contradict
or confirm him by your own actions, and not by what our friends
have said or done for us; for those things are other men's labours,
and do not satisfy the Americans, who are waiting for us to
prove to them ourselves, that we are MEN, before they will be
willing to admit the fact; for I pledge you my sacred word of
honour, that Mr. Jefferson's remarks respecting us, have sunk
deep into the hearts of millions of the whites, and never will
be removed this side of eternity.—For how can they, when we
are confirming him every day, by our *groveling submissions* and
treachery? I aver, that when I look over these United States of
America, and the world, and see the ignorant deceptions and
consequent wretchedness of my brethren, I am brought ofttimes
solemnly to a stand, and in the midst of my reflections I exclaim
to my God, "Lord didst thou make us to be slaves to our brethren, the whites?" But when I reflect that God is just, and that
millions of my wretched brethren would meet death with glory

—yea, more, would plunge into the very mouths of cannons and be torn into particles as minute as the atoms which compose the elements of the earth, in preference to a mean submission to the lash of tyrants, I am with streaming eyes, compelled to shrink back into nothingness before my Maker, and exclaim again, thy will be done, O Lord God Almighty.

Men of colour, who are also of sense, for you particularly is my APPEAL designed. Our more ignorant brethren are not able to penetrate its value. I call upon you therefore to cast your eyes upon the wretchedness of your brethren, and to do your utmost to enlighten them—*go to work and enlighten your brethren!*—Let the Lord see you doing what you can to rescue them and your selves from degradation. Do any of you say that you and your family are free and happy, and what have you to do with the wretched slaves and other people? So can I say, for I enjoy as much freedom as any of you, if I am not quite as well off as the best of you. Look into our freedom and happiness, and see of what kind they are composed!! They are of the very lowest kind—they are the very *dregs!*—they are the most servile and abject kind, that ever a people was in possession of! If any of you wish to know how FREE you are, let one of you start and go through the southern and western States of this country, and unless you travel as a slave to a white man (a servant is a slave to the man whom he serves) or have your free papers (which if you are not careful they will get from you), if they do not take you up and put you in jail, and if you cannot give good evidence of your freedom, sell you into eternal slavery, I am not a living man: or any man of colour, immaterial who he is, or where he came from, if he is not *the fourth from the negro race!!* (as we are called) the white Christians of America will serve him the same they will sink him into wretchedness and degradation for ever while he lives. And yet some of you have the hardihood to say that you are free and happy! May God have mercy on your freedom and happiness!!

I met a coloured man in the street a short time since, with a string of boots on his shoulders; we fell into conversation, and in course of which, I said to him, what a miserable set of people we are! He asked, why?—Said I, we are so subjected under the

whites, that we cannot obtain the comforts of life, but by cleaning their boots and shoes, old clothes, waiting on them, shaving
them &c. Said he (with the boots on his shoulders), "I am completely happy!!! I never want to live any better or happier than
when I can get a plenty of boots and shoes to clean!!!" Oh! how
can those who are actuated by avarice only, but think, that our
Creator made us to be an inheritance to them for ever, when
they see that our greatest glory is centered in such mean and
low objects? Understand me, brethren, I do not mean to speak
against the occupations by which we acquire enough and sometimes scarcely that, to render ourselves and families comfortable
through life. I am subjected to the same inconvenience, as you
all.—My objections are, to our *glorying* and being *happy* in such
low employments; for if we are men, we ought to be thankful
to the Lord for the past, and for the future. Be looking forward
with thankful hearts to higher attainments than *wielding the
razor* and *cleaning boots and shoes*. The man whose aspirations
are not *above,* and even *below* these, is indeed, ignorant and
wretched enough.

I advance it therefore to you, not as a *problematical,* but as
an unshaken and for ever immoveable *fact,* that your full glory
and happiness, as well as all other coloured people under
Heaven, shall never be fully consummated, but with the *entire
emancipation of your enslaved brethren all over the world.* You
may therefore, go to work and do what you can to rescue, or
join in with tyrants to oppress them and yourselves, until the
Lord shall come upon you all like a thief in the night. For I
believe it is the will of the Lord that our greatest happiness
shall consist in working for the salvation of our whole body.
When this is accomplished a burst of glory will shine upon
you, which will indeed astonish you and the world. Do any
of you say this never will be done? I assure you that God
will accomplish it—if nothing else will answer, he will hurl
tyrants and devils into *atoms* and make way for his people.
But O my brethren! I say unto you again, you must go to work
and prepare the way of the Lord.

There is a great work for you to do, as trifling as some of
you may think of it. You have to prove to the Americans and

the world, that we are MEN, and not *brutes,* as we have been
represented, and by millions treated. Remember, to let the
aim of your labours among your brethren, and particularly the
youths, be the dissemination of education and religion.[14] It is
lamentable, that many of our children go to school, from four
until they are eight or ten, and sometimes fifteen years of age,
and leave school knowing but a little more about the grammar
of their language than a horse does about handling a musket—
and not a few of them are really so ignorant, that they are unable to answer a person correctly, general questions in geography, and to hear them read, would only be to disgust a man
who has a taste for reading; which, to do well, as trifling as
it may appear to some (to the ignorant in particular), is a great
part of learning.

Some few of them, may make out to scribble tolerably well,
over a half sheet of paper, which I believe has hitherto been
a powerful obstacle in our way, to keep us from acquiring
knowledge. An ignorant father, who knows no more than what
nature has taught him, together with what little he acquires
by the senses of hearing and seeing, finding his son able to
write a neat hand, sets it down for granted that he has as good
learning as any body; the young, ignorant gump, hearing his
father or mother, who perhaps may be ten times more ignorant,
in point of literature, than himself, extolling his learning, struts
about, in the full assurance, that his attainments in literature
are sufficient to take him through the world, when, in fact, he
has scarcely any learning at all!!!!

I promiscuously fell in conversation once, with an elderly
coloured man on the topics of education, and of the great
prevalency of ignorance among us: Said he, "I know that our

[14] Never mind what the ignorant ones among us may say, many of whom
when you speak to them for their good, and try to enlighten their minds,
laugh at you, and perhaps tell you plump to your face, that they want no
instruction from you or any other Niger, and all such aggravating language.
Now if you are a man of understanding and sound sense, I conjure you in
the name of the Lord, and of all that is good, to impute their actions to
ignorance, and wink at their follies, and do your very best to get around
them some way or other, for remember they are your brethren; and I
declare to you that it is for your interests to teach and enlighten them.

people are very ignorant but my son has a good education: I spent a great deal of money on his education: he can write as well as any white man, and I assure you that no one can fool him," &c. Said I, what else can your son do, besides writing a good hand? Can he post a set of books in a mercantile manner? Can he write a neat piece of composition in prose or in verse? To these interrogations he answered in the negative. Said I, did your son learn, while he was at school, the width and depth of English Grammar? To which he also replied in the negative, telling me his son did not learn those things. Your son, said I, then has hardly any learning at all—he is almost as ignorant, and more so, than many of those who never went to school one day in all their lives. My friend got a little put out, and so walking off, said that his son could write as well as any white man. Most of the coloured people, when they speak of the education of one among us who can write a neat hand, and who perhaps knows nothing but to scribble and puff pretty fair on a small scrap of paper, immaterial whether his words are grammatical, or spelt correctly, or not; if it only looks beautiful, they say he has as good an education as any white man—he can write as well as any white man, &c. The poor, ignorant creature, hearing, this, he is ashamed, forever after, to let any person see him humbling himself to another for knowledge but going about trying to deceive those who are more ignorant than himself, he at last falls an ignorant victim to death in wretchedness.

I pray that the Lord may undeceive my ignorant brethren, and permit them to throw away pretensions, and seek after the substance of learning. I would crawl on my hands and knees through mud and mire, to the feet of a learned man, where I would sit and humbly supplicate him to instil into me, that which neither devils nor tyrants could remove, only with my life—for coloured people to acquire learning in this country, make tyrants quake and tremble on their sandy foundation. Why, what is the matter? Why, they know that their infernal deeds of cruelty will be made known to the world. Do you suppose one man of good sense and learning would submit himself, his father, mother, wife and children, to be slaves to a wretched man like himself, who, instead of compensating him for his labours, chains, hand-cuffs and beats him and family almost to death, leaving life enough in them, however, to work for, and call him master? No! no! he would cut his devilish throat from ear to ear, and well do slave-holders know it. The bare name of educating the coloured people, scares our cruel oppressors almost to death. But if they do not have enough to be frightened for yet, it will be, because they can always keep us ignorant, and because God approbates their cruelties, with which they have been for centuries murdering us. The whites shall have enough of the blacks, yet, as true as God sits on his throne in Heaven.

Some of our brethren are so very full of learning, that you cannot mention any thing to them which they do not know better than yourself!!—nothing is strange to them!!—they knew every thing years ago!—if any thing should be mentioned in company where they are, immaterial how important it is respecting us or the world, if they had not divulged it; they make light of it, and affect to have known it long before it was mentioned and try to make all in the room, or wherever you may be, believe that your conversation is nothing!!—not worth hearing! All this is the result of ignorance and ill-breeding; for a man of good-breeding, sense and penetration, if he had heard a subject told twenty times over, and should happen to be in company where one should commence telling it again, he would wait with patience on its narrator, and see if he would tell it as it was told in his presence before—paying the most strict attention to what is said, to see if any more light will be thrown on the subject: for all men are not gifted alike in telling, or even hearing the most simple narration. These ignorant, vicious, and wretched men, contribute almost as much injury to our body as tyrants themselves, by doing so much for the promotion of ignorance amongst us; for they, making such pretensions to knowledge, such of our youth as are seeking after knowledge, and can get access to them, take them as criterions to go by, who will lead them into a channel, where, unless the Lord blesses them with the privilege of seeing their folly, they will be irretrievably lost forever, while in time!!!

I must close this article by relating the very heart-rending fact, that I have examined school-boys and young men of colour in different parts of the country, in the most simple parts of Murray's English Grammar, and not more than one in thirty was able to give a correct answer to my interrogations. If anyone contradicts me, let him step out of his door into the streets of Boston, New-York, Philadelphia, or Baltimore (no use to mention any other, for the Christians are too charitable further south or west!)—I say, let him who disputes me, step out of his door into the streets of either of those four cities, and promiscuously collect one hundred school-boys, or young men of colour, *who have been to school,* and who are considered by the coloured people to have received an excellent education, because, perhaps, some of them can write a good hand, but who, notwithstanding their neat writing, may be almost as ignorant, in comparison, as a horse.—And, I say it, he will hardly find (in this enlightened day, and in the midst of this *charitable* people) five in one hundred, who, are able to correct the false grammar of their language.—The cause of this almost universal ignorance among us, I appeal to our school-masters to declare.

Here is a fact, which I this very minute take from the mouth of a young coloured man, who has been to school in this state (Massachusetts) nearly nine years, and who knows grammar this day, *nearly* as well as he did the day he first entered the school-house, under a white master. This young man says: "My master would never allow me to study grammar." I asked him, why? "The school committee," said he "forbid the coloured children learning grammar—they would not allow any but the white children to study grammar." It is a notorious fact, that the major part of the white Americans, have, ever since we have been among them, tried to keep us ignorant, and make us believe that God made us and our children to be slaves to them and theirs. *Oh! my God, have mercy on Christian Americans!!!*

Article III.

OUR WRETCHEDNESS IN CONSEQUENCE OF THE PREACHERS OF THE RELIGION OF JESUS CHRIST

Religion, my brethren, is a substance of deep consideration among all nations of the earth. The Pagans have a kind, as well as the Mahometans, the Jews and the Christians. But pure and undefiled religion, such as was preached by Jesus Christ and his apostles, is hard to be found in all the earth. God, through his instrument, Moses, handed a dispensation of his Divine will, to the children of Israel after they had left Egypt for the land of Canaan or of Promise, who through hypocrisy, oppression and unbelief, departed from the faith.—He then, by his apostles, handed a dispensation of his, together with the will of Jesus Christ, to the Europeans in Europe, who, in open violation of which, have made *merchandise* of us, and it does appear as though they take this very dispensation to aid them in their *infernal* depredations upon us. Indeed, the way in which religion was and is conducted by the Europeans and their descendants, one might believe it was a plan fabricated by themselves and the *devils* to *oppress* us. But hark! My master has taught me better than to believe it—he has taught me that his gospel as it was preached by himself and his apostles remains the same, notwithstanding Europe has tried to mingle blood and oppression with it.

It is well known to the Christian world, that Bartholomew Las Casas, that very very notoriously avaricious Catholic priest or preacher, and adventurer with Columbus in his second voyage, proposed to his countrymen, the Spaniards in Hispaniola to import the Africans from the Portuguese settlement in Africa, to dig up gold and silver, and work their plantations for them, to effect which, he made a voyage thence to Spain, and opened the subject to his master, Ferdinand then in declining health, who listened to the plan: but who died soon after, and left it in the hand of his successor, Charles V.[15] This wretch ("Las

[15] See Butler's History of the United States, vol. 1, page 24.—See also, page 25.

Casas, the Preacher"), succeeded so well in his plans of oppression, that in 1503, the first blacks had been imported into
the new world. Elated with this success, and stimulated by
sordid avarice only, he importuned Charles V. in 1511, to grant
permission to a Flemish merchant to import 4000 blacks at one
time.[16] Thus we see, through the instrumentality of a pretended
preacher of the gospel of Jesus Christ our common master, our
wretchedness first commenced in America—where it has been
continued from 1503, to this day, 1829. A period of three hundred and twenty-six years. But two hundred and nine, from
1620—when twenty of our fathers were brought into Jamestown, Virginia, by a Dutch man of war, and sold off like brutes
to the highest bidders; and there is not a doubt in my mind,
but that tyrants are in hope to perpetuate our miseries under
them and their children until the final consummation of all
things.—But if they do not get dreadfully deceived, it will be
because God has forgotten them.

The Pagans, Jews and Mahometans try to make proselytes
to their religions, and whatever human beings adopt their
religions they extend to them their protection. But Christian
Americans, not only hinder their fellow creatures, the Africans,
but thousands of them *will absolutely beat a coloured person
nearly to death, if they catch him on his knees, supplicating
the throne of grace.* This barbarous cruelty was by all the
heathen nations of antiquity, and is by the Pagans, Jews and

[16] It is not unworthy of remark, that the Portuguese and Spaniards, were
among, if not the very first Nations upon Earth, about three hundred and
fifty or sixty years ago—But see what those *Christians* have come to now in
consequence of afflicting our fathers and us, who have never molested, or
disturbed them or any other of the white *Christians*, but have they received
one quarter of what the Lord will yet bring upon them, for the murders
they have inflicted upon us?—They have had, and in some degree have now,
sweet times on our blood and groans, the time however, of bitterness have
sometime since commenced with them.—There is a God the Maker and
preserver of all things, who will as sure as the world exists, give all his
creatures their just recompense of reward in this and in the world to come,
—we may fool or deceive, and keep each other in the most profound ignorance, beat murder and keep each other out of what is our lawful rights,
or the rights of man, yet it is impossible for us to deceive or escape the
Lord Almighty.

Mahometans of the present day, left entirely to Christian Americans to inflict on the Africans and their descendants, that their cup which is nearly full may be completed. I have known tyrants or usurpers of human liberty in different parts of this country to take their fellow creatures, the coloured people, and beat them until they would scarcely leave life in them; what for? Why they say "The black devils had the audacity to be found *making prayers and supplications to the God who made them!!!!*"

Yes, I have known small collections of coloured people to have convened together, for no other purpose than to worship God Almighty, in spirit and in truth, to the best of their knowledge; when tyrants, calling themselves *patrols,* would also convene and wait almost in breathless silence for the poor coloured people to commence singing and praying to the Lord our God, as soon as they had commenced, the wretches would burst in upon them and drag them out and commence beating them as they would rattle-snakes—many of whom, they would beat so unmercifully, that they would hardly be able to crawl for weeks and sometimes for months. Yet the American ministers send out missionaries to convert the heathen, while they keep us and our children sunk at their feet in the most abject ignorance and wretchedness that ever a people was afflicted with since the world began. Will the Lord suffer this people to proceed much longer? Will he not stop them in their career? Does he regard the heathens abroad, more than the heathens among the Americans? Surely the Americans must believe that God is partial, notwithstanding his Apostle Peter, declared before Cornelius and others that he has no respect to persons, but in every nation he that feareth God and worketh righteousness is accepted with him.—"The word," said he, "which God sent unto the children of Israel, preaching peace, by Jesus Christ (he is Lord of all." [17]) Have not the Americans the Bible in their hands? Do they believe it? Surely they do not. See how they treat us in open violation of the Bible!!

They no doubt will be greatly offended with me, but if God

[17] See Acts of the Apostles, chap. xv.—25–27.

does not awaken them, it will be, because they are superior to other men, as they have represented themselves to be. Our divine Lord and Master said, "all things whatsoever ye would that men should do unto you, do ye even so unto them." But an American minister, with the Bible in his hand, holds us and our children in the most abject slavery and wretchedness. Now I ask them, would they like for us to hold them and their children in abject slavery and wretchedness? No says one, that never can be done—you are too abject and ignorant to do it— you are not men—you were made to be slaves to us, to dig up gold and silver for us and our children. Know this, my dear sirs, that although you treat us and our children now, as you do your domestic beast—yet the final result of all future events are known but to God Almighty alone, who rules in the armies of heaven and among the inhabitants of the earth, and who dethrones one earthly king and sits up another, as it seemeth good in his holy sight. We may attribute these vicissitudes to what we please, but the God of armies and of justice rules in heaven and in earth, and the whole American people shall see and know it yet, to their satisfaction.

I have known pretended preachers of the gospel of my Master, who not only held us as their natural inheritance, but treated us with as much rigor as any Infidel or Deist in the world—just as though they were intent only on taking our blood and groans to glorify the Lord Jesus Christ. The wicked and ungodly, seeing their preachers treat us with so much cruelty, they say: our preachers, who must be right, if any body are, treat them like brutes, and why cannot we?—They think it is no harm to keep them in slavery and put the whip to them, and why cannot we do the same!—They being preachers of the gospel of Jesus Christ, if it were any harm, they would surely preach against their oppression and do their utmost to erase it from the country; not only in one or two cities, but one continual cry would be raised in all parts of this confederacy, and would cease only with the complete overthrow of the system of slavery, in every part of the country.

But how far the American preachers are from preaching against slavery and oppression, which have carried their country to the brink of a precipice; to save them from plunging down the side of which, will hardly be affected, will appear in the sequel of this paragraph, which I shall narrate just as it transpired. I remember a Camp Meeting in South Carolina, for which I embarked in a Steam Boat at Charleston, and having been five or six hours on the water, we at last arrived at the place of hearing, where was a very great concourse of people, who were no doubt, collected together to hear the word of God (that some had collected barely as spectators to the scene, I will not here pretend to doubt, however, that is left to themselves and their God).

Myself and boat companions, having been there a little while, we were all called up to hear; I among the rest went up and took my seat—being seated, I fixed myself in a complete position to hear the word of my Saviour and to receive such as I thought was authenticated by the Holy Scriptures; but to my no ordinary astonishment, our Reverend gentleman got up and told us (coloured people) that slaves must be obedient to their masters—must do their duty to their masters or be whipped— the whip was made for the backs of fools, &c. Here I pause for a moment, to give the world time to consider what was my surprise, to hear such preaching from a minister of my Master, whose very gospel is that of peace and not of blood and whips, as this pretended preacher tried to make us believe. What the American preachers can think of us, I aver this day before my God, I have never been able to define. They have newspapers and monthly periodicals, which they receive in continual succession, but on the pages of which, you will scarcely ever find a paragraph respecting slavery, which is ten thousand times more injurious to this country than all the other evils put together; and which will be the final overthrow of its government, unless something is very speedily done; for their cup is nearly full.—Perhaps they will laugh at or make light of this; but I tell you Americans! that unless you speedily alter your course, *you* and your *Country are gone!!!!!!* For God Almighty will tear up the very face of the earth!!!

Will not that very remarkable passage of Scripture be fulfilled on Christian Americans? Hear it Americans!! "He that

is unjust, let him be unjust still:—and he which is filthy, let
him be filthy still: and he that is righteous, let him be righteous
still: and he that is holy, let him be holy still." [18] I hope that
the Americans may hear, but I am afraid that they have done
us so much injury, and are so firm in the belief that our Creator
made us to be an inheritance to them for ever, that their hearts
will be hardened, so that their destruction may be sure. This
language, perhaps is too harsh for the American's delicate ears.
But Oh Americans! Americans!! I warn you in the name of the
Lord (whether you will hear, or forbear), to repent and reform,
or you are ruined!!!

Do you think that our blood is hidden from the Lord, because you can hide it from the rest of the world, by sending
our missionaries, and by your charitable deeds to the Greeks,
Irish, &c.? Will he not publish your secret crimes on the house
top? Even here in Boston, pride and prejudice have got to
such a pitch, that in the very houses erected to the Lord, they
have built little places for the reception of coloured people,
where they must sit during meeting, or keep away from the
house of God, and the preachers say nothing about it—much
less go into the hedges and highways seeking the lost sheep
of the house of Israel, and try to bring them in to their Lord
and Master. There are not a more wretched, ignorant, miserable, and abject set of beings in all the world, than the blacks
in the Southern and Western sections of this country, under
tyrants and devils. The preachers of America cannot see them,
but they can send out missionaries to convert the heathens,
notwithstanding. Americans! unless you speedily alter your
course of proceeding, if God Almighty does not stop you, I say
it in his name, that you may go on and do as you please for
ever, both in time and eternity—never fear any evil at all!!!!!!!!

ADDITION.—The preachers and people of the United States
form societies against Free Masonry and Intemperance, and
write against Sabbath breaking, Sabbath mails, Infidelity, &c.
&c. But the fountain head,[19] compared with which, all those
other evils are comparatively nothing, and from the bloody

---

[18] See Revelation, chap. xxii. II.
[19] Slavery and oppression.

and murderous head of which, they receive no trifling support, is hardly noticed by Americans. This is a fair illustration of the state of society in this country—it shows what a bearing *avarice* has upon a people, when they are nearly given up by the Lord to a hard heart and a reprobate mind, in consequence of afflicting their fellow creatures. God suffers some to go on until they are ruined for ever!!!!! Will it be the case with the whites of the United States of America?—We hope not—we would not wish to see them destroyed notwithstanding, they have and do now treat us more cruel than any people have treated another, on this earth since it came from the hands of its Creator (with the exceptions of the French and the Dutch, they treat us nearly as bad as the Americans of the United States). The will of God must however, in spite of us, *be done.*

The English are the best friends the coloured people have upon earth. Though they have oppressed us a little and have colonies now in the West Indies, which oppress us *sorely.*— Yet notwithstanding they (the English) have done one hundred times more for the melioration of our condition, than all the other nations of the earth put together. The blacks cannot but respect the English as a nation, notwithstanding they have treated us a little cruel.

There is no intelligent *black man* who knows any thing, but esteems a real Englishman, let him see him in what part of the world he will—for they are the greatest benefactors we have upon earth. We have here and there, in other nations, good friends. But as a nation, the English are our friends.

How can the preachers and people of America believe the Bible? Does it teach them any distinction on account of man's colour? Hearken, Americans! to the injunctions of our Lord and Master, to his humble followers.

> And Jesus came and spake unto them, saying all power is given unto me in Heaven and in earth.
>
> Go ye, therefore, and teach all nations, baptizing them in the name of the Father, and of the Son, and of the Holy Ghost.[20]

[20] See St. Matthews' Gospel, chap. xxviii. 18, 19, 20. After Jesus was risen from the dead.

Teaching them to observe all things whatsoever I have commanded you; and lo, I am with you always, even unto the
end of the world. Amen.

I declare, that the very face of these injunctions appear to
be of God and not of man. They do not show the slightest degree of distinction. "Go ye therefore" (says my divine Master),
"and teach all nations" (or in other words, all people), "baptizing them in the name of the Father, and of the Son, and of
the Holy Ghost." Do you understand the above, Americans?

We are a people, notwithstanding many of you doubt it.
You have the Bible in your hands, with this very injunction.—
Have you been to Africa, teaching the inhabitants thereof the
words of the Lord Jesus? "Baptizing them in the name of the
Father, and of the Son, and of the Holy Ghost." Have you not,
on the contrary, entered among us, and learnt us the art of
throat-cutting, by setting us to fight, one against another, to
take each other as prisoners of war, and sell to you for small
bits of calicoes, old swords, knives, &c. to make slaves for you
and your children? This being done, have you not brought us
among you, in chains and hand-cuffs, like brutes, and treated
us with all the cruelties and rigour your ingenuity could invent, consistent with the laws of your country, which (for the
blacks) are tyrannical enough? Can the American preachers
appeal unto God, the Maker and Searcher of hearts, and tell
him, with the Bible in their hands, that they make no distinction on account of men's colour? Can they say, O God! thou
knowest all things—thou knowest that we make no distinction
between thy creatures, to whom we have to preach thy Word?
Let them answer the Lord; and if they cannot do it in the
affirmative, have they not departed from the Lord Jesus Christ,
their master?

But some may say, that they never had, or were in possession of a religion, which made no distinction, and of course they
could not have departed from it. I ask you then, in the name
of the Lord, of what kind can your religion be? Can it be that
which was preached by our Lord Jesus Christ from Heaven?
I believe you cannot be so wicked as to tell him that his Gos-

pel was that of *distinction.* What can the American preachers and people take God to be? Do they believe his words? If they do, do they believe that he will be mocked? Or do they believe, because they are whites and we blacks, that God will have respect to them? Did not God make us all as it seemed best to himself? What right, then, has one of us, to despise another, and to treat him cruel, on account of his colour, which none, but the God who made it can alter? Can there be a greater absurdity in nature, and particularly in a free republican country?

But the Americans, having introduced slavery among them, their hearts have become almost seared, as with an hot iron, and God has nearly given them up to believe a lie in preference to the truth!!! And I am awfully afraid that pride, prejudice, avarice and blood, will, before long prove the final ruin of this happy republic, or land of *liberty!!!!* Can any thing be a greater mockery of religion than the way in which it is conducted by the Americans?

It appears as though they are bent only on daring God Almighty to do his best—they chain and handcuff us and our children and drive us around the country like brutes, and go into the house of the God of justice to return him thanks for having aided them in their infernal cruelties inflicted upon us. Will the Lord suffer this people to go on much longer, taking his holy name in vain? Will he not stop them, PREACHERS and all? O Americans! Americans!! I call God—I call angels— I call men, to witness, that your DESTRUCTION *is at hand,* and will be speedily consummated unless you REPENT.

Article IV.

OUR WRETCHEDNESS IN CONSEQUENCE OF THE COLONIZING PLAN

My dearly beloved brethren: This is a scheme on which so many able writers, together with that very judicious coloured Baltimorean, have commented, that I feel my delicacy about touching it. But as I am compelled to do the will of my Master,

I declare, I will give you my sentiments upon it.—Previous, however, to giving my sentiments, either for or against it, I shall give that of Mr. Henry Clay, together with that of Mr. Elias B. Caldwell, Esq. of the District of Columbia, as extracted from the National Intelligencer, by Dr. Torrey, author of a series of "Essays on Morals, and the Diffusion of Useful Knowledge."

At a meeting which was convened in the District of Columbia, for the express purpose of agitating the subject of colonizing us in some part of the world, Mr. Clay was called to the chair, and having been seated a little while, he rose and spake, in substance, as follows: says he [21]—

> That class of the mixt population of our country [coloured people] was peculiarly situated; they neither enjoyed the immunities of freemen, nor were they subjected to the incapacities of slaves, but partook, in some degree, of the qualities of both. From their condition, and the unconquerable prejudices resulting from their colour, they never could amalgamate with the free whites of this country. It was desirable, therefore, as it respected them, and the residue of the population of the country, to drain them off. Various schemes of colonization had been thought of, and a part of our continent, it was supposed by some, might furnish a suitable establishment for them. But, for his part, Mr. C. said, he had a decided preference for some part of the Coast of Africa. There ample provision might be made for the colony itself, and it might be rendered instrumental to the introduction into that extensive quarter of the globe, of the arts, civilization, and Christianity.

[Here I ask Mr. Clay, what kind of Christianity? Did he mean such as they have among the Americans—distinction, whip, blood and oppression? I pray the Lord Jesus Christ to forbid it.]

"There," said he,

> was a peculiar, a moral fitness, in restoring them to the land of their fathers, and if instead of the evils and sufferings which

[21] See Dr. Torrey's Portraiture of Domestic Slavery in the United States, pages 85, 86.

we had been the innocent cause of inflicting upon the inhabitants of Africa, we can transmit to her the blessings of our arts, our civilization, and our religion. May we not hope that America will extinguish a great portion of that moral debt which she has contracted to that unfortunate continent? Can there be a nobler cause than that which, whilst it proposes, &c. . . . [you know what this means] contemplates the spreading of the arts of civilized life, and the possible redemption from ignorance and barbarism of a benighted quarter of the globe?

Before I proceed any further, I solicit your notice, brethren, to the foregoing part of Mr. Clay's speech, in which he says (look above), "and if, instead of the evils and sufferings, which we had been the innocent cause of inflicting," &c.—What this very learned statesman could have been thinking about, when he said in his speech, "we had been the innocent cause of inflicting," &c., I have never been able to conceive. Are Mr. Clay and the rest of the Americans, innocent of the blood and groans of our fathers and us, their children?—Every individual may plead innocence, if he pleases, but God will, before long, separate the innocent from the guilty, unless something is speedily done—which I suppose will hardly be, so that their destruction may be sure. Oh Americans! let me tell you, in the name of the Lord, it will be good for you, if you listen to the voice of the Holy Ghost, but if you do not, you are ruined!!! Some of you are good men; but the will of my God must be done. Those avaricious and ungodly tyrants among you, I am awfully afraid will drag down the vengeance of God upon you. When God Almighty commences his battle on the continent of America, for the oppression of his people, tyrants will wish they never were born.

But to return to Mr. Clay, whence I digressed. He says,

It was proper and necessary distinctly to state, that he understood it constituted no part of the object of this meeting, to touch or agitate in the slightest degree, a delicate question, connected with another portion of the coloured population of our country. It was not proposed to deliberate upon or consider at all, any question of emancipation, or that which was connected with the abolition of slavery. It was upon that condition alone, he was sure, that many gentlemen from the South and the West, whom he saw present, had attended, or could be expected to co-operate. It was upon that condition only, that he himself had attended.

That is to say, to fix a plan to get those of the coloured people, who are said to be free, away from among those of our brethren whom they unjustly hold in bondage, so that they may be enabled to keep them the more secure in ignorance and wretchedness, to support them and their children, and consequently they would have the more obedient slave. For if the free are allowed to stay among the slave, they will have intercourse together, and, of course, the free will learn the slaves *bad habits,* by teaching them that they are MEN, as well as other people, and certainly *ought* and *must* be FREE.

I presume, that every intelligent man of colour must have some idea of Mr. Henry Clay, originally of Virginia, but now of Kentucky; they know too, perhaps, whether he is a friend, or a foe to the coloured citizens of this country, and of the world. This gentleman, according to his own words, had been highly favoured and blessed of the Lord, though he did not acknowledge it; but, to the contrary, he acknowledged men, for all the blessings with which God had favoured him. At a public dinner, given him at Fowler's Garden, Lexington, Kentucky, he delivered a public speech to a very large concourse of people—in the concluding clause of which, he says,

> And now, my friends and fellow citizens, I cannot part from you, on possibly the last occasion of my ever publicly addressing you, without reiterating the expression of my thanks, from a heart overflowing with gratitude. I came among you, now more than thirty years ago, an orphan boy, pennyless, a stranger to you all, without friends, without the favour of the great, you took me up, cherished me, protected me, honoured me, you have constantly poured upon me a bold and unabated stream of innumerable favours, time which wears out every thing has increased and strengthened your affection for me.

When I seemed deserted by almost the whole world, and assailed by almost every tongue, and pen, and press, you have fearlessly and manfully stood by me, with unsurpassed zeal and undiminished friendship. When I felt as if I should sink beneath the storm of abuse and detraction, which was violently raging around me, I have found myself upheld and sustained by your encouraging voices and approving smiles. I have doubtless, committed many faults and indiscretions, over which you have thrown the broad mantle of your charity. But I can say, and in the presence of God and in this assembled multitude, I will say, that I have honestly and faithfully served my country—that I have never wronged it—and that, however unprepared, I lament that I am to appear in the Divine presence on other accounts, I invoke the stern justice of his judgment on my public conduct, without the slightest apprehension of his displeasure.

Hearken to this Statesman indeed, but no philanthropist, whom God sent into Kentucky, an orphan boy, pennyless, and friendless, where he not only gave him a plenty of friends and the comforts of life, but raised him almost to the very highest honour in the nation, where his great talents, with which the Lord has been pleased to bless him, has gained for him the affection of a great portion of the people with whom he had to do. But what has this gentleman done for the Lord, after having done so much for him? The Lord has a suffering people, whose moans and groans at his feet for deliverance from oppression and wretchedness, pierce the very throne of Heaven, and call loudly on the God of Justice, to be revenged. Now, what this gentleman, who is so highly favoured of the Lord, has done to liberate those miserable victims of oppression, shall appear before the world, by his letters to Mr. Gallatin, Envoy Extraordinary and Minister Plenipotentiary to Great Britain, dated June 19, 1826.—Though Mr. Clay was writing for the States, yet nevertheless, it appears, from the very face of his letters to that gentleman, that he was as anxious, if not more so, to get those free people and sink them into wretchedness, as his constituents, for whom he wrote.

The Americans of North and of South America, including the West India Islands—no trifling portion of whom were, for stealing, murdering, &c. compelled to flee from Europe, to save their necks or banishment, have effected their escape to this continent, where God blessed them with all the comforts of life—He gave them a plenty of every thing calculated to do them good—not satisfied with this, however, they wanted slaves, and wanted us for their slaves, who belong to the Holy Ghost, and no other, who we shall have to serve instead of tyrants.— I say, the Americans want us, the property of the Holy Ghost, to serve them.

But there is a day fast approaching, when (unless there is a universal repentance on the part of the whites, which will scarcely take place, they have got to be hardened in consequence of our blood, and so wise in their own conceit.) To be plain and candid with you, Americans! I say that the day is fast approaching, when there will be a greater time on the continent of America, than ever was witnessed upon this earth, since it came from the hand of its Creator. Some of you have done us so much injury, that you will never be able to repent. —Your cup must be filled.—You want us for your slaves, and shall have enough of us—God is just, *who will give you your fill of us.* But Mr. Henry Clay, speaking to Mr. Gallatin, respecting coloured people, who had effected their escape from the U. States (or to them *hell upon earth!!!*) to the hospitable shores of Canada,[22] from whence it would cause more than the lives of the Americans to get them, to plunge into wretchedness—he says:

> The General Assembly of Kentucky, one of the states which is most affected by the escape of slaves into Upper Canada, has again, at their session which has just terminated, invoked the interposition of the General Government. In the treaty which has been recently concluded with the United Mexican States, and which is now under the consideration of the Senate, provision is made for the restoration of fugitive slaves. As it appears from your statements of what passed on that subject,

[22] Among the English, our real friends and benefactors.

with the British Plenipotentiaries, that they admitted the correctness of the principle of restoration, it is hoped that you will
be able to succeed in making satisfactory arrangements.

There are a series of these letters, all of which are to the same
amount; some however, presenting a face more of his own responsibility. I wonder what would this gentleman think, if the
Lord should give him among the rest of his blessings enough
of slaves? Could he blame any other being but himself? Do we
not belong to the Holy Ghost. What business has he or any
body else, to be sending letters about the world respecting us?
Can we not go where we want to, as well as other people, only
if we obey the voice of the Holy Ghost? This gentleman (Mr.
Henry Clay), not only took an active part in this colonizing
plan, but was absolutely chairman of a meeting held at Washington, the 21st day of December 1816,[23] to agitate the subject
of colonizing us in Africa.—Now I appeal and ask every citizen
of these United States and of the world, both *white* and *black,*
who has any knowledge of Mr. Clay's public labor for these
States—I want you candidly to answer the Lord, who sees the
secrets of our hearts.—Do you believe that Mr. Henry Clay,
late Secretary of State, and now in Kentucky, is a friend to the
blacks, further, than his personal interest extends? Is it not his
greatest object and glory upon earth, to sink us into miseries
and wretchedness by making slaves of us, to work his plantation to enrich him and his family? Does he care a pinch of snuff
about Africa—whether it remains a land of Pagans and of blood,
or of Christians, so long as he get enough of her sons and
daughters to dig up gold and silver for him? If he had no slaves,
and could obtain them in no other way if it were not, repugnant
to the laws of his country, which prohibit the importation of
slaves (which act was, indeed, more through apprehension
than humanity) would he not try to import a few from Africa,
to work his farm? Would he work in the hot sun to earn his
bread, if he could make an African work for nothing, particularly, if he could keep him in ignorance and make him believe

[23] In the first edition of this work, it should read 1816, as above, and not
1826, as it there appears.

that God made him for nothing else but to work for him? Is not Mr. Clay a white man, and too delicate to work in the hot sun!! Was he not made by his Creator to sit in the shade, and make the blacks work without remuneration for their services, to support him and his family!!!

I have been for some time taking notice of this man's speeches and public writings, but never to my knowledge have I seen any thing in his writings which insisted on the emancipation of slavery, which has almost ruined his country. Thus we see the depravity of men's hearts, when in pursuit only of gain—particularly when they oppress their fellow creatures to obtain that gain—God suffers some to go on until they are lost forever. This same Mr. Clay, wants to know, what he has done, to merit the disapprobation of the American people. In a public speech delivered by him, he asked: "Did I involve my country in an unnecessary war?" to merit the censure of the Americans—"Did I bring obliquy upon the nation, or the people whom I represented—did I ever lose any opportunity to advance the fame, honor and prosperity of this State and the Union?" How astonishing it is, for a man who knows so much about God and his ways, as Mr. Clay, to ask such frivolous questions? Does he believe that a man of his talents and standing in the midst of a people, will get along unnoticed by the penetrating and all-seeing eye of God, who is continually taking cognizance of the hearts of men? Is not God against him, for advocating the murderous cause of slavery? If God is against him, what can the Americans, together with the whole world do for him? Can they save him from the hand of the Lord Jesus Christ?

I shall now pass in review the speech of Mr. Elias B. Caldwell, Esq. of the District of Columbia, extracted from the same page on which Mr. Clay's will be found. Mr. Caldwell, giving his opinion respecting us, at that ever memorable meeting, he says: "The more you improve the condition of these people, the more you cultivate their minds, the more miserable you make them in their present state. You give them a higher relish for those privileges which they can never attain, and turn what we intend for a blessing into a curse." Let me ask this benevolent man, what he means by a blessing intended for us?

Did he mean sinking us and our children into ignorance and wretchedness, to support him and his family? What he meant will appear evident and obvious to the most ignorant in the world. See Mr. Caldwell's intended blessings for us, O! my Lord!! "No," said he, "if they must remain in their present situation, keep them in the *lowest state of degradation and ignorance.* The nearer you bring them to the condition of brutes, the better chance do you give them of possessing their *apathy.*"

Here I pause to get breath, having labored to extract the above clause of this gentleman's speech, at that colonizing meeting. I presume that everybody knows the meaning of the word "apathy,"—if any do not, let him get Sheridan's Dictionary, in which he will find it explained in full. I solicit the attention of the world, to the foregoing part of Mr. Caldwell's speech, that they may see what man will do with his fellow men, when he has them under his feet. To what length will not man go in iniquity when given up to a hard heart, and reprobate mind, in consequence of blood and oppression? The last clause of this speech, which was written in a very artful manner, and which will be taken for the speech of a friend, without close examination and deep penetration, I shall now present. He says, "surely, Americans ought to be the last people on earth, to advocate such slavish doctrines, to cry peace and contentment to those who are deprived of the privileges of civil liberty, they who have so largely partaken of its blessings, who know so well how to estimate its value, ought to be among the foremost to extend it to others." The real sense and meaning of the last part of Mr. Caldwell's speech is, get the free people of colour away to Africa, from among the slaves, where they may at once be blessed and happy, and those who we hold in slavery, will be contented to rest in ignorance and wretchedness, to dig up gold and silver for us and our children. Men have indeed got to be so cunning, these days, that it would take the eye of a Solomon to penetrate and find them out.

ADDITION.—Our dear Redeemer said, "Therefore, whatsoever ye have spoken in darkness, shall be heard in the light; and that which ye have spoken in the ear in closets, shall be proclaimed upon the house tops."

How obviously this declaration of our Lord has been shown among the Americans of the United States. They have hitherto passed among some nations, who do not know any thing about their internal concerns, for the most enlightened, humane, charitable, and merciful people upon earth, when at the same time they treat us, the (coloured people) secretly more cruel and unmerciful than any other nation upon earth.

It is a fact, that in our Southern and Western States, there are millions who hold us in chains or in slavery, whose greatest object and glory is, centered in keeping us sunk in the most profound ignorance and stupidity, to make us work without remunerations for our services. Many of whom if they catch a coloured person, whom they hold in unjust ignorance, slavery and degradation, to them and their children, with a book in his hand, will beat him nearly to death. I heard a wretch in the state of North Carolina said, that if any man would teach a black person whom he held in slavery, to spell, read or write, he would prosecute him to the very extent of the law.—Said the ignorant wretch,[24] "a Nigar, ought not to have any more sense than enough to work for his master." May I not ask to fatten the wretch and his family?—These and similar cruelties these *Christians* have been for hundreds of years inflicting on our fathers and us in the dark, God has however, very recently published some of their secret crimes on the house top, that the world may gaze on their Christianity and see of what kind it is composed.

Georgia for instance, God has completely shown to the world, the *Christianity* among its white *inhabitants*. A law has recently passed the Legislature of this *republican* State (Georgia) prohibiting all free or slave persons of colour, from learning to read or write; another law has passed the *republican* House of Delegates (but not the Senate), in Virginia, to prohibit all persons of colour (free and slave), from learning to read or write, and even to hinder them from meeting together in order to

[24] It is a fact, that in all our Slave-holding States (in the countries) there are thousands of the whites, who are almost as ignorant in comparison as horses, the most they know, is to beat the coloured people, which some of them shall have their hearts full of yet.

worship our Maker!!!!!!—Now I solemnly appeal, to the most
skillful historians in the world, and all those who are mostly
acquainted with the histories of the Antideluvians, and of
Sodom and Gomorrah, to show me a parallel of barbarity.
Christians!! Christians!!! I dare you to show me a parallel of
cruelties in the annals of Heathens or of Devils, with those of
Ohio, Virginia and of Georgia—know the world that these
things were before done in the dark, or in a corner under a
garb of humanity and religion. God has however, taken off the
fig-leaf covering and make them expose themselves on the
house top. I tell you that God works in many ways his wonders
to perform, he will unless they repent, make them expose themselves enough more yet to the world.—See the acts of the *Christians* in FLORIDA, SOUTH CAROLINA, and KENTUCKY—
was it not for the reputation of the house of my Lord and
Master, I would mention here, an act of cruelty inflicted a few
days since on a black man, by the white *Christians* in the PARK
STREET CHURCH, in this (CITY) which is almost enough
to make Demons themselves quake and tremble in their FIERY
HABITATIONS.—Oh! my Lord how refined in iniquity the
whites have got to be in consequence of our blood[25]—what
kind!! Oh! what kind!!! of Christianity can be found this day
in all the earth!!!!!!
I write without the fear of man, I am writing for my God,
and fear none but himself; they may put me to death if they
choose—(I fear and esteem a good man however, let him be
black or white.) I forbear to comment on the cruelties inflicted
on this Black Man by the Whites, in the Park Street MEETING
HOUSE, I will leave it in the dark!!!!! But I declare that the
atrocity is really to Heaven daring and infernal, that I must
say that God has commenced a course of exposition among the
Americans, and the glorious and heavenly work will continue
to progress until they learn to do justice.

---

[25] The Blood of our fathers who have been murdered by the whites, and
the groans of our Brethren, who are now held in cruel ignorance, wretchedness and slavery by them, cry aloud to the Maker of Heaven and of earth,
against the whole continent of America, for redresses.

Extract from the Speech of Mr. John Randolph, of Roanoke. Said he:—

It had been properly observed by the Chairman, as well as by the gentleman from this District [meaning Messrs. Clay and Caldwell] that there was nothing in the proposition submitted to consideration which in the smallest degree touches another very important and delicate question, which ought to be left as much out of view as possible [Negro Slavery.][26]

There is no fear [Mr. R. said], that this proposition would alarm the slave-holders; they had been accustomed to think seriously of the subject.—There was a popular work on agriculture, by John Taylor of Caroline, which was widely circulated, and much confided in, in Virginia. In that book, much read because coming from a practical man, this description of people [referring to us half free ones] were pointed out as a great evil. They had indeed been held up as the greater bugbear to every man who feels an inclination to emancipate his slaves, not to create in the bosom of his country so great a nuisance. If a place could be provided for their reception, and a mode of sending them hence, there were hundreds, nay thousands of citizens who would, by manumitting their slaves, relieve themselves from the cares attendant on their possession. The great slave-holder [Mr. R. said], was frequently a mere sentry at his own door—bound to stay on his plantation to see that his slaves were properly treated, &c. [Mr. R. concluded by saying] that he had thought it necessary to make these remarks being a slave-holder himself, to shew that, so far from being connected with abolition of slavery, the measure proposed would prove one of the greatest securities to enable the master to keep in possession his own property.

Here is a demonstrative proof, of a plan got up, by a gang of slave-holders to select the free people of colour from among

[26] "Niger," is a word derived from the Latin, which was used by the old Romans, to designate inanimate beings, which were black; such as soot, pot, wood, house, &c. Also, animals which they considered inferior to the human species, as a black horse, cow, hog, bird, dog, &c. The white Americans have applied this term to Africans, by way of reproach for our colour, to aggravate and heighten our miseries, because they have their feet on our throats.

the slaves, that our more miserable brethren may be the better secured in ignorance and wretchedness, to work their farms and dig their mines, and thus go on enriching the Christians with their blood and groans. What our brethren could have been thinking about, who have left their native land and home and gone away to Africa, I am unable to say. This country is as much ours as it is the whites, whether they will admit it now or not, they will see and believe it by and by. They tell us about prejudices—what have we to do with it? Their prejudices will be obliged to fall like lightning to the ground, in succeeding generations; not, however, with the will and consent of all the whites, for some will be obliged to hold on to the old adage, viz.: the blacks are not men, but were made to be an inheritance to us and our children for ever!!!!!! I hope the residue of the coloured people, will stand still and see the salvation of God and the miracle which he will work for our delivery from wretchedness under the Christians!!!!!!

ADDITION.—If any of us see fit to go away, go to those who have been for many years, and are now our greatest earthly friends and benefactors—the English. If not so, go to our brethren, the Haytians, who, according to their word, are bound to protect and comfort us. The Americans say, that we are ungrateful—but I ask them for heaven's sake, what should we be grateful to them for—for murdering our fathers and mothers? —Or do they wish us to return thanks to them for chaining and hand-cuffing us, branding us, cramming fire down our throats, or for keeping us in slavery, and beating us nearly or quite to death to make us work in ignorance and miseries, to support them and their families. They certainly think that we are a gang of fools. Those among them, who have volunteered their services for our redemption, though we are unable to compensate them for their labours, we nevertheless thank them from the bottom of our hearts, and have our eyes steadfastly fixed upon them, and their labours of love for God and man.—But do slave-holders think that we thank them for keeping us in miseries, and taking our lives by the inches?

Before I proceed further with this scheme, I shall give an extract from the letter of that truly Reverent Divine (Bishop

Allen), of Philadelphia, respecting this trick. At the instance of the editor of the Freedom's Journal, he says,

> Dear Sir, I have been for several years trying to reconcile my mind to the Colonizing of Africans in Liberia, but there have always been, and there still remain great and insurmountable objections against the scheme. We are an unlettered people, brought up in ignorance, not one in a hundred can read or write, not one in a thousand has a liberal education; is there any fitness for such to be sent into a far country, among heathens, to convert or civilize them, when they themselves are neither civilized or Christianized? See the great bulk of the poor, ignorant Africans in this country, exposed to every temptation before them: all for the want of their morals being refined by education and proper attendance paid unto them by their owners, or those who had the charge of them. It is said by the Southern slave-holders, that the more ignorant they can bring up the Africans, the better slaves they make ["go and come."] Is there any fitness for such people to be colonized in a far country to be their own rulers? Can we not discern the project of sending the free people of colour away from their country? Is it not for the interest of the slave-holders to select the free people of colour out of the different states, and send them to Liberia? Will it not make their slaves uneasy to see free men of colour enjoying liberty? It is against the law in some of the Southern States, that a person of colour should receive an education, under a severe penalty. Colonizationists speak of America being first colonized; but is there any comparison between the two? America was colonized by as *wise, judicious* and *educated* men as the world afforded. WILLIAM PENN did not want for *learning, wisdom,* or *intelligence.* If all the people were as ignorant and in the same situation as our brethren, what would become of the world? Where would be the principle or piety that would govern the people? We were *stolen* from our mother country, and brought *here.* We have *tilled* the ground and made fortunes for thousands, and still they are not weary of our services. *But they who stay to till the ground must be slaves.* Is there not land enough in America, or "corn enough in

Egypt"? Why should they send us into a far country to die?
See the thousands of foreigners emigrating to America every
year: and if there be ground sufficient for them to cultivate,
and bread for them to eat, why would they wish to send the
first tillers of the land away? Africans have made fortunes for
thousands, who are yet unwilling to part with their services; but
the free must be sent away, and those who remain, must be
slaves. I have no doubt that there are many good men who do
not see as I do, and who are sending us to Liberia; but they
have not duly considered the subject—they are not men of
colour.—This land which we have watered with our *tears* and
our blood, is now our *mother country,* and we are well satisfied
to stay where wisdom abounds and the gospel is free.

> RICHARD ALLEN,
> *Bishop of the African Methodist Episcopal*
> *Church in the United States*[27]

I have given you, my brethren, an extract verbatim, from
the letter of that godly man, as you may find it on the afore-
mentioned page of Freedom's Journal. I know that thousands,
and perhaps millions of my brethren in these States, have never
heard of such a man as Bishop Allen—a man whom God many
years ago raised up among his ignorant and degraded brethren,
to preach Jesus Christ and him crucified to them—who notwithstanding, had to wrestle against principalities and the powers
of darkness to diffuse that gospel with which he was endowed
among his brethren—but who having overcome the combined
powers of devils and wicked men, has under God planted a
Church among us which will be as durable as the foundation
of the earth on which it stands. Richard Allen! O my God!!
The bare recollection of the labours of this man, and his ministers among his deplorably wretched brethren (rendered so
by the whites), to bring them to a knowledge of the God of
Heaven, fills my soul with all those very high emotions which
would take the pen of an Addison to portray.

It is impossible my brethren for me to say much in this
work respecting that man of God. When the Lord shall raise

[27] See Freedom's Journal for Nov. 2d, 1827—vol. 1, No. 34.

up coloured historians in succeeding generations, to present the crimes of this nation, to the then gazing world, the Holy Ghost will make them do justice to the name of Bishop Allen, of Philadelphia. Suffice it for me to say, that the name of this very man (Richard Allen) though now in obscurity and degradation, will notwithstanding, stand on the pages of history among the greatest divines who have lived since the apostolic age, and among the Africans, Bishop Allen's will be entirely pre-eminent. My brethren, search after the character and exploits of this godly man among his ignorant and miserable brethren, to bring them to a knowledge of the truth as it is in our Master. Consider upon the tyrants and false Christians against whom he had to contend in order to get access to his brethren. See him and his ministers in the States of New York, New Jersey, Pennsylvania, Delaware and Maryland, carrying the gladsome tidings of free and full salvation to the coloured people.

Tyrants and false Christians however, would not allow him to penetrate far into the South, for fear that he would awaken some of his ignorant brethren, whom they held in wretchedness and misery—for fear, I say it, that he would awaken and bring them to a knowledge of their Maker. O my Master! my Master! I cannot but think upon Christian Americans!!!—What kind of people can they be? Will not those who were burnt up in Sodom and Gomorrah rise up in judgment against Christian Americans with the Bible in their hands, and condemn them? Will not the Scribes and Pharisees of Jerusalem, who had nothing but the laws of Moses and the Prophets to go by, rise up in judgment against Christian Americans and condemn them,[28] who, in addition to these have a revelation from Jesus Christ the Son of the Living God?

In fine, will not the Antideluvians, together with the whole heathen world of antiquity, rise up in judgment against Christian Americans and condemn them? The Christians of Europe and America go to Africa, bring us away, and throw us into

[28] I mean those whose labours for the good, or rather destruction of Jerusalem, and the Jews. Ceased before our Lord entered the Temple, and overturned the tables of the Money Changers.

the seas, and in other ways murder us, as they would wild beasts. The Antideluvians and heathens never dreamed of such barbarities.—Now the Christians believe, because they have a name to live, while they are dead, that God will overlook such things. But if he does not deceive them, it will be because he has overlooked it sure enough.

But to return to this godly man, Bishop Allen. I do hereby openly affirm it to the world, that he has done more in a spiritual sense for his ignorant and wretched brethren than any other man of colour has, since the world began. And as for the greater part of the whites, it has hitherto been their greatest object and glory to keep us ignorant of our Maker, so as to make us believe that we were made to be slaves to them and their children, to dig up gold and silver for them. It is notorious that not a few professing Christians among the whites, who profess to love our Lord and Saviour Jesus Christ, have assailed this man and laid all the obstacles in his way they possibly could, consistent with their profession—and what for? Why, their course of proceeding and his, clashed exactly together—they trying their best to keep us ignorant, that we might be the better and more obedient slaves—while he, on the other hand, doing his very best to enlighten us and teach us a knowledge of the Lord.

And I am sorry that I have it to say, that many of our brethren have joined in with our oppressors, whose dearest objects are only to keep us ignorant and miserable against this man to stay his hand.—However, they have kept us in so much ignorance, that many of us know no better than to fight against ourselves, and by that means strengthen the hands of our natural enemies, to rivet their infernal chains of slavery upon us and our children. I have several times called the white Americans our *natural enemies*—I shall here define my meaning of the phrase. Shem, Ham and Japheth, together with their father Noah and wives, I believe were not natural enemies to each other. When the ark rested after the flood upon Mount Arrarat, in Asia, they (eight) were all the people which could be found alive in all the earth—in fact if Scriptures be true (which I believe are), there were no other living men in all

the earth, notwithstanding some ignorant creatures hesitate
not to tell us that we (the blacks) are the seed of Cain the
murderer of his brother Abel.

But where or of whom those ignorant and avaricious wretches
could have got their information, I am unable to declare. Did
they receive it from the Bible? I have searched the Bible as
well as they, if I am not as well learned as they are, and have
never seen a verse which testifies whether we are the seed of
Cain or of Abel. Yet those men tell us that we are the seed of
Cain, and that God put a dark stain upon us, that we might be
known as their slaves!!! Now, I ask those avaricious and ignorant wretches, who act more like the seed of Cain, by
murdering the whites or the blacks? How many vessel loads of
human beings, have the blacks thrown into the seas? How many
thousand souls have the blacks murdered in cold blood, to
make them work in wretchedness and ignorance, to support
them and their families? [29]

However, let us be the seed of *Cain, Harry, Dick,* or *Tom!!!*
God will show the whites what we are, yet. I say, from the
beginning, I do not think that we were natural enemies to
each other. But the whites having made us so wretched, by
subjecting us to slavery, and having murdered so many millions
of us, in order to make us work for them, and out of devilishness—and they taking our wives, whom we love as we do ourselves—our mothers, who bore the pains of death to give us
birth—our fathers and dear little children, and ourselves, and
strip and beat us one before the other—chain, hand-cuff, and
drag us about like rattle-snakes—shoot us down like wild bears,
before each other's faces, to make us submissive to, and work
to support them and their families. They (the whites) know
well, if we are *men*—and there is a secret monitor in their
hearts which tells them we are—they know, I say, if we *are*

---

[29] How many millions souls of the human family have the blacks beat
nearly to death, to keep them from learning to read the Word of God, and
from writing. And telling lies about them, by holding them up to the world
as a tribe of TALKING APES, void of INTELLECT!!! *incapable* of
LEARNING, &c.

men, and see them treating us in the manner they do, that there can be nothing in our hearts but death alone, for them, notwithstanding we may appear cheerful, when we see them murdering our dear mothers and wives, because we cannot help ourselves.

Man, in all ages and all nations of the earth, is the same. Man is a peculiar creature—he is the image of his God, though he may be subjected to the most wretched condition upon earth, yet the spirit and feeling which constitute the creature, man, can never be entirely erased from his breast, because God who made him after his own image, planted it in his heart; he cannot get rid of it. The whites knowing this, they do not know what to do; they know that they have done us so much injury, they are afraid that we, being men, and not brutes, will retaliate, and woe will be to them; therefore, that dreadful fear, together with an avaricious spirit, and the natural love in them, to be called masters (which term will yet honour them with to their sorrow), bring them to the resolve that they will keep us in ignorance and wretchedness, as long as they possibly can,[30] and make the best of their time, while it lasts. Consequently they, themselves (and not us), render themselves our natural enemies, by treating us so cruel.

They keep us miserable now, and call us their property, but some of them will have enough of us by and by—their stomachs shall run over with us; they want us for their slaves, and shall

---

[30] And still hold us up with indignity as being incapable of acquiring knowledge!!! See the inconsistency of the assertions of those wretches—they beat us inhumanely, sometimes almost to death, for attempting to inform ourselves, by reading the *Word* of our Maker, and at the same time tell us, that we are beings *void of intellect*!!! How admirably their practices agree with their professions in this case. Let me cry shame upon you Americans, for such outrages upon human nature!!! If it were possible for the whites always to keep us ignorant and miserable, and make us work to enrich them and their children, and insult our feelings by representing us as *talking Apes,* what would they do? But glory, honour and praise to Heaven's King, that the sons and daughters of Africa, will, in spite of all the opposition of their enemies, stand forth in all the dignity and glory that is granted by the Lord to his creature man.

have us to their fill. We are all in the world together!!—I said above, because we cannot help ourselves (viz. we cannot help the whites murdering our mothers and our wives), but this statement is incorrect—for we can help ourselves; for, if we lay aside abject servility, and be determined to act like men, and not brutes—the murderers among the whites would be afraid to show their cruel heads. But O, my God!—in sorrow I must say it, that my colour, all over the world, have a mean, servile spirit. They yield in a moment to the whites, let them be right or wrong—the reason they are able to keep their feet on our throats. Oh! my coloured brethren, all over the world, when shall we arise from this death-like apathy?—And be men!! You will notice, if ever we become men (I mean *respectable* men, such as other people are), we must exert ourselves to the full.

For remember, that it is the greatest desire and object of the greater part of the whites, to keep us ignorant, and make us work to support them and their families.—Here now, in the Southern and Western sections of this country, there are at least three coloured persons for one white, why is it, that those few weak, good-for-nothing whites, are able to keep so many able men, one of whom, can put to flight a dozen whites, in wretchedness and misery? It shows at once, what the blacks are, we are ignorant, abject, servile and mean—and the whites know it—they know that we are too servile to assert our rights as men—or they would not fool with us as they do. Would they fool with any other people as they do with us? No, they know too well, that they would get themselves ruined. Why do they not bring the inhabitants of Asia to be body servants to them? They know they would get their bodies rent and torn from head to foot. Why do they not get the Aborigines of this country, to be slaves to them and their children, to work their farms and dig their mines? They know well that the Aborigines of this country, (or Indians) would tear them from the earth. The Indians would not rest day or night, they would be up all times of the night, cutting their cruel throats. But my colour (some, not all), are willing to stand still and be murdered by the cruel whites. In some of the West-India Islands, and over a large part of South America, there are six or eight coloured persons for one white.[31] Why do they not take possession of those places? Who hinders them? It is not the avaricious whites—for they are too busily engaged in laying up money—derived from the blood and tears of the blacks. The fact is, they are too servile, they love to have Masters too well!!

Some of our brethren, too, who seeking more after self aggrandisement, than the glory of God, and the welfare of their brethren, join in with our oppressors, to ridicule and say all manner of evils falsely against our Bishop. They think, that they are doing great things, when they can get in company with the whites, to ridicule and make sport of those who are labouring for their good. Poor ignorant creatures, they do not

[31] For instance in the two States of Georgia, and South Carolina, there are, perhaps, not much short of six or seven hundred thousand persons of colour; and if I was a gambling character, I would not be afraid to stake down upon the board FIVE CENTS against TEN, that there are in the single State of Virginia, five or six hundred thousand Coloured persons. Four hundred and fifty thousand of whom (let them be well equipt for war) I would put against every white person on the whole continent of America. (Why? Why because I know that the Blacks, once they get involved in a war, had rather die than to live, they either kill or be killed.) The whites know this too, which make them quake and tremble. To show the world further, how servile the coloured people are, I will only hold up to view, the one Island of Jamaica, as a specimen of our meanness.

In that Island, there are three hundred and fifty thousand souls—of whom fifteen thousand are whites, the remainder, three hundred and thirty-five thousand are coloured people and this Island is ruled by the white people!!! (15,000) ruling and tyrannizing over 335,000 persons!—O! coloured men! O! coloured men!! O! coloured men!! Look!! look!! at this!! and, tell me if we are not abject and servile enough, how long, O! how long my colour shall we be dupes and dogs to the cruel whites?—I only passed Jamaica, and its inhabitants, in review as a specimen to show the world, the condition of the Blacks at this time, now coloured people of the whole world, I beg you to look at the (15,000 white), and (Three Hundred and Thirty-five Thousand coloured people) in that Island, and tell me how can the white tyrants of the world but say that we are not men, but were made to be slaves and Dogs to them and their children forever!!!—why my friends only look at the thing!!! (15,000) whites keeping in wretchedness and degradation (335,000, viz. 22 coloured persons for one white!!!) when at the same time, an equal number (15,000) Blacks would almost take the whole of South America, because where they go as soldiers to fight death follows in their train.

know that the sole aim and object of the whites, are only to make fools and slaves of them, and put the whip to them, and make them work to support them and their families.

But I do say, that no man, can well be a despiser of Bishop Allen, for his public labours among us, unless he is a despiser of God and of Righteousness. Thus, we see, my brethren, the two very opposite positions of those great men, who have written respecting this "Colonizing Plan." (Mr. Clay and his slave-holding party,) men who are resolved to keep us in eternal wretchedness, are also bent upon sending us to Liberia. While the Reverend Bishop Allen, and his party, men who have the fear of God, and the welfare of their brethren at heart. The Bishop, in particular, whose labours for the salvation of his brethren, are well known to a large part of those, who dwell in the United States, are completely opposed to the plan—and advise us to stay where we are. Now we have to determine whose advice we will take respecting this all important matter, whether we will adhere to Mr. Clay and his slave holding party, who have always been our oppressors and murderers, and who are for colonizing us, more through apprehension than humanity, or to this godly man who has done so much for our benefit, together with the advice of all the good and wise among us and the whites. Will any of us leave our homes and go to Africa? I hope not.[32] Let them commence their attack upon us as they did on our brethren in Ohio, driving and beating us from our country, and my soul for theirs, they will have enough of it. Let no man of us budge one step, and let slave-holders come to beat us from our country. America is more our country, than it is the whites—we have enriched it with our *blood and tears*. The greatest riches in all America have arisen from our blood and tears:—and will they drive us from our property and homes, which we have earned with our *blood?* They must look sharp or this very thing will bring swift destruction upon them. The Americans

[32] Those who are ignorant enough to go to Africa, the coloured people ought to be glad to have them go, for if they are ignorant enough to let the whites *fool* them off to Africa, they would be no small injury to us if they reside in this country.

have got so fat on our blood and groans, that they have almost forgotten the God of armies. But let them go on.

ADDITION.—I will give here a very imperfect list of the cruelties inflicted on us by the enlightened Christians of America.—First, no trifling portion of them will beat us nearly to death, if they find us on our knees praying to God,—They hinder us from going to hear the word of God—they keep us sunk in ignorance, and will not let us learn to read the word of God, nor write—If they find us with a book of any description in our hand, they will beat us nearly to death—they are so afraid we will learn to read, and enlighten our dark and benighted minds—They will not suffer us to meet together to worship the God who made us—they brand us with hot iron—they cram bolts of fire down our throats—they cut us as they do horses, bulls, or hogs—they crop our ears and sometimes cut off bits of our tongues—they chain and hand-cuff us, and while in that miserable and wretched condition, beat us with cow-hides and clubs—they keep us half naked and starve us sometimes nearly to death under their infernal whips or lashes (which some of them shall have enough of yet)—They put on us fifty-sixes and chains, and make us work in that cruel situation, and in sickness, under lashes to support them and their families.—They keep us three or four hundred feet under ground working in their mines, night and day to dig up gold and silver to enrich them and their children.—They keep us in the most death-like ignorance by keeping us from all source of information, and call us, who are free men and next to the Angels of God, their property!!!!!! They make us fight and murder each other, many of us being ignorant, not knowing any better.—They take us (being ignorant), and put us as drivers one over the other, and make us afflict each other as bad as they themselves afflict us—and to crown the whole of this catalogue of cruelties, they tell us that we the (blacks) are an inferior race of beings! incapable of self government!!— We would be injurious to society and ourselves, if tyrants should loose their unjust hold on us!!! That if we were free we would not work, but would live on plunder or theft!!!! that we are the meanest and laziest set of beings in the world!!!!! That they are obliged to keep us in bondage to do us good!!!!!!—That we are satisfied to rest in slavery to them and their children!!!!!! —That we ought not to be set free in America, but ought to be sent away to Africa!!!!!!!!—That if we were set free in America, we would involve the country in a civil war, which assertion is altogether at variance with our feeling or design, for we ask them for nothing but the rights of man, viz. for them to set us free, and treat us like men, and there will be no danger, for we will love and respect them, and protect our country— but cannot conscientiously do these things until they treat us like men.

How cunning slave-holders think they are!!!—How much like the king of Egypt who, after he saw plainly that God was determined to bring out his people, in spite of him and his, as powerful as they were. He was willing that Moses, Aaron and the Elders of Israel, but not all the people should go and serve the Lord. But God deceived him as he will Christian Americans, unless they are very cautious how they move. What would have become of the United States of America, was it not for those among the whites, who not in words barely, but in truth and in deed, love and fear the Lord?—Our Lord and Master said:—[33] "Whoso shall offend one of these little ones which believe in me, it were better for him that a millstone were hanged about his neck, and that he were drowned in the depth of the sea."

But the Americans with this very threatening of the Lord's, not only beat his little ones among the Africans, but many of them they put to death or murder. Now the avaricious Americans, think that the Lord Jesus Christ will let them off, because his words are no more than the words of a man!!! In fact, many of them are so avaricious and ignorant, that they do not believe in our Lord and Saviour Jesus Christ. Tyrants may think they are so skillful in State affairs is the reason that the government is preserved. But I tell you, that this country would have been given up long ago, was it not for the lovers of the Lord. They are indeed, the salt of the earth. Remove the people of God

[33] See St. Matthew's Gospel, chap. xviii. 6.

among the whites, from this land of blood, and it will stand until they cleverly get out of the way.

I adopt the language of the Rev. Mr. S. E. Cornish, of New-York, editor of the Rights of All, and say: "Any coloured man of common intelligence, who gives his countenance and influence to that colony, further than its missionary object and interest extend, should be considered as a traitor to his brethren, and discarded by every respectable man of colour. And every member of that society, however pure his motive, whatever may be his religious character and moral worth, should in his efforts to remove the coloured population from their rightful soil, the land of their birth and nativity, be considered as acting gratuitously unrighteous and cruel."

Let me make an appeal brethren, to your hearts, for your cordial co-operation in the circulation of "The Rights of All," among us. The utility of such a vehicle if rightly conducted, cannot be estimated. I hope that the well informed among us, may see the absolute necessity of their co-operation in its universal spread among us. If we should let it go down, never let us undertake any thing of the kind again, but give up at once and say that we are really so ignorant and wretched that we cannot do any thing at all!!—As far as I have seen the writings of its editor, I believe he is not seeking to fill his pockets with money, but has the welfare of his brethren truly at heart. Such men, brethren, ought to be supported by us.

But to return to the colonizing trick. It will be well for me to notice here at once, that I do not mean indiscriminately to condemn all the members and advocates of this scheme, for I believe that there are some friends to the sons of Africa, who are laboring for our salvation, not in words only but in truth and in deed, who have been drawn into this plan.—Some, more by persuasion than any thing else; while others, with humane feelings and lively zeal for our good, seeing how much we suffer from the afflictions poured upon us by unmerciful tyrants, are willing to enroll their names in any thing which they think has for its ultimate end our redemption from wretchedness and miseries; such men, with a heart truly overflowing with gratitude for their past services and zeal in our cause, I humbly beg to examine this plot minutely, and see if the end which they have in view will be completely consummated by such a course of procedure. Our friends who have been imperceptibly drawn into this plot I view with tenderness, and would not for the world injure their feelings, and I have only to hope for the future, that they will withdraw themselves from it;—for I declare to them, that the plot is not for the glory of God, but on the contrary the perpetuation of slavery in this country, which will ruin them and the country forever, unless something is immediately done.

Do the colonizationists think to send us off without first being reconciled to us? Do they think to bundle us up like brutes and send us off, as they did our brethren of the State of Ohio? [34] Have they not to be reconciled to us, or reconcile us to them, for the cruelties with which they have afflicted our fathers and us? Methinks colonizationists think they have a set of brutes to deal with, sure enough. Do they think to drive us from our country and homes, after having enriched it with our blood and tears, and keep back millions of our dear brethren, sunk in the most barbarous wretchedness, to dig up gold and silver for them and their children? Surely, the Americans must think that we are brutes, as some of them have represented us to be. They think that we do not feel for our brethren, whom they are murdering by the inches, but they are dreadfully deceived.

I acknowledge that there are some deceitful and hypocritical wretches among us, who will tell us one thing while they mean another, and thus they go on aiding our enemies to oppress themselves and us. But I declare this day before my Lord and

[34] The great slave-holder, Mr. John Randolph, of Virginia, intimated in one of his *great, happy* and *eloquent* HARRANGUES, before the Virginia Convention, that Ohio is a slave State, by ranking it among other Slaveholding States. This probably was done by the HONORABLE Slave-holder to deter the minds of the ignorant; to such I would say, that Ohio always was and is now a free State, that it never was and I do not believe it ever will be a Slave-holding State; the people I believe, though some of them are hard hearted enough, detest Slavery too much to admit an evil into their bosom, which gnaws into the very vitals, and sinews of those who are now in possession of it.

Master, that I believe there are some true-hearted sons of Africa, in this land of oppression, but pretended *liberty*!!!!!— who do in reality feel for their suffering brethren, who are held in bondage by tyrants. Some of the advocates of this cunningly devised plot of Satan represent us to be the greatest set of cut-throats in the world, as though God wants us to take his work out of his hand before he is ready. Does not vengeance belong to the Lord? Is he not able to repay the Americans for their cruelties, with which they have afflicted Africa's sons and daughters, without our interference, unless we are ordered?

It is surprising to think that the Americans, having the Bible in their hands, do not believe it. Are not the hearts of all men in the hands of the God of battles? And does he not suffer some, in consequence of cruelties, to go on until they are ir-recoverably lost? Now, what can be more aggravating, than for the Americans, after having treated us so bad, to hold us up to the world as such great throat-cutters? It appears to me as though they are resolved to assail us with every species of afflic-tion that their ingenuity can invent. See the African Repository and Colonial Journal, from its commencement to the present day—see how we are through the medium of that periodical, abused and held up by the Americans, as the greatest nuisance to society, and throat-cutters in the world. But the Lord sees their actions.

Americans! notwithstanding you have and do continue to treat us more cruel than any heathen nation ever did a people it had subjected to the same condition that you have us. Now let us reason—I mean you of the United States, whom I believe God designs to save from destruction, if you will hear. For I declare to you, whether you believe it or not, that there are some on the continent of America, who will never be able to repent. God will surely destroy them, to show you his disap-probation of the murders they and you have inflicted on us. I say, let us reason; had you not better take our body, while you have it in your power, and while we are yet ignorant and wretched, not knowing but a little, give us education, and teach us the pure religion of our Lord and Master, which is calculated to make the lion lay down in peace with the lamb, and which millions of you have beaten us nearly to death for trying to obtain since we have been among you, and thus at once, gain our affection while we are ignorant? Remember Americans, that we must and shall be free and enlightened as you are, will you wait until we shall, under God, obtain our liberty by the crushing arm of power? Will it not be dreadful for you? I speak Americans for your good. We must and shall be free I say, in spite of you. You may do your best to keep us in wretchedness and misery, to enrich you and your children, but God will deliver us from under you. And wo, wo, will be to you if we have to obtain our freedom by fighting. Throw away your fears and prejudices then, and enlighten us and treat us like men, and we will like you more than we do now hate you,[35] and tell us now no more about colonization, for America is as much our country, as it is yours.—

Treat us like men, and there is no danger but we will all live in peace and happiness together. For we are not like you, hard hearted, unmerciful, and unforgiving. What a happy country this will be, if the whites will listen. What nation under heaven, will be able to do any thing with us, unless God gives us up into its hand? But Americans, I declare to you, while you keep us and our children in bondage, and treat us like brutes, to make us support you and your families, we cannot be your friends. You do not look for it, do you? Treat us then like men, and we will be your friends. And there is not a doubt in my mind, but that the whole of the past will be sunk into oblivion, and we yet, under God, will become a united and happy people. The whites may say it is impossible, but remember that nothing is impossible with God.

The Americans may say or do as they please, but they have to raise us from the condition of brutes to that of respectable men, and to make a national acknowledgement to us for the wrongs they have inflicted on us. As unexpected, strange, and wild as these propositions may to some appear, it is no less a fact, that unless they are complied with, the Americans of the United States, though they may for a little while escape, God

[35] You are not astonished at my saying we hate you, for if we are men, we cannot but hate you, while you are treating us like dogs.

will yet weigh them in a balance, and if they are not superior to other men, as they have represented themselves to be, he will give them wretchedness to their very heart's content.

And now brethren, having concluded these four Articles, I submit them, together with my Preamble, dedicated to the Lord, for your inspection, in language so very simple, that the most ignorant, who can read at all, may easily understand—of which you may make the best you possibly can.[36] Should tyrants take it into their heads to emancipate any of you, remember that your freedom is your natural right. You are men, as well as they, and instead of returning thanks to them for your freedom, return it to the Holy Ghost, who is our rightful owner. If they do not want to part with your labours, which have enriched them, let them keep you, and my word for it, that God Almighty, will break their strong band. Do you believe this, my brethren?—See my Address, delivered before the General Coloured Association of Massachusetts, which may be found in Freedom's Journal, for Dec. 20, 1828.—See the last clause of that Address. Whether you believe it or not, I tell you that God will dash tyrants, in combination with devils, into atoms, and will bring you out from your wretchedness and miseries under these *Christian People*!!!!!!

Those philanthropists and lovers of the human family, who have volunteered their services for our redemption from

[36] Some of my brethren, who are sensible, do not take an interest in enlightening the minds of our more ignorant brethren respecting this BOOK, and in reading it to them, just as though they will not have either to stand or fall by what is written in this book. Do they believe that I would be so foolish as to put out a book of this kind without strict—ah! very strict commandments of the Lord?—Surely the blacks and whites must think that I am ignorant enough.—Do they think that I would have the audacious wickedness to take the name of my God in vain?

Notice, I said in the concluding clause of Article 3—I call God, I call Angels, I call men to witness, that the destruction of the Americans is at hand, and will be speedily consummated unless they repent. Now I wonder if the world think that I would take the name of God in this way in vain? What do they think I take God to be? Do they suppose that I would trifle with that God who will not have his Holy name taken in vain?—He will show you and the world, in due time, whether this book is for his glory, or written by me through envy to the whites, as some have represented.

wretchedness, have a high claim on our gratitude, and we should always view them as our greatest earthly benefactors.

If any are anxious to ascertain who I am, know the world, that I am one of the oppressed, degraded and wretched sons of Africa, rendered so by the avaricious and unmerciful, among the whites.—If any wish to plunge me into the wretched incapacity of a slave, or murder me for the truth, know ye, that I am in the hand of God, and at your disposal. I count my life not dear unto me, but I am ready to be offered at any moment. For what is the use of living, when in fact I am dead. But remember, Americans, that as miserable, wretched, degraded and abject as you have made us in preceding, and in this generation, to support you and your families, that some of you (whites), on the continent of America, will yet curse the day that you ever were born. You want slaves, and want us for your slaves!!! My colour will yet, root some of you out of the very face of the earth!!!!!! You may doubt it if you please. I know that thousands will doubt—they think they have us so well secured in wretchedness, to them and their children, that it is impossible for such things to occur.[37] So did the antideluvians

[37] Why do the Slave-holders or Tyrants of America and their advocates fight so hard to keep my brethren from receiving and reading my Book of Appeal to them?—Is it because they treat us so well?—Is it because we are satisfied to rest in Slavery to them and their children?—Is it because they are treating us like men, by compensating us all over this free country!! for our labours?—But why are the Americans so very fearfully terrified respecting my Book?—Why do they search vessels, &c. when entering the harbours of tyrannical States, to see if any of my Books can be found, for fear that my brethren will get them to read. Why, I thought the Americans proclaimed to the world that they are a happy, enlightened, humane and Christian people all the inhabitants of the country enjoy equal Rights!! America is the Asylum for the oppressed of all nations!!!

Now I ask the Americans to see the fearful terror they labor under for fear that my brethren will get my Book and read it and tell me if their declaration is true—viz. if the United States of America is a Republican Government?—Is this not the most tyrannical, unmerciful, and cruel government under Heaven—not excepting the Algerines, Turks and Arabs?—I believe if any candid person would take the trouble to go through the Southern and Western sections of this country, and could have the heart to see the cruelties inflicted by these *Christians* on us, he would say, that the Algerines, Turks and Arabs treat their dogs a thousand times better than

doubt Noah, until the day in which the flood came and swept them away. So did the Sodomites doubt, until Lot had got out of the city, and God rained down fire and brimstone from Heaven upon them, and burnt them up. So did the king of Egypt doubt the very existence of a God; he said, "who is the Lord, that I should let Israel go?" Did he not find to his sorrow, who the Lord was, when he and all his mighty men of war, were smothered to death in the Red Sea? So did the Romans doubt, many of them were really so ignorant, that they thought the whole of mankind were made to be slaves to them; just as many of the Americans think now, of my colour. But they got dreadfully deceived. When men got their eyes opened, they made the murderers scamper. The way in which they cut

---

we are treated by the *Christians.*—But perhaps the Americans do their very best to keep my Brethren from receiving and reading my "Appeal" for fear they will find in it an extract which I made from their Declaration of Independence, which says, "we hold these truths to be self-evident, that all men are created equal," &c. &c. &c.—If the above are not the causes of the alarm among the Americans, respecting my Book, I do not know what to impute it to, unless they are possessed of the same spirit with which Demetrius the Silversmith was possessed—however, that they may judge whether they are of the same avaricious and ungodly spirit with that man, I will give here an extract from the Acts of the Apostles, chapter xix.—verses 23, 24, 25, 26, 27.

"And the same time there arose no small stir about that way. For a certain *man* named Demetrius, a silversmith, which made silver shrines for Diana, brought no small gain unto the craftsmen; whom he called together with the workmen of like occupation, and said, Sirs, ye know that by this craft we have our wealth: moreover, ye see and hear, that not alone at Ephesus, but almost throughout all Asia, this Paul hath persuaded and turned away much people, saying, that they be no gods which are made with hands: so that not only this our craft is in danger to be set at nought; but also that the temple of the great goddess Diana should be despised, and her magnificence should be destroyed, whom all Asia and the world worshippeth."

I pray you Americans of North and South America, together with the whole European inhabitants of the world, (I mean Slave-holders and their advocates) to read and ponder over the above verses in your minds, and judge whether or not you are of the infernal spirit with that Heathen Demetrius, the Silversmith: In fine I beg you to read the whole chapter through carefully.

their tyrannical throats, was not much inferior to the way the Romans or murderers, served them, when they held them wretchedness and degradation under their feet. So would Christian Americans doubt, if God should send an Angel from Heaven to preach their funeral sermon. The fact is, the Christians having a name to live, while they are dead, think that God will screen them on that ground.

See the hundreds and thousands of us that are thrown into the seas by Christians, and murdered by them in other ways. They cram us into their vessel holds in chains and in handcuffs—men, women and children, all together!! O! save us, we pray thee, thou God of Heaven and of earth, from the devouring hands of the white Christians!!!

> Oh! thou Alpha and Omega!
> The beginning and the end,
> Enthron'd thou art in Heaven above,
> Surrounded by Angels there:
>
> From whence thou seest the miseries
> To which we are subject;
> The whites have murder'd us, O God!
> And kept us ignorant of thee.
>
> Not satisfied with this, my Lord!
> They throw us in the seas:
> Be pleas'd, we pray, for Jesus' sake,
> To save us from their grasp.
>
> We believe that, for thy glory's sake,
> Thou wilt deliver us;
> But that thou may'st effect these things,
> Thy glory must be sought.

In conclusion, I ask the candid and unprejudiced of the whole world, to search the pages of historians diligently, and see if the Antideluvians—the Sodomites—the Egyptians—the Babylonians—the Ninevites—the Carthagenians—the Persians—the Macedonians—the Greeks—the Romans—the Mahometans—the Jews—or devils, ever treated a set of human beings, as the white

Christians of America do us, the blacks, or Africans. I also ask the attention of the world of mankind to the declaration of these very American people, of the United States.

A declaration made July 4, 1776.

It says,

When in the course of human events, it becomes necessary for one people to dissolve the political bands which have connected them with another, and to assume among the Powers of the earth, the separate and equal station to which the laws of nature and of nature's God entitle them. A decent respect for the opinions of mankind requires, that they should declare the causes which impel them to the separation.—We hold these truths to be self evident—that all men are created equal, that they are endowed by their Creator with certain unalienable rights: that among these, are life, liberty, and the pursuit of happiness that, to secure these rights, governments are instituted among men, deriving their just powers from the consent of the governed; that when ever any form of government becomes destructive of these ends, it is the right of the people to alter or to abolish it, and to institute a new government laying its foundation on such principles, and organizing its powers in such form, as to them shall seem most likely to effect their safety and happiness. Prudence, indeed, will dictate, that governments long established should not be changed for light and transient causes; and accordingly all experience hath shewn, that mankind are more disposed to suffer, while evils are sufferable, than to right themselves by abolishing the forms to which they are accustomed. But when a long train of abuses and usurpations, pursuing invariably the same object, evinces a design to reduce them under absolute despotism, it is their right, it is their duty to throw off such government, and to provide new guards for their future security.[38]

See your Declaration Americans!!! Do you understand your own language? Hear your language, proclaimed to the world, July 4th, 1776—

[38] See the Declaration of Independence of the United States.

> We hold these truths to be self evident—that ALL men are
> created EQUAL!! that they *are endowed by their creator with
> certain unalienable rights;* that among these are life, *liberty,*
> and the pursuit of happiness!!

Compare your own language above, extracted from your
Declaration of Independence, with your cruelties and murders
inflicted by your cruel and unmerciful fathers and yourselves
on our fathers and on us—men who have never given your
fathers or you the least provocation!!!!!!
Hear your language further!

> But when a long train of abuses and usurpation, pursuing
> invariably the same object, evinces a design to reduce them
> under absolute despotism, it is their *right,* it is their *duty,* to
> throw off such government, and to provide new guards for
> their future security.

Now, Americans! I ask you candidly, was your sufferings
under Great Britain, one hundredth part as cruel and tyrannical
as you have rendered ours under you? Some of you, no doubt,
believe that we will never throw off your murderous government and "provide new guards for our future security." If
Satan has made you believe it, will he not deceive you?[39] Do
the whites say, I being a black man, ought to be humble, which
I readily admit? I ask them, ought they not to be as humble as
I? or do they think that they can measure arms with Jehovah?
Will not the Lord yet humble them? or will not these very
coloured people whom they now treat worse than brutes, yet
under God, humble them low down enough? Some of the
whites are ignorant enough to tell us, that we ought to be submissive to them that they may keep their feet on our throats.
And if we do not submit to be beaten to death by them, we are
bad creatures and of course must be damned, &c.
If any man wishes to hear this doctrine openly preached to

[39] The Lord has not taught the Americans that we will not some day or
other throw off their chains and hand-cuffs from our hands and feet, and
their devilish lashes (which some of them shall have enough of yet) from
off our backs.

us by the American preachers, let him go into the Southern and Western sections of this country—I do not speak from hear say—what I have written, is what I have seen and heard myself. No man may think that my book is made up of conjecture—I have travelled and observed nearly the whole of those things myself, and what little I did not get by my own observation, I received from those among the whites and blacks, in whom the greatest confidence may be placed.

The Americans may be as vigilant as they please, but they cannot be vigilant enough for the Lord, neither can they hide themselves, where he will not find and bring them out.

> 1 Thy presence why withdraw'st, Lord?
>   Why hid'st thou now thy face,
>   When dismal times of deep distress
>   Call for thy wonted grace?
>
> 2 The wicked, swell'd with lawless pride,
>   Have made the poor their prey;
>   O let them fall by those designs
>   Which they for others lay.
>
> 3 For straight they triumph, if success
>   Their thriving crimes attend;
>   And sordid wretches, whom God hates,
>   Perversely they command.
>
> 4 To own a pow'r above themselves
>   Their haughty pride disdains;
>   And, therefore, in their stubborn mind
>   No thought of God remains.
>
> 5 Oppressive methods they pursue,
>   And all their foes they slight;
>   Because thy judgments, unobserv'd,
>   Are far above their sight.
>
> 6 They fondly think their prosp'rous state
>   Shall unmolested be;
>   They think their vain designed shall thrive,
>   From all misfortune free.

7 Vain and deceitful is their speech,
      With curses fill'd, and lies;
   By which the mischief of their heart
      They study to disguise.

8 Near public roads they lie conceal'd
      And all their art employ,
   The innocent and poor at once
      To rifle and destroy.

9 Not lions, crouching in their dens,
      Surprise their heedless prey
   With greater cunning, or express
      More savage rage than they.

10 Sometimes they act the harmless man,
       And modest looks they wear;
    That so, deceiv'd the poor may less
       Their sudden onset fear.

PART II.

11 For, God, they think, no notice takes,
       Of their unrighteous deeds;
    He never minds the suff'ring poor,
       Nor their oppression heeds.

12 But thou, O Lord, at length arise,
       Stretch forth thy mighty arm,
    And, by the greatness of thy pow'r,
       Defend the poor from harm.

13 No longer let the wicked vaunt,
       And, proudly boasting, say,
    "Tush, God regards not what we do;
       "He never will repay."—*Common Prayer Book.*

1 Shall I for fear of feeble man,
   The spirit's course in me restrain?
   Or, undismay'd in deed and word,
   Be a true witness of my Lord.

2 Aw'd by mortal's frown, shall I
   Conceal the word of God Most High!
   How then before thee shall I dare
   To stand, or how thy anger bear?

3 Shall I, to soothe th' unholy thong,
   Soften the truth, or smooth my tongue,
   To gain earth's gilded toys or, flee
   The cross endur'd, my Lord, by thee?

4 What then is he whose scorn I dread?
   Whose wrath or hate makes me afraid
   A man! an heir of death! a slave
   To sin! a bubble on the wave!

5 Yea, let men rage, since thou will spread
   Thy shadowing wings around my head:
   Since in all pain thy tender love
   Will still my sure refreshment prove.

Wesleys Collection.

It may not be understood, when I say my Third and last Edition, I mean to convey the idea, that there will be no more Books of this Third Edition printed, but to notify that there will be no more addition in the body of this Work, or additional Notes to this "Appeal."

THE END

3

TEN LETTERS BY AUGUSTINE:
MORAL WORK FOR COLORED MEN

Pittsburgh, November 3, 1837

MR. EDITOR:—Since the commencement of the great abolition movement in our country, many highly respectable and intelligent colored men have fallen into the opinion, that we have less to do in our own moral elevation, and that it will require less to raise us to respectability and usefulness now, than formerly. There are also others, who think it impolitic and improper for us to acknowledge and speak of ourselves as a distinct class, in the community in which we live. Both these I conceive to be errors of considerable magnitude.

Our abolition friends may adduce to the world unanswerable proof of the great sin of slavery, as it now exists in the United States and of the sin of that prejudice which grows out of slavery.—Nay more; they may procure the abolition of both, and still the colored population be as low and degraded as they now are. The mere circumstance of our not being slaves, and of other people's not being prejudiced against us, does not necessarily constitute us elevated and worthy. All moral worth is inherent, and never entirely depends for its existence on external circumstances. Consequently, unless we within and among ourselves become elevated and worthy, we should still be cut off from polite and elevated society, though all the world around us were in our favor.

The relation in which we have for generations been held in this land, constitutes us a distinct class. We have been held as slaves, while those around us have been free. They have been our holders, and we the held. Every power and privilege have been invested with them, while we have been divested of every right. The distinction of our classification is as wide as freedom and slavery, and of a wider than that, my mind has no conception. That it is at all expedient or necessary that this classification and distinction should continue in its present form, I do not by any means desire or allow. But of the fact and reality of its existence, I cannot see how any rational mind could entertain a single doubt.

To adduce all the arguments which might be brought to establish these two positions (that we are a distinct class, and that our moral elevation is a work of our own), would require much more room than is allowed for a single letter in your excellent little paper. I must, therefore, at present, take them for granted, and adduce my further arguments in succeeding letters.

If, then, we form a distinct class, and our present condition be not as we could wish it, and the bettering of that condition be a work of our own, what shall we do for its accomplishment? To every end, there are appropriate means: and if these be not employed, the end cannot be attained. That the general diffusion of useful knowledge is the great means of our moral elevation, is well known and fully appreciated by many. And that the *school,* the *pulpit,* and the *press* are the natural and proper channels through which to communicate this knowledge, is also known;—but I fear the influence of the pulpit, which lies below and beyond both the others, is not so fully appreciated as it should be. Such is the influence of the clergy upon the church, and the church upon the world, that he who commences any great work, with their opposition, commences but to be defeated. A just conception of the magnitude of the influence of the church, is necessary to the mind of every one who would commence the work of our elevation with any hope of success. And as it is a matter of such importance, I shall reserve the arguments in its favor for a future letter.

If the *school,* the *pulpit,* and the *press* be the natural and legitimate means of our moral elevation, and that elevation, to be effectual, must be *general,* how shall these be brought to bear upon every individual of our race in this land? I answer, by

ORGANIZED and *systematic* effort. Every youth should be educated; every minister should be a fountain of light; and a copy of the "Colored American" should be put into the hands of every family. To accomplish these, or either of them, requires organization and the concentration of our whole moral and pecuniary power. And as to our possessing the requisite power and means, I have not the shadow of a doubt. All that is requisite to effect it, is the will.

As to the best mode of organization, whether in a Society or a Convention, I shall not at present undertake to determine. That organization which will be the most general in its composition, the most effective in its operation, and will do the greatest amount of good to the greatest number, is certainly the best. The failures in our attempts at previous organizations, should be no obstacle to future efforts. The young colored men of the United States are our present hope: and it is to them I chiefly address myself. Brethren, shall we, notwithstanding our superior advantages, do no more than our fathers have done before us?— Shall we live and shall we die, without leaving a single monument of our existence behind, to beckon our children on to further and higher moral improvement?

Augustine

From *The Colored American,* December 2, 1837

Pittsburgh, November 30, 1837

MR. EDITOR:—In my first letter to you, under the above caption, I announced my apprehension that some highly respectable and intelligent colored men had fallen into the mistaken opinion [that we have less to do in our] own moral elevation, since the commencement of the great Abolition movement in our country, than before; and, also, that we do not form a distinct class in the community in which we live, and consequently need no separate set of means for our moral elevation. Beside these, I brought forward some other propositions, among which was this, that our moral elevation, in order to its being effectual, should be general, and that its accomplishment is a work of our own; to offer some remarks upon which, I proceed, in this my second letter.

The general character of any nation or class of men, is determined by the private character of a majority of the individuals who compose it. A few individuals of any class of men, being civilized, enlightened and refined, does not procure for their class such a character. This is the case with Ireland, Spain, Turkey and Russia. Not but that there may be found in all these countries, many who excel in whatever is elegant, polite and refined; but because a majority of their population are low, ignorant and degraded, it establishes for them a corresponding national character. So on the contrary; France is characterised for her politeness; Scotland for her morality and attention to the duties of religion; Germany for her gravity and profound learning; and England for her true greatness and national pride. Not but that there may be found in all these nations, many individuals differing essentially from these national characteristics; but because a majority of the individuals who compose them, are such, it establishes for the whole, such a national character.

So it is, and so it will continue to be, with regard to the colored population of the U. States. A majority of them are now in a most degraded condition; and this has stamped the character of degradation upon the whole race. The few who have risen above the condition of the many, are not regarded; nor need they expect to be. Their virtues and attainments will never be fully appreciated, until the majority of the class with whom they are identified, have risen to something like a level with themselves. Hence, the necessity of making an adequate effort for *general* moral improvement. And that that improvement is, and ought so to be considered, by us all, a work of our own. I next proceed to show—

And, in the first place, to desire or admit of others doing for us that which by any possible means we can do for ourselves, is contrary to the manifest design of the Almighty in our original creation. In the beginning God created but one man, and one woman. By this, He no doubt intended to establish the identity and sameness of the whole human family. But, although He has thus made to be of one blood the whole family of man, and constituted them one great brotherhood; yet, in this act, He has clearly shown that it is His will, that each individual of that great family and brotherhood, should take care of himself. This I conceive to be the grand design in the original creation of man; nor does any of the advantages or pleasures which grow out of society, of which I am exceedingly fond, go to the subversion of this design, but rather to its establishment. If, when God created the first man, He had created a number of others to administer to his wants and pleasures, there would have been some ground for the doctrine of dependence, and even slavery itself; but as He acted entirely otherwise, we infer from thence, that originally He intended no dependence.

Secondly, it is a tacit acknowledgment of the want of capacity and nobleness of mind. If we have the capacity to devise the means, and prosecute the end of our moral elevation, what but the want of a right and noble mind, could hinder us from doing it? What better argument could our enemies desire, to establish the doctrine, of our intellectual inferiority, than this, that when ourselves acknowledge, and even feel, our present low and un-desirable condition, we make no general effort, on our own part, to rise above it?

Thirdly, it not only degrades us in the eyes of our opponents, but also in the eyes of our friends. Whenever we are called upon to assist or take care of those who are unable to provide for them-selves, they necessarily lose in our estimation, all considerations of rank and equality. Equality of privilege is a sentiment on which many of us have often dwelt, with much apparent fond-ness, and for the enjoyment of which we have seemed ardently to wish; but we can never rationally expect its attainment, until the majority of our brethren have risen above a state of dependence.

Fourthly, and lastly. So long as we admit of others taking the lead in our moral improvement and elevation, we never can expect it to be done according to our wish or desire. This naturally results from our assuming the attitude of dependents;

and from the inferior consideration in which we are necessarily held, by our benefactors.

This much I have said, not as desiring to discard the assistance of friends, to whom I cling with most unyielding tenacity, but as showing the proper and lawful use of them. To inspire us with a desire to rise above the condition of wards and minors, and assume the rank of *responsible* MEN. Nature, reason, and God Himself, conspire to teach us that it is our duty; and how may we expect to escape the unmingled execration of the present and succeeding generations, if we neglect its performance.

Augustine

From *The Colored American,* December 9, 1837

- -

Pittsburgh, December 15, 1837

Mr. Editor:—In my third letter, I gave it as my opinion that a combination of the moral and pecuniary power of the free colored people of the United States, under the name of a *Convention,* would be, all things considered, best adapted to the general welfare. In this, my fourth letter, I propose to make some remarks on the members who should compose such a body; and on its general utility.

The great object in forming a *General Convention,* or *national meeting* of any kind, should be, to obtain the collected *wisdom, integrity* and *patriotism,* of our race in this land. It needs no argument to show, that these are best qualified to devise the means of the general welfare. Nor need I detain the reader, for the purpose of bringing from past history, unquestionable evidence, that while the destinies of any people have been guided by such men, they have always been prosperous. Whatever want of ability and qualification they experience in the beginning, is more than made up in their integrity of purpose and uprightness of soul. Their patriotism prompts them soon to learn whatever pertains to the general good; and having learned, they certainly do it. No matter can be too great for them; for the minds of such men always experience an elevation and expansion commensurate with the object before them. But, to obtain such a body of men, is a matter of no ordinary difficulty.

As a class, our condition is a very peculiar one. The great body of us are not, at present, sufficiently enlightened to see or appreciate our own best interest. And, as is the case with all people thus circumstanced, our best men are far from being the most popular: the light of example which shines in the wise and good, is intolerable to those whose ignorance has made them vicious; and whose state of moral feeling, for want of cultivation, has necessarily become low. Such men, let their extraction be what it may, could scarcely be expected to come together; and at once, voluntarily from among themselves, elect such public servants as we have before mentioned. That men by any course of policy should be thus incapacitated, is a matter of the deepest regret. But that such cases may, and do exist, must be admitted by the most devoted lover of his country and his kind. The doctrine that men need qualification for self government, has been established in the history of modern France. The lovers of self government in that quarter, thought they could secure its enjoyment without the requisite qualification; they tried, but they failed.—Such an example should be sufficient to determine the conduct of every wise and prudent man in regard to ourselves.

If then it cannot be hoped, that in our present condition, we will voluntarily from among ourselves, elect men the most eminent for their wisdom, integrity and patriotism; and if it be desirable that such, and such only, should compose the *national meeting*, whose sole object should be the general welfare, by what means may such a meeting be obtained? To whatever answer we may propose to this question, there arise numberless objections; and, therefore, whilst I attempt it, I ask the indulgence and candour of every young man, who may have taken any interest in these letters.

And, *in the first place,* I would answer, let all those whose love of country and kindred might prompt them to such a course, voluntarily associate. Into such an association, every colored American who has in any way distinguished himself in behalf of his countrymen, should be admitted. The terms of admission should be a lawful character, and a reasonable pecuniary consideration. If it be objected that too many would thus associate, for the convenience of transacting business in the annual meeting; the answer is, that the expense of such attendance is sufficient to guard it from all superfluity. And even if this were not the case, such regulations could easily be made, as would free it from all excess. Thus an opportunity would be afforded for all our wisest and best men to associate themselves for the general good.

Secondly. Let the people in their respective districts *select delegates* to represent them in their national meeting. I need scarcely add, that delegates elected by the people should, as soon as practicable, entirely supersede the voluntarily associated.

The utility of a General Convention is apparent from various reasons. As I observed in a previous letter, that the elevation of a few *individuals* of a particular class, does not obtain for that class the character of elevation; so, in like manner does it apply to the elevation of a few individual *districts* of a whole nation. It is necessary that a majority of all its *districts*, as well as its individuals, should be elevated, enlightened and refined, in order to its obtaining a like general character. Hence, the necessity of *general action* on our part. Those gentlemen who labor for one city or one state alone, without any regard to uniting the whole in that labor, show themselves to be short sighted; and if they could trace out the result of their labors, would find them imperfect indeed. He who labors not for the general good of his *whole* country, deserves not the name of patriotism.

A General Convention is necessary to the full development of our intellectual powers. It is one of the laws of nature, to furnish just so much material as is brought into actual requisition, and no more. Consequently if there be no means with us, of bringing into requisition the great and noble powers of the soul, they must necessarily greatly diminish, if not become entirely extinct. And there are no means of developing these mighty powers, like that of great and popular assemblies. Ancient Greece owes her greatness and glory more to the eloquence of her orators, than the swords of her warriors.

It would create *national feeling* and *intensity* of *interest;* inspire *confidence, energy* and *self respect.* The want of these qualities, among the detached portions of our race in this land, is apparent to the most careless observer; and is deeply lamented by every patriot with whom I have ever conversed. Without them, nothing honorable or worthy can ever be expected. Men will never respect themselves, much less be respected by others, until they are conscious of some moral worth or consideration; nor will they ever aim at high and exalted action, without a consciousness of the ability.

Augustine

From *The Colored American,* December 30, 1837

Pittsburgh, December 29, 1837

MR. EDITOR:—Those young men whose attention and interest I have been so happy as to secure, will recollect, that in the first of my four preceding letters, I stated that the only efficient means of our moral elevation is the general diffusion of useful knowledge; and that the proper and legitimate channels of its diffusion are the *school,* the *pulpit,* and the *press.* The vast importance of these is self-evident to every one who reads and *thinks;* and therefore requires no pause for elucidation. But of the three, the importance and influence of the *pulpit* is the greatest; lying below and beyond both the others—controlling and ultimately triumphing over them. And accordingly, as I promised in a preceding letter, I now proceed to make some observations on this mighty influence, as it may be made to apply to our condition in the United States.

Devotion is one of the constituent principles of our nature. Let us cast our eyes on whatever portion of the earth's surface we may, there we find the *priest,* the *altar,* the *offering,* and the *devoted.* From the freezing pole to the burning zone, and around the entire circle, we may follow its deep traces, and witness the signs of its triumph. Men of every nation, language, country and clime, are alike subject to its sway. Those who have been for unknown ages cut off from all connection with the rest of their species, are as deeply imbued with it, as those who have enjoyed the most unbounded intercourse. Nor can it, by any course of instruction, be wholly eradicated—being by the utmost stretch of human effort, merely modified. And although it is often made to assume a variety of *forms,* yet the *principle* is the same among all classes of men.

To deny the fact of the predominance of this principle, is but to show our ignorance of the philosophy of our own nature. And to assert that it has been imposed upon us by a crafty priesthood, is but to show our ignorance of the history of our race. It is the foundation of the moral world, and the chief corner stone on which all its superstructures are built. It is the nucleus around which all the affairs of mortality revolve; and upon its purity or corruption ever has, and ever will depend the purity or corruption of all human society.

In all countries where devotion has been qualified and regulated by the light of revelation from God, there we find a more or less pure and exalted state of society; but where it has been left to the light of unaided reason, there we find society more or less corrupt and degenerate. The state of morals among all classes of men is in an exact ratio to the amount of useful knowledge which they possess; and their idea of the moral character of the Deity whom they worship. In all the passions, appetites and desires, of which they suppose him capable, they will freely indulge; and to all the high and holy attributes which they suppose him to possess, they will ardently aspire. What he has enjoined, they will do; and from what he has forbidden they will refrain. All aberrations from this principle are but transitory —lasting only while the sunshine of prosperity gilds our path. For when the ills of mortality crowd upon us, we invariably seek for relief in acts of devotion, and endeavor to assimilate our own character to that of the object whom we worship.

Hence the importance of getting hold of this great leading principle in our nature, and giving it a proper direction; for in doing this we secure the control of all others.

From all which I have said, from the commencement of these letters, the attentive reader will have but little difficulty in determining what pulpits I expect to constitute the channel for the diffusion of useful knowledge, among all classes of our people in this land. The motto under which I have written, pre-supposes them to be *our own*. All hopes of any general benefit from the pulpits of others, are without any rational foundation. Prejudice, the offspring of slavery, shuts us out alike from the pulpit and the house of God, with our fairer brethren; —it shuts their eyes, stops their ears, steels their hearts against us, and cuts us off from all friendly intercourse with them—and leaves it with ourselves alone to sink to perdition, or rise to immortality. It is to the pulpits of our own congregations that I wish to direct the attention of the reader, as being the only source from which shall issue those fountains of knowledge, virtue and piety, that shall cause the moral regeneration of our race.

The priesthood are as much the repository of knowledge, as the standard of morals among all classes of men. And it is as much their duty to enlighten the understanding, as to purify the heart. This truth has been established by the example of God Himself, in the government of His chosen people. For among the Jews, it was as much the duty of the tribe of Levi to instruct the people, as to administer at the altar. This example, in itself, is sufficient to silence every objection, and dispel every doubt. But if there is one who yet doubts its wisdom and truth, let him cast his eyes over our present world, and contemplate its condition. Wherever there is an enlightened and pious priesthood, there he beholds all the advantages of civilization, and Christianity blessing mankind with the glories of her reign. But wherever there is an ignorant priesthood, there he beholds all the horrors of heathenism, and the reign of idolatry, entailing all the curses incident to frail and deluded mortality. With these facts before him, who can doubt the utility of interesting the priesthood in the great work of our moral regeneration?—qualifying them for the discharge of the high and solemn duties for which they are ordained, and urging them to their performance?

After duly considering what has been said, I would ask

my attentive reader, on what does he found his hopes of any permanent success in our moral elevation, without the co-operation of the priesthood? And what assurance has he for his expectation, that our moral character will ever be what it should, unless we have a competent priesthood to supply our intellectual wants? That such a priesthood may be attained and their co-operation secured, I have no hesitation in believing; and as the space allowed me is now filled, I must leave the further observa-tions on this subject for my next letter.

In concluding this letter, I most solemnly disclaim all ill or irreverent feeling towards the most unqualified brother who now ministers at the altar of God, in any of our congregations. The God whom I desire to serve is witness, that I have no hostility against a single being on the whole earth. My only inducement to write is, a humble, though ardent desire to do good.

Augustine

From *The Colored American,* January 13, 1838

- -

Pittsburgh, January 17, 1838

MR. EDITOR:—In the last of my five preceding letters, I made some observations on the universal prevalence of devotional feeling, and on its controlling influence over all others. In this my *sixth* letter, I proceed to conclude the observations which I there began.

The want of a competent clergy to supply the intellectual wants of the colored population of the United States, has long been seriously felt and deeply deplored, by all our most en-lightened and patriotic fellow citizens. It is the source of in-numerable evils, delinquencies, and derelictions from the paths of honor and rectitude; an admitted evil by all who have either spoken or written upon it; lying in the way, as a great stumbling block, of every effort for our moral elevation. It sits as a mighty incubus upon our moral energies—paralyzing and rendering them wholly inadequate to those herculean efforts which are necessary to break down the walls with which we have been so long surrounded.

No people has ever yet arose to any eminence, without a clergy competent to their intellectual wants. And the highest period in the history of every nation, is that in which the greatest attention was paid to the duties of religion. Thus it was with the Jews in the days of Solomon; for while the *wealth of the world* was being poured into their coffers, at the same time their *Temple* was adorned with the greatest glory and grandeur, and their *altar* smoked with the most numerous victims. Let the intelligent reader cast his eyes over the society by which he is surrounded, and see who it is that have the most wealth, talent, and power in their hands:—it is those who are most noted for their attendance on the administration of a *pious and enlightened clergy*. Indeed, our most enlightened and patriotic statesmen attribute the imparalleled (sic) prosperity of our country, more to the services of an enlightened clergy, than to all our natural advantages combined.

The spirit of our free institutions is traced by every *American,* to the *"Pilgrim Fathers,"* who fled from *religious* intolerance in Europe to the wilds of America, that they might worship God according to the dictates of their own consciences—and not according to the dictates of others. These men, in being accompanied by their pious and enlightened clergy, brought with them all the elements of true greatness and successful enterprise.—From a handful, who were soon expected to perish among the desolations of the wilderness, they have become the mightiest republic on the face of the globe—the spirit of freedom still living in the bosoms of their sons, who are foremost in the ranks of those who fight for universal liberty, and are first to die in its defence. But I must come to the more immediate subject of my letter.—How are we to obtain a competent clergy to supply our intellectual wants?

Those who have preceded me in answering this question, have generally failed in this one point: they have never proposed a remedy commensurate with the evil of which they complain. My talented and learned friend, "A COLORED BALTI-

MOREAN," was especially defective in this particular. He proposed a remedy for *his own city*, while the evil of which he complained exists every where; nor did he even tell us what was the literary *"standard"* to which he would have his theological students aspire. At the time of his writing, I felt much disappointed at the limited view which he took of a subject of such importance—well knowing the power of his eloquent pen, and his entire competency to have pointed out a *commensurate remedy*.

Every *remedy* which is not commensurate with the evil for which it is proposed, is essentially defective;—for although it may mitigate the disease, it never can produce an *effectual cure*. To have a competent clergy to supply the intellectual wants of *one city*, is indeed excellent, so far as it goes; but it does not go far enough; we want a like supply for the intellectual wants of ALL our cities. We wish to see our whole race in this land formed into congregations for the worship of GOD, and every congregation supplied with a competent clergyman.

Although *devotion* is the controlling influence of our nature, yet it is not of such a kind that it may not itself be controlled and modified by other influences. The pulpit acts upon and controls the press; and so does the press act upon and control the pulpit. The pulpit and the press are the proper regulators of *public opinion;*—and again, public opinion may be made to regulate them both. *Combination* is the genius of all the institutions of this country, whether civil, social, or religious; and is the great secret of its unparalleled achievements. This much I have said, as showing the efficiency of the means which I would enjoy in the attainment of a competent clergy.

Hence I would say, let all who are fully impressed with the importance of our having such a clergy, *combine* for its attainment. Let as many of our ministers as already possess the usual literary qualifications of ministers, in the more popular branches of the Christian church in this country, begin to *preach* pointedly and clearly on the importance of young men preparing for the duties of the sacred office. Let those who are not ministers, *speak* of it at all proper times and places, in a mild and affectionate manner. And let them lay by a reasonable sum monthly, out of that with which the Lord hath blessed them, to constitute a FUND for the promotion of this object. Let all who have the ability, *write* on this subject, and bring the PRESS with all its influence to bear upon it. Thus our people would soon be brought to see its importance and feel an interest in it. Public opinion would demand it, AND THEN IT MUST BE HAD.

But, says one, "This is a delicate question;—you wish to stop those who are already in the ministry, whom you think not sufficiently qualified for the office." Not so;—we only wish to prevent any more unqualified ones from getting in. It is the young, who are just coming forward, that we hope to have prepared; so that when the old are gone, they may fill up their places with honor to themselves, and usefulness to the world.

The "standard" to which I would have all our young candidates for the ministry aspire, is a thorough classical education, and a life of spotless piety. Nor would I stop at educating those only who have an eye to the sacred office; we want a great number to teach our schools, and to heal our diseases, and for many other purposes. Slavery must soon be abolished; and if so, where are the men to supply the wants that will then be created? Brethren, we are far behind the spirit of the age. God is holding out his blessings to us, and we are not preparing to receive them. When HE calls for us, will we be ready? When HE demands our action, will we be prepared?

In concluding this letter, may I be allowed to indulge the hope, that I have drawn the attention of at least a few patriotic brethren, to this important subject—and that they will bring it with them to our next "*national meeting*," for its final settlement.

Augustine

From *The Colored American,* January 27, 1838

Pittsburgh, January 25, 1838

MR. EDITOR:—Having in my *six* preceding letters hastily glanced at the great work which is necessary to be done, in order to our moral elevation in this land, the persons by whom it is chiefly to be performed, and the means to be employed for its accomplishment, in this my *seventh* letter, I proceed to close the series.

As I observed in the commencement of these letters, I am fully aware of my inability to do justice to a subject of such grave importance. The elevation of three millions of immortal beings from the lowest depths of moral degradation, to the proper level of humanity, is a work to which the head and pen of the mightiest sage is barely adequate.

To produce a moral revolution, such as is needed in our case, has ever been found a work of the greatest difficulty, even when every facility for its accomplishment was afforded. But how much more difficult must it be with us, when a thousand obstacles are thrown in the way; the very contemplation of which is enough to still the tongue, and stop the pen, of the most ardent patriotism? And had no others presented themselves to my mind, considerations of this nature would have entirely deterred me from writing. But I remembered that man, though ever so degraded, is still possessed of an immortal SOUL, having stamped on it the impress of DIVINITY. And although it may be long borne down with the casualties of the body, yet the *divinity* within it is sufficient to enable it to rise above all external circumstances, and regain its native dignity. Hence arose the hope which prompted me to write; feeling well assured, that if our case were a thousand times worse than it really is, it were not yet hopeless; our resources being more than sufficient for every thing, provided each one would do his part.

Nothing is more apparent at the present time, than the want of union and concert of action among us.—We are scattered over a vast surface of country, and settled in small communities at a great distance from each other, knowing little of each other, and feeling but little interest in each other's welfare. While at the same time, that prejudice which is the offspring of slavery, and is equally our enemy in all places, unites its votaries to cut us off from all privileges in the society by which we are surrounded, whether civil, social, or religious. It separates us into a distinct class; not for the purpose of elevating and doing us good, but for the purpose of degrading and doing us evil. It never has sought, nor never intends to seek, our welfare. And if we sit down and fold our hands together, under the expectation that all the blessings of enlightened freedom will come upon us of themselves, or be put upon us solely by the labor of others, our expectation will never be realized.

Our moral elevation is a work in which we may be *assisted*, and in which we *need* much assistance, in which much assistance is *owed* us, but which never can be done for us. We must become alive to its importance on our own part, and acquaint ourselves of its true nature. And if ever we expect its accomplishment, we must engage in it with a zeal and energy commensurate with its magnitude. We should form an institution that will bring the most distant and detached portions of our people together, embrace their varied interests, and unite their whole moral power. Our collected wisdom should be assembled, to consult on measures pertaining to the general welfare; and so direct our energies, as to do the greatest amount of good to the greatest number. Thus *united*, and thus directed, every weapon that prejudice has formed against us, would be rendered powerless; and our moral elevation would be as rapid, as it would be certain.

Without a national institution of some description, our affairs can never attain any degree of consistence or permanence. There can be no *head* or *centre* around which we may rally. Our *numbers, means* and *capacity*, will remain useless, for want of something to combine and concentrate them. The high intellectual powers must diminish, if not become entirely extinct, for want of the means of their development. The noble and praiseworthy efforts of the *few*, must continue to be partial, imperfect, and unsuccessful, for want of the support and cooperation of the *many*. I have already expressed myself in favor of a *Convention*, but if a society can be so modified as to meet our wants, I shall be perfectly willing to acquiesce. I will not object to any institution which may meet the views of a majority, provided it will unite and harmonize the distant and discordant parts of our population.

I have said but little in regard to the importance of the *Press*, because it was not necessary; its importance having been already set before us with much more ability than that of which I am capable. But in my conviction of its importance, and devotion to its interest, I yield to none. Since its commencement, the "*Colored American*" has done more for the establishment of our intellectual character, than all other papers, lecturers, and friends combined. It is our moral oregis; and the inscriptions of *intellect* upon it, are more terrible to our enemies than the Gorgon's head.

Nor was it necessary that I should say much in regard to the importance of *Schools*. Most of our leading men, and especially those who *read,* are fully impressed with their importance. It were happy for us, did our clergy and church every where take a deeper interest in this important matter. *The general diffusion of useful knowledge,* is the certain and sure means of our real elevation; and every channel should not only be kept open, but made to flow. Without a more general diffusion of useful knowledge, we need never expect to obtain that *liberty* and *equality* for which we all so ardently wish.—And even if we could obtain it, we never could realise its enjoyment, in our present unqualified state, in all its fulness and purity.

Throughout these letters I have endeavored to treat of things as they *really are,* and not as I would *wish* them to be. My recognition of ourselves as "*a distinct class,*" is not in consequence of my approbation of the wicked spirit which has produced it. No man on earth can more cordially abhor the spirit of "caste" than I do. And I treat of it, not for the purpose of its continuance, but for the purpose of its most speedy abolition.

My quotations have been chiefly from the Bible, not only because it is the best book, but the most common, being, as I trust, in the hands of all my readers.

A thousand thanks to you, Mr. Editor, for your prompt insertion of my letters, and for your flattering notice of them; as, also, my acknowledgments to the indulgent reader; and, with these, the series is concluded.

Augustine

From *The Colored American,* February 10, 1838

- -

Pittsburgh, July 13, 1838

Mr. Editor:—I thank you for the kind and courteous manner in which you noticed my letter in your paper of the 23rd of June, and for the freedom and independence with which you have been pleased to remark upon it.—And had your remarks been altogether free from "error" or "mistake," I should not have found it necessary to trouble you with this letter.

And before I proceed, allow me to assure you that it is no love of controversy which prompts me to write, for I have neither the talent nor the disposition for it. My sole object is, to assist in carrying forward that great work of moral reformation, which we all agree is so much needed among our race in this land. In doing this, I have always endeavored to lay aside all personal feeling, and advocate such measures as were not merely to me *desirable,* but such as were actually and generally *practicable;* such as were calculated not to benefit only the *few,* but the *many.* I believe in, and would desire to practice upon, that philosophy which aims to do the greatest amount of good to the greatest number.

We agree that too many of our people have crowded themselves into the larger towns and cities of the free States; and we also agree in the necessity of their removing to, and settling in the country. But about the *mode* of that settlement we disagree. *You* would have them leave the cities and towns, where they are already "mixed" and "scattered" among the whites, and in which situation you acknowledge the many hardships and inconveniences which prejudice has caused them, and "mix" and "scatter" themselves among the whites in the country, where you suppose their condition would be much improved. But your authority for supposing that there is less prejudice in the country than in the city, and that there are better accommodations for us in the churches, and greater facilities for our children's getting into good schools there, you have not been kind enough to give us. *I* would have them leave the cities where they are now "scattered" and "mixed" among the whites, whose prejudices exclude them from equal privileges in society, churches and schools, and settle themselves in communities in the country, and establish society, churches and schools of their own.

Your arguments against separate settlements are far from being conclusive or satisfactory. In one place you tell us that *"contact"* is the most powerful engine in wearing out prejudices;—if so, why has it not worn out the prejudices of the whites in the cities, where the contact is daily and continued? If this argument be true, prejudice in the country must be far greater than in the city, for in the country there has been little or no *"contact."* And this argument you say is sustained by the history and experience of all ages; but you have not been kind enough to cite us to a single passage. Separation has been resorted to as a means of curing antipathies, by older and better men than me. When there was strife between the herdmen of Lot's cattle and those of Abraham's, that good man and "father of the faithful"—that "friend of God" proposed to heal the strife by separation.—Gen. 13 chapt. 9 v. This I consider a fair quotation, and to the point. And if following such an illustrious example renders me "weak and foolish," I am perfectly content to be considered so. If I, with even this my "foolishness," may ultimately find a resting place in the bosom of Abraham, *wise men* shall be welcome to rest where they can.

When you asserted that the whole history of the past was in favor of "contact," as being the most powerful means of destroying antipathies, the history of *our own country* must have entirely escaped your memory. The very act which gave it political existence, was an act of separation. Is the DECLARATION OF INDEPENDENCE therefore, a "weak and foolish" document, and were its framers "weak and foolish" men? Have you forgotten the history of the separation of the Friends, the Methodists, and even the Presbyterians? Of the utility of these several separations I do not now pretend to speak. My object in referring to them is, to show that other men than me, or old father Abraham, have been "weak and foolish" enough to resort to separation, and the formation of societies of their own, as a means of curing existing antipathies.

The *principle* which I have endeavored to maintain . . . on separate settlements is this, that it is right, and in accordance with the mind of God, for men whose condition has been rendered unhappy in one place, to better it if they can, by removing to another; and that the *manner, time,* and *place* of such removal, should be exclusively matters of their own choice. And through what kind of glasses you were looking, Mr. Editor, when this simple principle appeared to you like *"colonization magnified,"* I am at a loss to know. Those which I use are a plain pair of Parisian manufacture;—and when I look at it through them, it has no such appearance. Purchasing contiguous tracts of land from the Congress of our native country, and settling upon them, so as to have society, churches, and schools of our own, without being subject to the humiliation of begging them from others, looks very much like being *exiled* to the cheerless coast of Africa, don't it? Surely your readers will be able to distinguish the difference.

In the third paragraph of your remarks, you say, "If we or our posterity ever possess the inalienable rights of American citizens, it must be in identity of interests, and consequently in identity of communities and of intercourse with our white brethren." This is an "error," as I shall endeavor to show very plainly.—The people of Georgia, Alabama and Mississippi form three distinct communities, and yet their interests are so closely identified as scarcely to admit of a contrast. Moreover, more than half the individuals of any one of these three distinct communities, never see or have any intercourse with those of the others, and yet they are American citizens. And for any thing that I know, the same may be said of the people of the Western, or of the New England States. Hence you see there can be an identity of *interest*, without an identity of *community*, and that men may be American citizens without having any *intercourse* with each other. And this I hold would be the case with ourselves, though we even composed a separate State in this great confederacy. For the right to the title of American citizen, depends not upon the circumstances of interest, location, or intercourse, but upon having been born and reared upon the soil, and contributed to the general welfare.

In the fifth paragraph of your remarks, you say I am "mistaken" in saying that our friends contend not for our social equality or intercourse. I shall be very happy to find myself mistaken; but where is your authority for charging me with "mistake"? Our bare assertions will certainly have equal credit with all candid

readers, until the weight of authority shall turn the balance in
favor of either the one or the other. This is a point on which I
have bestowed particular attention, from the commencement of
the Anti-Slavery operations; and I have never seen any thing
from the pen of a single popular writer, which led me to believe
that they considered such intercourse at all desirable, much less
to be "sought after."—If you know of any *standard work* recommending such intercourse, cite me to it, and I will thank you
most heartily.

In calling upon you, Mr. Editor, for *authority* to sustain the
opinions which you have advanced, no disrespect whatever of
your integrity is intended. The only presumption is, that a
multiplicity of other cares, as well as an opposite "feeling," has
prevented you from bestowing that attention on this subject
which its importance demands. It may also be a subject of
novelty to you, and merely on that account may not have your
approbation. But I can assure you that in the West it is not
merely a matter of theory; it has long since been reduced to
practice. My father now resides, and has been for the last eight
years residing in such a settlement, in Jackson county, Ohio.
The settlement is highly prosperous and happy. They have a
church, day and Sabbath school of their own. The people of this
settlement cut their own harvests, roll their own logs, and raise
their own houses, just as well as though they had been assisted
by white friends. They find just as ready and as high market for
their grain and cattle, as their white neighbors. They take the
newspapers and read many useful books, and are making as
rapid advancement in intelligence and refinement as any people
in the country generally do. And when they travel out of their
settlement, no colored people, let them reside where or among
whom they may, are more respected, or treated with greater
deference than they are.

This is certainly a subject of vast importance; because it
directly concerns the happiness and prosperity of a majority of
all our people in the free States. Their condition in the towns
and cities is miserable and degraded to the last extreme. We see,
I trust we feel, the necessity of their removing to the country;
and in urging them to do so, we take upon ourselves a vast

amount of responsibility. It is our duty to provide, not only for their *physical*, but for their *mental* wants. We should not seek to have them located in such a manner, that their children would grow up as rude and ignorant as the horses and oxen on their pastures; but so that they might grow up under all the advantages of literature, religion, and civil society.

In conclusion, I would say to those who fear that the adoption of this plan would so thin our numbers in the cities, as to render us unable to maintain our present necessary moral institutions, there need be no fear. The increased facilities for the acquisition of means, by those left behind, would more than fill the vacuum. A whole State might be formed, without any *perceptible* diminution of our numbers.

I have been rather more lengthy, I fear, than is pleasant to some of your readers and correspondents. But this is a subject in which I, as well as many others of my acquaintance, feel such a deep interest, that I could not well dismiss it sooner. And to ensure from them, and you, Mr. Editor, a more ready pardon, I promise you that I shall not soon again write such a long letter.

Augustine

From *The Colored American,* July 28, 1838

- -

Pittsburgh, January 22, 1839

THE WEST NO. 1.

MESSRS. EDITORS:—So much has been already written, and written well, on the climate, soil, productions, and scenery of the West, that nothing in these respects which may be interesting to your readers, is left for me to write. Its colored population has seldom employed the pen of any one; and even when employed, it has been mostly in misrepresentation. A consideration of this fact has induced me to contribute a few numbers for your paper, giving a true and impartial representation of this class of population.

The territory to which my remarks are intended to apply, is all that of the free States, west of the Allegheny mountains. Of the *present* number of colored persons included within this territory, I have no means of ascertaining. Since 1830, its increase has been very great, and it now very probably amounts to thirty thousand.

This population is made up chiefly of emigrants from the Southern and South-western States. There, in almost every place, are vastly more than those born upon the soil. Most of the men are hardy and robust; capable of enduring the severest labor, having been accustomed to it from childhood; but too many of them are unfortunately wanting in that intelligence, which is necessary to give to their labor a proper direction, and render it most *productive*.

INTELLIGENCE is as necessary to *productive* industry, as the genial co-operation of the natural elements. The earth may present her fruitful surface, the pearly dews and refreshing showers may distil, and the sun may send down his fructifying rays: but all in vain, if man be destitute of a knowledge of the wonderful advantages which they offer him. This consideration fully accounts for the poverty of many, who might otherwise be vastly rich.

Many of them are settled in the country, and own the farms on which they live. This, I think, is far more generally the case than at the North and East.—In some of the large towns, a majority of its colored inhabitants are the owners of lots. When I lived in Columbus, Ohio, in 1830, there were 34 colored families in the place, of whom 30 were the owners of lots; some of which were very valuable, being within a square and a square and a half of the State House.—But this happy proportion of landholders is far less in some other equally favored places; and its cause may almost invariably be traced to a want of intelligence and enterprise in its inhabitants.

A colored farmer has just the same chance of getting along that a white one has. In this department of industry, if in no other, he is on perfect equality. Nature has no prejudice in her heart. With the same equal hand she lavishes her rewards on all who are willing to earn them, whether white or colored. He finds just as ready market for all his produce, of the same quality, as any body else. I never knew of any one having a good lot of wheat, butter, feathers, cattle, hogs, sheep or horses, and could not dispose of them at the market price. Some of them do not take the newspapers, and are often ignorant of the improvements that are making in agriculture; and consequently do not sometimes bring so good an article to market, as their more intelligent and enterprising neighbors, and of course must take a less price for it, if they sell it at all. These are apt to grumble, and charge their *color* with being the cause of this difference, when the true cause is, their own obstinate stupidity. When they employ the same means that others do, they never fail of realizing the same result.

In most of the small towns and country places there is little prejudice against colored mechanics. I never knew a first-rate workman, in any of the mechanical departments, who need go idle a single week, in the whole year, for want of work. Mechanics are often in great demand, and at such times gentlemen think very little about *color*. A good workman, who can push their business *"ahead,"* is what they want. The general reason why colored mechanics complain of want of work, is because they do not *assiduously* apply themselves to the acquisition of skill in their trades and are lacking in the true mechanic *"quick step."*

As I observed before, at some seasons of the year mechanical labor is in great demand. Many manufactured articles are wanting, and the highest price is offered. Manufacturers then become urgent for work, and are willing to give the highest wages. If at such a time a hand is dull, and will not exert himself to the utmost, they become irritated and disgusted at him, and turn him off. I have known some to refuse to work at night, in time of a great throng, although they were offered double pay; because they thought it a little hard. I know that it is hard, and too hard to be long sustained, by the most robust constitution, to work night and day; but when double wages are offered, the hardship is greatly mitigated, and might be sustained for a short time, by almost any one. I have known white mechanics to work eighteen hours, out of the twenty-four, for a whole week at a time.

In some places, ten hours a day is the usual time of labor. And if a man only labor during this time, his wages will be just sufficient to keep him decently, without any surplus at the end of the year. Now suppose he were working at a dollar a day, which is the same as ten cents an hour, and would extend his labor to twelve hours; in this case he would gain twenty cents a day, over and above his decent maintenance—and allowing three hundred working days in a year, this would amount to sixty dollars. But suppose he would extend his labor to fifteen hours a day; his surplus production would amount in a year to one hundred and fifty dollars. This sum at the end of ten years would be a sufficient capital whereon to commence the acquisition of a fine fortune.

But a dollar a day is the very lowest wages offered our mechanics; they mostly get from a dollar and a quarter to a dollar and a half; and hence have so much the better chance of enriching themselves by extra labor.

Augustine

From *The Colored American,* February 9, 1839

- -

Pittsburgh, February 1, 1839

THE WEST NO. 2.

Messrs. Editors:—My last letter closed with some remarks on colored mechanics in the west. My present will commence with some allusion to those engaged in merchandise or exchange.

The number of these is necessarily very small. The intelligence and skill which is necessary for conducting the business of exchange, is possessed by few colored persons. This, in most cases, is more their misfortune than their fault. They have been brought up without the necessary training. Those who had charge of their youth, in most cases, intended them, in after life, for none but the most common employments and lowest drudgery; and hence adapted all their instruction to this end. It is not then to be wondered at, that so few attain to the intelligence and skill which is necessary to the successful conduct of commercial operations.

I have often heard many, even of our friends, wonder why more of our people do not aspire to the higher employments of society. This wonder is founded on that absurdity, which looks for the *end,* without considering the *means.* By them, qualification has been overlooked. They expect us to perform successfully, without any previous preparation, that which they can only perform successfully, after a preparation of years. This absurd notion cannot be too deeply reprobated, or too soon discarded. If ever we attain to any eminence in agriculture, commerce, or the arts, it will be by the same course of previous training, which experience has proven to be absolutely necessary to every body else.

A few individuals have engaged in some small land speculations, from which they have realized considerable profit; and a few others have realized considerable from the grocery business; besides these I know of none who have done any business worth mentioning.

It may be very properly asked by some, what success would colored men have, possessing the necessary capital, skill, and intelligence for conducting commercial operations. I answer, that in some places they would have just the same success that others would have; while in others they would meet with much opposition. But even in the most prejudiced places, a man of pleasing address, polished manners, and unquestionable integrity could get along. Some time since, a very respectable man opened a very large grocery store in this city, nearly opposite my own business place. It was thought by some that he could not succeed—that his house would be stoned; and all such stuff as that. But the man went on; and in his daily transactions soon proved himself to be a gentleman, and a man of business. All his neighbors esteemed him, and seemed just as anxious for his success, as any gentleman in the street. Many of his customers were among our most respectable citizens; and up to the time of his removing to one of our neighboring towns, I never heard any one wish him any harm as a merchant.

In the West, like every other part of this country, prejudice exists; in some places with much virulence, in others with so much mildness as to be scarcely perceptible. In all places where there are a number of highly respectable colored persons, maintaining a healthy state of morals among the majority, there colored men are respected and encouraged. But where there are a number of profligate ones, and the morals of the majority are corrupt, there is much prejudice against color, and a strong desire for colonization.

The observance of this fact, for the last fifteen years, has entirely satisfied my mind that CONDITION and not *color,* is the chief cause of the prejudice, under which we suffer. I have noticed that the intelligent colored man, of polished manners, and pleasing address, is always well received and well treated; while some others, who were even wealthy, but who had paid no attention to the cultivation of the manners and habits of polished society, were rejected. I have seen some men grossly insulted, and abused, by attempting to *push* themselves, as it is called, forward in society. In some cases this is far from being their own fault; but in many others it is almost entirely so. It mostly originates in the mistaken idea that a man can be either welcome or happy in that society, to get into which, requires of him extraordinary effort. I admit that the *qualifications* for admission into polished society are not to be attained without great effort; both moral and physical; but when the qualification is consummated, a man slides into his proper circle, with as much ease as he sits down to rest, or lies down to sleep.

I would that I were able 'to fasten the importance of this truth upon the mind of every young man in our land. We should then cease to be disgusted with the exhibitions of their ignorance and folly. They would then find that elegant language and polished manners, would give them greater currency in society, than a smooth beaver, or a golden headed rattan; and that a cultivated mind is of higher consideration than dollars and cents. They would cease to haunt our church doors and the corners of our streets, offending the moral sense of all who go in and out or that pass by, and crowd into the lecture room or library; and instead of drinking grog or smoking tobacco, they would read the newspaper.

What I have written, I am satisfied differs in many respects, from the accounts of those who have preceded me. But had I written any thing else, I should have written that which my own experience and observation has satisfied me is not the truth.

Augustine

From *The Colored American*, February 16, 1839

- -

Pittsburgh, February 26, 1841

THE RIGHT OF SUFFRAGE IN PENNSYLVANIA

In my previous letter on the right of suffrage in Pennsylvania, I made some remarks on the meeting in Philadelphia of the 13th of January, in which I did not notice their resolution to petition the Legislature, for the passage of a law granting a jury trial, to all such persons as may be claimed as fugitive slaves. Of the justice and reality of such a law I have no doubt. Nay, I go farther. A law should be passed *prohibiting*, under severe penalties, the arrest of all persons charged with no other offence than fleeing from slavery. Freedom is the natural inherent right of all men. No law or power under heaven can justly deprive the innocent and unoffending of this right. And when deprived of it, the law of nature, and the law of God, not only allow, but impel them to, the use of all just and fair means to obtain it; and I know of no means more just, more harmless, more in accordance with the spirit of the Gospel, for men to relieve themselves from slavery, than by fleeing from its horrors to a land of freedom. And I believe that the law or the land that hinders him in such a flight, or arrests and returns him to such slavery, is, to say the least of it, equal in atrocity to the land and the law which first held him.

But good policy often shows that it is better to bear our wrongs in silence, than to aggravate them by fruitless attempts at their overthrow, when we are destitute of the power. Such I consider to be the present case with the colored citizens of Pennsylvania. Divested of many civil, and of all political immunities, by those who are unwilling to grant them the smallest favor, on the most just ground; good policy would seem to dictate, that it were best for them to endeavor to secure their rights, in their own state, before they begin to contend for the rights of citizens of other states. When a skillful General is about to engage a superior force, he is always careful to guard against two things:—1. Of engaging too many points at once; thereby dividing and weakening his forces, and rendering them more liable to defeat. 2. Of engaging on such ground as will admit of too great an extent of front; giving the enemy the double advantage of either outflanking him, or of breaking his too far extended lines. Our forces are weak, our enemy is powerful; let us therefore avoid these errors, and attack and carry a single object at a time; and then we may hope ultimately to carry the whole.

I am fully aware that my opinion in regard to fugitives, is contrary to the terms of the *"national compact,"* but this *"compact"* I do not regard, because it is an unrighteous one; and therefore not binding on those who fear God, and love their neighbor as themselves. I shall never render *active* obedience to it; but on the contrary, shall ever lend a helping hand to the fugitive; being heartily conscious of a triumphant acquittal before my final Judge in the Great Day.

Having bestowed this much attention on the proceedings of my fellow citizens of Philadelphia, towards whom I entertain none but the most friendly feeling, I now return to the main object of my letters, which is, to show that one of the most powerful means of obtaining the right of suffrage is the holding of a STATE CONVENTION.

The great moving cause of all that is done under a Republican Government, is the will of the people. Before the representative can feel himself free to act, he wishes, in some, to ascertain the will of those for whom he is to act. This usage prevails generally throughout our country. When the people have made up their will that such a thing shall be done, they immediately take some method of showing that will; and this is oftener than in any other way, done by holding a convention. This measure possesses the double advantage:—1. Of expressing the will. 2. Of arousing the sympathies. Ancient Greece owes her fame as much to the eloquence of her orators, as to the swords of her warriors. And may we not say with fidelity to the truth, that the eloquence of Henry, contributed as much towards the Independence of this country, as the sword of Washington. In short, I believe that such is the natural constitution of man that he can not obtain his liberties, or preserve them when obtained, without the aid of popular assemblies.

If a majority of the colored people in Pennsylvania desire the right to vote, they must show it in some way. The white people are compelled to submit to this course. When they wish to express their will in favor of a certain individual for President, or Governor, or in favor of any great measure, they must subject themselves to the expense and trouble of holding great convention; and I cannot see upon what ground the colored people expect to succeed by easier and cheaper means.

We have long been charged, and I fear with too much justice, with careless indifference about our rights; and we owe it to ourselves, to our friends, to posterity, to do something to wipe off their foul disgrace. Let us do something to show to the world, that if we do not enjoy our rights, we at least deserve them.

Augustine

From *The Colored American,* March 13, 1841

- -

4

FOUR LETTERS BY SIDNEY

Mr. Editor:—It is alike the product of reflection, and the testimony of experience, that weakness occasions misery. And their teachings are equally explicit upon a like subject; that power, unconcentrated, divided, is often as much to be lamented as the want of it, and that frequently, it is the direct means of weakness.

We are told that at the battle of Bothwell Bridge, in the time of Charles 2d, the chief cause of the defeat of the Presbyterians, was the bitter divisions in their army, even when in sight of the advancing columns of well-trained regulars of the Royalists. The milder and more reasonable part of them were willing to make gentle concessions to their aggrieved associates in arms, the Cameronians, who, nevertheless, insisted upon the general acknowledgment of fierce and unreasonable sentiments. As might be expected, their internal dissensions were the seal of their defeat. They were shamefully defeated, and cruelly treated; and the cause of freedom in that country, though destined, as it ever is, to a triumphant issue, yet by the folly of its professed leagued friends, met with severe hindrance and was long retarded.

It is to be feared, we are placing ourselves in like jeopardy, in this country. For the last half century, and especially during the immediate twelve years, we have been putting forth direct, harmonious, and effectual effort for the enfranchisement of our people. During this time we have done well. Our efforts have not been those of babes. They are characterized by their clearness of design, and strength of manliness. Living in connection with their planning and operation, we cannot so well remark concerning them. History will exhibit their judiciousness, and award the meed of praise.

But of late we have been divided. The harmonious accents of numerous men joining in a common effort, without discordant tones, are no longer heard among us. The work is going on, but sympathy and uniformity have measurably departed. We now look in vain for that unity of purpose and operation, which once marked the carrying out of our convictions. We hear, now, in different places, strange and dissimilar sounds, one calling to this peculiar course, and another inciting to that, and no two alike in tone.

I have noticed, of late, two letters in the *Colored American*, from Mr. Wm. Whipper, of Columbia, Pa., which contain sentiments singular and unfortunate, though by no means novel and unheard of. They represent the views of a very respectable portion of our people. They are the sentiments which have characterised the controversy, which has been carried between many of our brethren, and in which the *Colored American* and *National Reformer* have been interested.

The entire point of this controversy, which has been carried on for the last three or four years with singular earnestness, and at times, with warm pertinacity, seems to me, to lie in a very small compass.

There are some things upon which we have no disagreement. The bitter portion and cheerless heritage of our race on this continent, beget universal sorrow and lament.

Casting our eyes in the retrospect, we behold our ancestors in their earliest situation in the country, subjected to the most cruel wrongs and inhuman severities. Tracing their condition through successive generations, each and every succeeding one receiving to itself the accumulated sufferings and indignities of all the preceding . . . ; we come down to our times, and find ourselves enfeebled in soul, power, and capacity, with minds without culture, and wills deprived of their native energetic power; with such an amount of oppression upon us, as to awaken a bitter sense and consciousness of degradation, and to reveal the alarming nature of that oppression which is destroying with fearful certainty and unerring precision.

But nature, even in the worst circumstances, is ever true to herself, and in all conditions of society, among the most abject of races, she retains her vindicators.—The best spirits among us, looking at their people's condition, the necessity of their amelioration, and the adaptedness of truth to quicken and invigorate the crushed and enfeebled, have determined upon the vigorous use of means for our common elevation. And this has become a common feeling, a general desire, and, as the promptings of duty, almost universal. As a people, then, we entertain no chimeras concerning our *actual condition*; we feel, that though not chattels, yet we are slaves. The *necessity* of effort to extricate ourselves from the deep pitfalls, and the loathsome cells of the dark prison-house of oppression, is a common conviction. And the determination, we think, is fully made, to hurl from us every vestige of proscription and degradation. In all this, we all agree.

But there are differences among us. From whence do they proceed? Of what nature are they? They do not resolve themselves into *what* we shall do, neither *for whom* we shall do. The condition of our people, either in gentle or severe accents, incites us to effort, and for the upraising of wronged, and pent up, and straitened humanity, as seen in the persons and condition of the *colored people* of this country. Do not the differences arise, then, let me respectfully ask, from the *mode of operation* —the *how* of the matter? This, *we* think, is the cause of controversy.

Our purpose is not to animadvert upon all the different topics presented in Mr. Whipper's letters, but to notice this particular one, "The mode of operation for the elevation of our people." In doing so, we shall most certainly vindicate the plan for the Albany Convention—the good old way of blessed memory—the time-sanctioned course of our sires, approved by them in their earliest efforts, and confirmed by the reflection and experience, and the rich fruits of successive generations; the course hallowed by the efforts, and prayers, and benedictions of receding age, and the living energy and undying fervor of youth—the mode in which our best men, the living and the dead, have labored—not ineffectually—for years, in behalf of the rights of the people.

Sidney,
A Member of the Convention

From *The Colored American,* February 13, 1841, Vol. I, No. 50

"Trust not the stale fallacious cry
Of foreign aid, or friendly dole,
But timely will alone rely
On means within our own control:
So shall success your efforts crown,
And recreant friends your merits own."—*Anon.*

"Resolved, That the way to obtain rights that have been
wrested from a depressed people is by the continual presentation of the first principles of political freedom, truth and justice,
accompanied by corresponding efforts on the part of the proscribed."—*Albany Con*

It is the irrevocable decree of nature, that our main hope of
progress and elevation through life, shall depend upon our own
energy and activity. The growth and development of our nature, rests mainly upon the putting forth of whatever powers
we possess. We cannot make this exertion by the employment
of foreign aid. Activity on the part of others, though it may
produce important results; yet neither brings forth our latent
energies, nor can be imputed to us.

Our individual well being, depends upon the vigorous and
judicious employment of our various faculties. This is the dictate alike of common sense and experience. In the way of
analogy we might produce and reproduce facts, thick and mul-
titudinous, to illustrate and prove this position. It is one of the
most prominent and beautiful features manifested in the divine
economy, running through the entire web of existence, developing itself in all the multiform operations of nature; and even in
civil, domestic, or political life—in the unfoldings of Science or
the teachings of Philosophy, as well as from the text of Holy
Writ, affirming the great universal truth—"Whosoever hath
(useth) to him shall be given."

The sentiment herein expressed is of equal applicability to a
class, as to one of the species; and for this reason:—there is no
general principle which relates to individuals respectively, but
what pertains to men in the aggregate. Shall an outraged and
insulted people intent upon their disenthralment, come forth by

themselves, express their convictions and commence their operations? In reply, we adduce the general principle, as of primary import—self-exertion the great law of our being. And history in myriad forms, and enlivening hues, attests its truth and affirms its beauty.

We know not where to begin in availing ourselves of the rich and abundant testimonials with which its pages teem. They rise up before us, clothed in antique sanctity, or invested with modern truthfulness and grandeur. The great Exodus from Egypt, the atmosphere of patriotic inspirations which hangs around Marathon, and Bannockburn, and Bunker Hill,—every struggle for human rights, whether marked by sanguinary features, or purified by mental energy—the self-devotedness and patriotic nationality of Tell and De Witt, of Washington and Bolivar, and La Overture, give verity to our position, and elevate it above the changeful influence of temporary opinion, or dubitable disputation, and invest it with the purity majesty and universality of a PRINCIPLE.

There is an illustration to which our mind now recurs which we think of peculiar and striking force—a people subjected to a deep and long-lasting prejudice, oppressed, disfranchised. We refer to the Irish. What has been the course of that long-insulted and deeply injured people? In their great contest for Catholic emancipation were associations among themselves condemned, and denounced as savoring of exclusiveness or as abandoning principle on their part? Nay, verily. The immortal patriots of Erin, from Fitzgerald to O'Connell, have sent forth their trumpet-calls, sounding over heath and bog, heard in the antiquated castle and in the lowly hut, by lord and peasant; invoking the entire people to organize themselves into associations for the freedom of Ireland. And by this system of operation they effected their emancipation—by this system, they gained seats in the Commons of Britain; by this system they have made their voice heard in the national councils, and caused themselves to be respected; and by this system of *exclusive effort* they will eventually throw off every hindrance to a free and unrestrained employment of British law and British freedom, and stand up before the world, the greatest spectacle in modern times of one of the most debased and abject of races, revested by their own exertions and the energy of active determination into a nation of brave and enlightened freemen, attained to respect, dignity, and manhood.

And look at our brethren in the British West Indies. How was the emancipation of the slave, and the enfranchisement of the free colored people effected there? We unhesitatingly affirm, that it was chiefly through the influence of colored men—the oppressed; by that restless discontent that changed deeply injured slaves into insurgent runaways, by that manly bearing and living purpose, with which the free people of color contended for their rights, and which, especially in Jamaica, led the noble JORDON and his compeers to some of the most daring and heroic acts in the annals of the race; which confer honor upon the people who seconded him, and which ultimately will give him an emblazoned immortality.[1]

In these, and all similar cases, the legislation was effected, it is true, by those in power; but they were compelled, forced to it, by the combined exertions of the oppressed.

The testimony of history upon this point is distinctly harmonious, univocal. Its affirmations are strong and emphatic. Its teachings clear and explicit. The history of the human race is but one continued struggle for rights; and though there is constantly associated with it the jarring sounds, the deep din and clamorous uproar of contending elements; yet, there is a profound, a lucid current of Philosophy running through the whole; as if heaven purposed, these continual providences to inwomb the will and teachings of the Infinite for the instruction of after ages. The position we maintain is one of the brightest offspring, and most precious fruits it presents. It is as clear as the sun in heaven. It has the living effulgence of eternal truth.

The stirring anxieties and deep intensities, the inflexible purpose, the indomitable will and the decided action of the oppressed; give indubitable evidence to the oppressor of a common nature in both, are an emphatic affirmance of like tendencies of soul, awaken a consciousness of those upward unquench-

----

[1] See Thmoe and Kimball's Journal, p. 88.

able aspirations, that our motherly humanity universally begets; and these brushing away the accumulated rubbish of old dusty cobweb prejudices, and penetrating the dark meshes of error and sophistry, touch the seal enclosing the sympathies and affections of our common-brotherhood, which, bursting forth into the deep stream flowing from the long pent-up but now out-gushing hearts of the oppressed, together form an irresistible current sweeping away the strong barriers, and deep obstructions of time-sanctioned oppression and aged tyranny.

Sidney

From *The Colored American,* February 20, 1841, Vol. I, No. 51

- -

Ought they not (the free people of color), to make one weak effort; nay, one strong, one mighty, moral effort to roll off the burden that crushes them?—*Wm. Hamilton*

THE CORRECTNESS OF OUR VIEWS will further appear from a consideration of the essentially peculiar ability of the oppressed, and the necessary incapability of all others, even of the best of friends.

In an effort for freedom, there are several important and indispensable qualifications, which the oppressed alone can possess.

There must be, primarily, a keen sense of actual suffering, and a fixed consciousness that it is no longer sufferable. These are requisite, both to unite the entire feeling and purpose of those who suffer, and likewise to awaken the sympathy of those in power. It is absolutely important that there should be *such* a presentation of wrongs as may reveal to the power-holding body the enormity of their oppression; and at the same time, acquaint them that their outrages have so proved the vital seat of suffering, as to arouse the deepest feelings and most inflexible determination of their insulted victims. Now, from the nature of the case, this statement of grievance in all its fulness and power, can come from none other than those conscious of suffering. How is it possible, we ask, for men who know nothing of oppression, who have always enjoyed the blessedness of freedom, by any effort of imagination, by any strength of devotedness, by any depth of sympathy, so fully and adequately to express the sense of wrong and outrage, as the sorrowful presence and living desire of us who have drank the dregs of the embittered chalice?

The oppressed are ever their best representatives. Their short and even abrupt expression of intense feeling, is more effectual than the most refined and polished eloquence, prompted though it be, by deep humanity and strong human-heartedness. Sterne's description of slavery has always been considered very graphic; we can bring three millions of men who can give one still more natural and touching. Hence the expression of Mr. Buxton, in his recent letter upon Colonization, in which he calls us "the *natural* allies, and ABLEST CHAMPIONS of the slave!" And why? Because we are the oppressed, and know what slavery is.

Again; it is one of the most malignant features of slavery, that it leads the oppressor to stigmatise his victim with inferiority of nature, after he himself has almost brutalized him. This is an universal fact. Hence the oppressed must vindicate their character. No abstract disquisitions from sympathising friends, can effectually do this. The oppressed themselves must manifest energy of character and elevation of soul. Oppression never quails until it sees that the down trodden and outraged

"Know their rights, and knowing, dare maintain."

This is a radical assurance, a resistless evidence both of worth and manliness, and of earnest intention and deep determination.

We maintain that these evidences—these feelings, desires, and capacities, must stand out prominently, as coming from their proper source, to have their rightful influence. Thus exhibited, they can be employed with prodigious effect. But on the other hand, experience proves, that they lose by retailment or admixture. Let an expression of our wants and feelings be produced by others, and should there be anything of character, intellect, or dignity connected with it, it is not predicated of our ability. How pregnant with verification are facts in our history!

where documents setting forth our views and demanding our rights, which were ostensibly the productions of colored men, have proved to have been written by whites. The base suspicion (to say nothing of the real knowledge of the fact), has caused the effort to fall powerless to the ground.

The elevation of a people is not measurably dependent upon external relations or peculiar circumstances, as it is upon the inward rational sentiments which enable the soul to change circumstances to its own temper and disposition. Without these, the aids of sympathising friends, the whisperings of hope, the power of eternal truth, are of but little advantage. We take the case of an individual. His ancestors have been the objects of wrong and violence. In consequence, they became degraded. At the season of thought and reflection he feels a desire to escape from the degradation of his sires, and the oppressions of the many. The sympathy of friends is excited, and they make active exertions.

Now we affirm that their efforts and influence may be as potent as angels; yet vain that influence, vain their efforts, vain

> . . . The sayings of the wise,
> In ancient and in modern books enrolled.
>
> . . .
>
> Unless he feel within himself,
> Secret refreshings that repair his strength
> And fainting spirits uphold.

It must exist in the man. The spirit that would elevate him above his circumstances, and gain him respect and manhood, must have all the strength of personal character.

And the same it is with a people. Our friends, abolitionists, may redouble their efforts, they may lavishly expend their means, they may strew their pamphlets over the country, thick as the leaves in some primeval forest, where the soil is undistinguishable from their thickly bedded masses—they may add to their numbers, and fill up their ranks, until they become as numerous as that

. . . Pitchy cloud
of locusts,
That o'er the realm of impious Pharaoh hung
Like night.

Yet our condition will remain the same, our sufferings will be unmitigated, until we awaken to a consciousness of a momentous responsibility, which we shall manifest by giving it actuality. We occupy a position, and sustain relations which they cannot possibly assume. *They* are our allies—OURS is the battle.

In coming forth as colored Americans, and pleading for our rights, we neither preclude the necessity, nor forbid the action of our friends, no more than the Americans forbade the help of their French allies. We ask their sympathy, and entreat their prayers and efforts. The Americans received the aid and co-operation of their French allies; but they kept the idea of *American* resistance to oppression distinct and prominent. As wise men, they knew much depended on that. They know not what evils—perhaps failure—might result from an admixture of extraneosities.

So the convention at Albany acted. They interdicted the presence and co-operation of no set of men, but they called for the exertion of a people peculiarly interested in its objects.

The necessity, nay, the DUTY of peculiar activity on the part of an aggrieved people, we conclude, is the dictate of reason and common sense, and the testimony of history.

And thus thought our fathers. In this way they acted for years. It was this conviction that led to the concentration of their energies in the annual conventions. The people generally acquiesce in their judgment, and follow in their wise and rational footsteps. Thus, throughout the country, we hear the sounds of their hearty, earnest labor. But lo! in the midst of our energetic and effectual exertions, we are called off from our efforts, when we have made considerable progress in undermining our great Bastile, a LEADER informs us, that not only we, but our fathers, yea, all mankind, have gone wrong, and that he has found out a better plan—a new *theory*.

He bids us disregard the voice of principle, to pay no heed to its historic affirmations, to repudiate the dictates of *reason* and common sense, to leave the path of our sires, and adopt a new theory, alike unsupported by reason, and unaffirmed by experience.

In speculating upon "heaven-born truth," he comes to despising all specific actions or means, and can deal in nothing but generalities—universalities.

We differ from him. We do not think that by watering and preserving the plant that perfumes our room, that *therefore* we dislike all other plants in the world. We do not believe that in loving our own mother's sons, our brothers, that therefore we create a cord of caste, and exclude mankind from our rights. In fine, we have no sympathy with that cosmopoliting disposition which tramples upon all nationality, which encircles the universe, but at the same time theorises away the most needed blessings, and blights the dearest hopes of a people.

And pray, for what are we to turn around and bay the whole human family? In the name of common sense, we ask for what have we to make this great radical change in our operations? Why are we to act different from all others in this important matter? Why, because we *happen* to be—COLORED—which we shall endeavor to look into by and by.

Sidney

From *The Colored American,* March 6, 1841, Vol. II, No. 1

- -

IT HAS BEEN OUR PURPOSE, in our last two preceding articles, to answer, in a summary manner the questions and objections proposed by Mr. Whipper in his letters, to show the duty and necessity of special exertions on the part of the oppressed, as a principle—that it is identical with the testimony of history, and that, inasmuch as it comported with the peculiar relations of the oppressed, it was in accordance with common sense.

It is a remarkable fact, that obstreperous as have been the friends of this new theory, in their advocacy of it, yet they have never attempted to show its feasibility in the light of history. Now, we always suspect any theory that cannot be supported by facts. The world is old enough, the human family have had sufficient experience to give some few illustrations of any principle of importance, that may be proposed for the benefit of man. And although new combinations of known truth may be made, and thus originality be produced, yet, save in this way, there is nothing new under the sun. How unreasonable, then, in such a matter as this—a matter so practical in its nature, so begirt by the teachings and supports of common sense, and in the light of history, so luminous—a matter upon which the human family have been schooled for centuries; how unreasonable it is, we say, for gentlemen to come forward and require us to leave a well known and long tried course, for which we have the authority of the wisest and best of all ages, to enter upon a vain and untried expedient, merely on account of the marvellous, hidden virtues of a new theory.

It has been our object in our former communications, to defend the measures of our fathers, in past time, of our brethren of the present day in their laudable self-exertion to elevate themselves, and especially the "Albany Convention," in its "call" and its after measures. It will be seen that we have argued the matter thus far, without any reference to *color*. The relative position and the relative duties and responsibilities of the oppressed and the oppressors; being, in our opinion, the only grounds upon which any argument was predictable. This endless clamoring about "color," is alike devoid of reason, as it is disreputable to us as a people. The people are perishing by oppression, and our leaders, one opposing the other, upon a *word;* they are metaphysicising upon *things,* when they should be using the resistless energy of principle, to vindicate their wronged and deeply injured brethren; and instead of giving living, productive action—proposing idle theories! We would discontinue the matter here, were it not that there are some minor points in Mr. W.'s letters, which demand some notice.

We come now to the term "colored."

We would premise here, that we are not frightened at the portentous phrase—"Complexionally distinctive organizations"

—not in the least. But we regard it as a "nise deguerre." Is it a want of kindness, or a want of clear vision, that leads our brethren to charge us with preferring our mode of operation, to devotion to color? Our argument is this:—Whenever a people are oppressed, peculiarly (not complexionally), distinctive organization or action, is required on the part of the oppressed, to destroy that oppression. The colored people of this country are oppressed; therefore the colored people are required to act in accordance with this fundamental principle.

If Mr. W. can, for a few minutes, get clear of the idea of color, perhaps he will then be able to understand us.

But to the term "colored." That we are colored, is a fact, an undeniable fact. That we are descendants of Africans—colored people—negroes if you will, is true. We affirm there is nothing in it that we need be ashamed of, yea, rather much that we may be proud of. There is, then, on our part, as identified with the negro race, no reason why the term should be repudiated.

The bearing of this fact (of color), on the whites, does *it* present any sufficient and adequate cause why we should desire the use of the term to be discontinued? Let us see. Prejudice is a moral phenomenon, a wrong exercise of the sentiments and sympathies, a disease of the will. Now, Mr. W. should know enough of human nature to be aware, that repugnances of such a character, are to be met and cured by something entirely diverse from a—term. "As the diseases of the mind are invisible, invisible must the remedies likewise be. Those who have been entrapped by false opinions, are to be liberated by convincing truths."—*Tertullian.*

Discontinue the use of the term—does prejudice die? Oh no, Leviathan is not so tamed. But Mr. W. may say, prejudice is the result of color, and *therefore* we should not use the term "colored." But look again at the matter. If it is the result of *color,* then it does *not* proceed from the word; and if *that* (color) is the cause, and Mr. W. desires to act upon the cause, then let him commence his operations upon the color. For ourselves, we are quite well satisfied. And we intend, in all our public effort, to go [to] the power-holding body, and tell them, "Colored as we are, *black* though we may be, yet we demand our rights, the same rights other citizens have"; and to Christians, "We demand it of you in the name of Christ our common master, to give us as large a share in your affections and sympathies as you give to the rest of the Saviour's fold."

We say our people should not give way the least to the stout-heartedness of our oppressors in this matter. If they have prejudices, they must get over them. As for our color, as God has given it to us, thus we are pleased with it—and so must they get to be. Surely the term colored is not disgusting to Mr. W. and his friends? They cannot be ashamed of their identity with the negro race!

But in the different relations, the two people sustain to each other, some terms are to be used by which each may be known. A definition is correct and proper, when it distinguishes its object or class from all others. The term "colored," then, is a very good one. It has this very commendable qualification, and that there is nothing objectionable in it, is evident from the fact that from time immemorial, different races of men have been distinguished according to their color, and thus not from bad and bitter feelings, as white men, black men, red men, olive, &c., &c. When the English, French, Spanish, and others use these terms, do the *terms* create prejudice, or are they employed from prejudice? Neither one. There is, then, no such marvellous power in the *word* as to make it so repugnant to the tender sensibilities of Mr. W.

To Mr. Whipper's vision, there is but one thing visible—COLOR. For a long period this, apparently, has been his Alpha and Omega. It has been a ghost, haunting him in the day time, and in the night season—a ghost that would not down at his bidding; or rather, we are inclined to think, he is not so displeased with the ghostly presence, from the deep thought and intense feelings with which he regards it.

So potent and peculiar has its influence been upon him, that it has deprived him of much of that clear thought and peculiar discrimination that generally characterises Mr. Whipper. Objects appear before *him*, confused and disarranged, which to others, and the general mind, are clear and distinct. See, for instance, his second letter (*Colored American*, Feb. 20th), wherein he warns you not to advocate our call and measures on the ground of *necessity*. Why, they can be defended on that ground, and ably and triumphantly. If he will consult but the primer of philosophy, he will discover that much that is fair, and beautiful, and beneficial—some of the brightest features of law, and of the entire frame work of civil polity—are the product of necessity. Observe again how blurred is Mr. Whipper's vision. In the same letter, speaking of the similar "broad platform principle" of the Anti Slavery Society, and the American Moral Reform Society, he remarks: "I maintain whatever is morally right for a white man to do, is morally right for a colored man to do, and vice versa. If this position be correct, and I presume you will not gainsay it," &c., &c. Gainsay it! Most certainly we do, if we understand Mr. W. to say that the moral duties of men are equally and universally alike and the same. On the contrary, we maintain that what is morally right for one man to do, may be morally wrong for another; and thus of entire classes of a whole people. Duties arise from relations. Our responsibilities and obligations receive their hue and coloring from the situation we may maintain, and the connections we may have. Moral right is manifested in innumerable forms. The sun is fixed in the solar system, and the light he imparts is one in nature; yet how diverse in their hues and tints are the rays that come streaming down upon us! And thus is it in the manifestations of duty.

No. We sustain relations to our own people, so peculiar that white men cannot assume them, and according to these relations are our attending duties.

Finally, Mr. Whipper says, "As a people we are deeply afflicted with 'colorphobia.' " True, true! we are deeply afflicted with colorphobia, at least *some of us*. It *is* a "phobia," and it (color) has so perturbed some of our brethren, that they have devoted a paper to do away with the nuisance; and have written long articles to banish the designating term into oblivion.

For ourselves, we plead *"not guilty"* to the charge. Whatever other phobia we may have, "colorphobia" has not yet afflicted us with its sore and rabid influences. The color God has given us, we are satisfied with; and it is a matter of but little moment to us, who may be displeased with it.

We *are* afflicted with colorphobia, and it is going to work wonders with us—wonders like those Moses wrought in Egypt —of fearful nature, and destructive tendency; unless the right means are used to effect a radical cure, so that henceforth, neither the fact, nor the term indicative of it, shall excite convulsions, nor create a MONOMANIA.

Sidney

From *The Colored American*, March 13, 1841, Vol. II, No. 2

- -

5

AN ADDRESS

To the Slaves of the United States of America (rejected by the National Convention, held in Buffalo, N. Y., 1843), by Henry Highland Garnet.

Brethren and Fellow-Citizens:—Your brethren of the North, East, and West have been accustomed to meet together in National Conventions, to sympathize with each other, and to weep over your unhappy condition. In these meetings we have addressed all classes of the free, but we have never, until this time, sent a word of consolation and advice to you. We have been contented in sitting still and mourning over your sorrows, earnestly hoping that before this day your sacred liberties would have been restored. But, we have hoped in vain. Years have rolled on, and tens of thousands have been borne on streams of blood and tears, to the shores of eternity. While you have been oppressed, we have also been partakers with you; nor can we be free while you are enslaved. We, therefore, write to you as being bound with you.

Many of you are bound to us, not only by the ties of a common humanity, but we are connected by the more tender relations of parents, wives, husbands, children, brothers, and sisters, and friends. As such we most affectionately address you.

Slavery has fixed a deep gulf between you and us, and while it shuts out from you the relief and consolation which your friends would willingly render, it afflicts and persecutes you with a fierceness which we might not expect to see in the fiends of hell. But still the Almighty Father of mercies has left to us a glimmering ray of hope, which shines out like a lone star in a cloudy sky. Mankind are becoming wiser, and better—the oppressor's power is fading, and you, every day, are becoming better informed, and more numerous. Your grievances, brethren, are many. We shall not attempt, in this short address, to present to the world all the dark catalogue of this nation's sins, which have been committed upon an innocent people. Nor is it indeed necessary, for you feel them from day to day, and all the civilized world look upon them with amazement.

Two hundred and twenty-seven years ago, the first of our injured race were brought to the shores of America. They came not with glad spirits to select their homes in the New World. They came not with their own consent, to find an unmolested enjoyment of the blessings of this fruitful soil. The first dealings they had with men calling themselves Christians, exhibited to them the worst features of corrupt and sordid hearts: and convinced them that no cruelty is too great, no villainy and no robbery too abhorrent for even enlightened men to perform, when influenced by avarice and lust. Neither did they come flying upon the wings of Liberty, to a land of freedom. But they came with broken hearts, from their beloved native land, and were doomed to unrequited toil and deep degradation. Nor did the evil of their bondage end at their emancipation by death. Succeeding generations inherited their chains, and millions have come from eternity into time, and have returned again to the world of spirits, cursed and ruined by American slavery.

The propagators of the system, or their immediate ancestors, very soon discovered its growing evil, and its tremendous wickedness, and secret promises were made to destroy it. The gross inconsistency of a people holding slaves, who had themselves "ferried o'er the wave" for freedom's sake, was too apparent to be entirely overlooked. The voice of Freedom cried, "Emancipate your slaves." Humanity supplicated with tears for the deliverance of the children of Africa. Wisdom urged her solemn plea. The bleeding captive plead his innocence, and pointed to Christianity who stood weeping at the cross. Jehovah frowned upon the nefarious institution, and thunderbolts, red with vengeance, struggled to leap forth to blast the guilty wretches who maintained it. But all was vain. Slavery had stretched its dark wings of death over the land, the Church stood silently by—the priests prophesied falsely, and the people loved to have it so. Its throne is established, and now it reigns triumphant.

Nearly three millions of your fellow-citizens are prohibited by law and public opinion (which in this country is stronger than law), from reading the Book of Life. Your intellect has been destroyed as much as possible, and every ray of light they have attempted to shut out from your minds. The oppressors themselves have become involved in the ruin. They have become weak, sensual, and rapacious—they have cursed you—they have cursed themselves—they have cursed the earth which they have trod.

The colonists threw the blame upon England. They said that the mother country entailed the evil upon them, and that they would rid themselves of it if they could. The world thought they were sincere, and the philanthropic pitied them. But time soon tested their sincerity. In a few years the colonists grew strong, and severed themselves from the British Government. Their independence was declared, and they took their station among the sovereign powers of the earth. The declaration was a glorious document. Sages admired it, and the patriotic of every nation reverenced the God-like sentiments which it contained. When the power of Government returned to their hands, did they emancipate the slaves? No; they rather added new links to our chains. Were they ignorant of the principles of Liberty? Certainly they were not. The sentiments of their revolutionary orators fell in burning eloquence upon their hearts, and with one voice they cried, LIBERTY OR DEATH. Oh what a sentence was that! It ran from soul to soul like electric fire, and nerved the arm of thousands to fight in the holy cause of Freedom. Among the diversity of opinions that are entertained in regard to physical resistance, there are but a few found to gainsay that stern declaration. We are among those who do not.

SLAVERY! How much misery is comprehended in that single word. What mind is there that does not shrink from its direful effects? Unless the image of God be obliterated from the soul, all men cherish the love of Liberty. The nice discerning political economist does not regard the sacred right more than the untutored African who roams in the wilds of Congo. Nor has the one more right to the full enjoyment of his freedom than the other. In every man's mind the good seeds of liberty are planted, and he who brings his fellow down so low, as to make him contented with a condition of slavery, commits the highest crime against God and man. Brethren, your oppressors aim to do this. They endeavor to make you as much like brutes as possible. When they have blinded the eyes of your mind—when they have embittered the sweet waters of life—when they have shut out the light which shines from the word of God—then, and not till then, has American slavery done its perfect work.

To such Degradation it is sinful in the Extreme for you to make voluntary Submission. The divine commandments you are in duty bound to reverence and obey. If you do not obey them, you will surely meet with the displeasure of the Almighty. He requires you to love him supremely, and your neighbor as yourself—to keep the Sabbath day holy—to search the Scriptures—and bring up your children with respect for his laws, and to worship no other God but him. But slavery sets all these at nought, and hurls defiance in the face of Jehovah. The forlorn condition in which you are placed, does not destroy your moral obligation to God. You are not certain of heaven, because you suffer yourselves to remain in a state of slavery, where you cannot obey the commandments of the Sovereign of the universe. If the ignorance of slavery is a passport to heaven, then it is a blessing, and no curse, and you should rather desire its perpetuity than its abolition. God will not receive slavery, nor ignorance, nor any other state of mind, for love and obedience to him. Your condition does not absolve you from your moral obligation. The diabolical injustice by which your liberties are cloven down, neither God, nor angels, or just men, command you to suffer for a single moment. Therefore it is your solemn and imperative duty to use every means, both moral, intellectual, and physical, that promises success. If a band of heathen men should attempt to enslave a race of Christians, and to place their children under the influence of some false religion, surely, Heaven would frown upon the men who would not resist such aggression, even to death. If, on the other hand, a band of Christians should attempt to enslave a race of heathen men, and to entail slavery upon them, and to keep them in heathenism in the midst of Christianity, the God of heaven would smile upon every effort which the injured might make to disenthral themselves.

Brethren, it is as wrong for your lordly oppressors to keep you in slavery, as it was for the man thief to steal our ancestors from the coast of Africa. You should therefore now use the same manner of resistance, as would have been just in our ancestors, when the bloody foot-prints of the first remorseless soul-thief was placed upon the shores of our fatherland. The humblest peasant is as free in the sight of God as the proudest monarch that ever swayed a sceptre. Liberty is a spirit sent out from God, and like its great Author, is no respecter of persons.

Brethren, the time has come when you must act for yourselves. It is an old and true saying that, "if hereditary bondmen would be free, they must themselves strike the blow." You can plead your own cause, and do the work of emancipation better than any others. The nations of the old world are moving in the great cause of universal freedom, and some of them at least will, ere long, do you justice. The combined powers of Europe have placed their broad seal of disapprobation upon the African slave-trade. But in the slave-holding parts of the United States, the trade is as brisk as ever. They buy and sell you as though you were brute beasts. The North has done much—her opinion of slavery in the abstract is known. But in regard to the South, we adopt the opinion of the *New York Evangelist*—"We have advanced so far, that the cause apparently waits for a more effectual door to be thrown open than has been yet." We are about to point you to that more effectual door. Look around you, and behold the bosoms of your loving wives heaving with untold agonies! Hear the cries of your poor children! Remember the stripes your fathers bore. Think of the torture and disgrace of your noble mothers. Think of your wretched sisters, loving virtue and purity, as they are driven into concubinage and are exposed to the unbridled lusts of incarnate devils. Think of the undying glory that hangs around the ancient name of Africa:— and forget not that you are native-born American citizens, and as such, you are justly entitled to all the rights that are granted to the freest. Think how many tears you have poured out upon the soil which you have cultivated with unrequited toil and enriched with your blood; and then go to your lordly enslavers and tell them plainly, that you *are determined to be free.* Appeal to their sense of justice, and tell them that they have no more right to oppress you, than you have to enslave them. Entreat them to remove the grievous burdens which they have imposed upon you, and to remunerate you for your labor. Promise them renewed diligence in the cultivation of the soil, if they will render to you an equivalent for your services. Point them to the increase of happiness and prosperity in the British West-Indies since the Act of Emancipation. Tell them in language which they cannot misunderstand, of the exceeding sinfulness of slavery, and of a future judgment, and of the righteous retributions of an indignant God. Inform them that all you desire is FREEDOM, and that nothing else will suffice. Do this, and for ever after cease to toil for the heartless tyrants, who give you no other reward but stripes and abuse. If they then commence the work of death, they, and not you, will be responsible for the consequences. You had far better all die—*die immediately,* than live slaves, and entail your wretchedness upon your posterity. If you would be free in this generation, here is your only hope. However much you and all of us may desire it, there is not much hope of redemption without the shedding of blood. If you must bleed, let it all come at once—rather *die freemen, than live to be the slaves.* It is impossible, like the children of Israel, to make a grand exodus from the land of bondage. The Pharaohs are on both sides of the blood-red waters! You cannot move *en masse,* to the dominions of the British Queen—nor can you pass through Florida and overrun Texas, and at last find peace in Mexico. The propagators of American slavery are spending their blood and treasure, that they may plant the black flag in the heart of Mexico and riot in the halls of the Montezumas. In the language of the Rev. Robert Hall, when addressing the volunteers of Bristol, who were rushing forth to repel the invasion of Napoleon, who threatened to lay waste the fair homes of England, "Religion is too much interested in your behalf, not to shed over you her most gracious influences."

You will not be compelled to spend much time in order to become inured to hardships. From the first moment that you breathed the air of heaven, you have been accustomed to nothing else but hardships. The heroes of the American Revolution were never put upon harder fare than a peck of corn and a few herrings per week. You have not become enervated by the luxuries of life. Your sternest energies have been beaten out upon the anvil of severe trial. Slavery has done this, to make you subservient to its own purposes; but it has done more than this, it has prepared you for any emergency. If you receive good treatment, it is what you could hardly expect; if you meet with pain, sorrow, and even death, these are the common lot of the slaves.

Fellow-men! patient sufferers! behold your dearest rights crushed to the earth! See your sons murdered, and your wives, mothers and sisters doomed to prostitution. In the name of the merciful God, and by all that life is worth, let it no longer be a debatable question, whether it is better to choose *Liberty* or *death*.

In 1822, Denmark Veazie, of South Carolina, formed a plan for the liberation of his fellow-men. In the whole history of human efforts to overthrow slavery, a more complicated and tremendous plan was never formed. He was betrayed by the treachery of his own people, and died a martyr to freedom. Many a brave hero fell, but history, faithful to her high trust, will transcribe his name on the same monument with Moses, Hampden, Tell, Bruce and Wallace, Toussaint L'Ouverture, Lafayette and Washington. That tremendous movement shook the whole empire of slavery. The guilty soul-thieves were overwhelmed with fear. It is a matter of fact, that at that time, and in consequence of the threatened revolution, the slave States talked strongly of emancipation. But they blew but one blast of the trumpet of freedom, and then laid it aside. As these men became quiet, the slaveholders ceased to talk about emancipation: and now behold your condition to-day! Angels sigh over it, and humanity has long since exhausted her tears in weeping on your account!

The patriotic Nathaniel Turner followed Denmark Veazie. He was goaded to desperation by wrong and injustice. By despotism, his name has been recorded on the list of infamy, and future generations will remember him among the noble and brave.

Next arose the immortal Joseph Cinque, the hero of the Amistad. He was a native African, and by the help of God he emancipated a whole ship-load of his fellow men on the high seas. And he now sings of liberty on the sunny hills of Africa and beneath his native palm-trees, where he hears the lion roar and feels himself as free as that king of the forest.

Next arose Madison Washington, that bright star of freedom, and took his station in the constellation of true heroism. He was a slave on board the brig Creole, of Richmond, bound to New Orleans, that great slave mart, with a hundred and four others. Nineteen struck for liberty or death. But one life was taken, and the whole were emancipated, and the vessel was carried into Nassau, New Providence.

Noble men! Those who have fallen in freedom's conflict, their memories will be cherished by the true-hearted and the God-fearing in all future generations; those who are living, their names are surrounded by a halo of glory.

Brethren, arise, arise! Strike for your lives and liberties. Now is the day and the hour. Let every slave throughout the land do this, and the days of slavery are numbered. You cannot be more oppressed than you have been—you cannot suffer greater cruelties than you have already. *Rather die freemen than live to be slaves*. Remember that you are FOUR MILLIONS!

It is in your power so to torment the God-cursed slaveholders, that they will be glad to let you go free. If the scale was turned, and black men were the masters and white men the slaves, every destructive agent and element would be employed to lay the oppressor low. Danger and death would hang over their heads day and night. Yes, the tyrants would meet with plagues more terrible than those of Pharaoh. But you are a patient people. You act as though you were made for the special use of these devils. You act as though your daughters were born to pamper the lusts of your masters and overseers. And worse than all, you tamely submit while your lords tear your wives from your embraces and defile them before your eyes. In the name of God, we ask, are you men? Where is the blood of your fathers? Has it all run out of your veins? Awake, awake; millions of voices are calling you! Your dead fathers speak to you from their graves. Heaven, as with a voice of thunder, calls on you to arise from the dust.

Let your motto be resistance! *resistance!* RESISTANCE! No oppressed people have ever secured their liberty without resistance. What kind of resistance you had better make, you must decide by the circumstances that surround you, and according to the suggestion of expediency. Brethren, adieu! Trust in the living God. Labor for the peace of the human race, and remember that you are FOUR MILLIONS.

6

HENRY HIGHLAND GARNET'S SPEECH
AT AN ENTHUSIASTIC MEETING
OF THE COLORED CITIZENS OF BOSTON

REMARKS OF REV. J. SELLA MARTIN—SPEECH OF REV. HENRY
HIGHLAND GARNET—TRIUMPHANT RESOLUTIONS IN FAVOR OF
MR. GARNET.

TUESDAY EVENING, 29th ult., the citizens of Boston assembled in
the Joy Street Baptist Church to hear a lecture by Rev. Henry
Highland Garnet, on African Civilization. He was introduced
to the audience by Rev. J. Sella Martin, who remarked as
follows:

Ladies and gentlemen: In introducing our staunch friend and
able advocate, I feel that it would be superfluous for me to
utter one word of eulogy upon his character, or one sentence
in commendation of his course (*Applause*). I am confident that
the generosity and wisdom of this audience will accord to him
all that he wishes or needs, both in respect and courtesy and
justice. But, while this is true, I feel it incumbent upon me to
remove some unfavorable impressions which others (and I
know not but he) may entertain in regard to the conduct of
some of the leading men of the Twelfth (colored) Baptist
Church of this city. When Mr. Garnet's personal friends applied
for that church for him to speak in, the reason assigned for the
refusal to open it to him was that the citizens of Boston did not
wish to hear him, because they were tired of the discussion of
the African civilization question. Now, without stopping to refute these reasons, admitting that they were true, it may not be
out of place for me to state that I did all that I could, in one of
the preliminary meetings which were taking measures for the
success of the Convention, to dissuade the originators of the

Convention from introducing that subject as a matter of discussion; but all to no purpose. Not that I feared discussion, but because I did not wish to interrupt more important objects of the Convention by the introduction of a topic which I know would not benefit our people generally, as the Convention would not have time to examine the merits of the question.

Now, my friends, no matter what the self-elected guardians of the colored people of Boston may say, I feel that I am prepared to deny the charge that the colored people of Boston are so unjust and uncourteous as to refuse to hear any man in his defense and efforts to remove imputations cast upon his character in his absence by those who disagree with him (*Applause*). I know too much about the generosity of the colored people of this city to allow our *dear friend,* Mr. Garnet, to go away with the impression that you are enemies to free discussion. During my labors in Tremont Temple, where the largest white congregation in New England assembles, I have been cheered by the presence of our most intelligent and respectable colored friends, and when, during the week I have been out among you, you have given me words of sympathy and encouragement (*Applause*). And if you have acted thus kindly towards me in my humbleness and obscurity, I know you will not depart from this course when the character of H. H. Garnet is at stake and submitted to your just judgment (*Applause*). A man who is celebrated for his charity towards both his friends and his enemies, as he is admired for the ability with which he defends the one and overthrows the other when they dare to meet him (*Applause*). Could it be possible for Boston, with all its talent and respectability, with courtesy and love of freedom, to act worse than the slave-holder does toward his slave? When a slave is tried in the South they will at least allow him the privilege of pleading guilty or not guilty. I repeat, it has not been done by the colored people of Boston (*Applause*). A few men, whose minds and hearts melted into one would find room to rattle in the shell of a mustard seed (*Laughter*), whose perceptions are as dull as their conscience are elastic, and whose highest sense of right is to go with what may for the time appear popular, and the utmost of whose usefulness is measured by the power of their lungs (*Laughter*); these men are the only persons to be blamed in Boston, and upon these the blame shall fall (*Applause*). Mr. Grimes knew, when he refused to open his church, and his satellites, when they refused to hire the church (notwithstanding it has been hired to every and any man who could command five dollars to pay for it), they knew that the people, had they known of it at the time, as they have done since, would have given expression to their just indignation at this ostracism and unmanliness. I, for one, am not sorry for the state of shame and confusion into which his contemptible unkindness has precipitated him (*Applause*). A man who would violate the courtesy which he owed to a brother minister, with so little compunction of conscience as to go to every colored church to get them to act as he had done in refusing his church—a man who would outrage every claim of hospitality in the person of a man from whom he had enjoyed hospitable entertainment, by refusing his church and his house to one who took him for a friend up to the moment of refusal, simply because that man differed with him in opinion—a man who would strike down freedom of speech in the person of a great leader among colored people, while he affects to condemn the same thing among pro-slavery white people, is at once too contemptible for condemnation and too hypocritical to secure confidence (*Applause and laughter*). Had I a dog who should treat another dog in this manner, I don't know but what I should swap him off for a snake, and then kill the snake (*Applause and laughter*). The time is coming, my friends, when the deeds of our people in regard to the great cause of human liberty, are to be committed to the historian's page, and upon the exercise of justice, which we owe to our leading men, depends the beauty of the portrait which shall be drawn of the people in Boston. Respecting the African Civilization Society, and my connection with it, I have this to say: The cloud of revolution is ascending, and the great spirit of Liberty enthroned upon it is hurling his thunderbolts thick and hot against the garrisons of slavery and of wrong; and if that society is wrong it will not escape, and if it is right God will do with it what we cannot do without it— make it a mighty instrument of the overthrow of slavery. Another among the many reasons why I support it is, that here I see a man who has made twenty-five years of sacrifice to the cause of colored people in this country, who stands today as much respected and as dearly beloved as any man among us, who is as calm in his judgment, as zealous in his advocacy, and as eloquent and efficient in his efforts as he has been unchanging and unchanged in his fidelity, who advocates the movement, who has given his time and talent to it without reward, and who now comes to remove the aspersions cast upon him in the late New England Convention, and to vindicate, by his own statements, the position he occupies with regard to this movement. Allow me, then, to introduce to you the Rev. Henry Highland Garnet (*Prolonged applause*).

MR. GARNET SPOKE AS FOLLOWS:

I am happy that one impression, unfavorable to the liberality of the sentiment of the people of Boston, which, for a little while, had rested on my mind; has been altogether removed.

On the first day of August, when the Convention was held here, I was engaged in the State of Pennsylvania, away down almost on the borders of Maryland. I was lifting up my feeble voice in behalf of my oppressed and down-trodden brethren. I had been engaged to labor there at that time, eighteen months previous. Had my engagement been of such a character that I could easily have broken it, I should have foregone the pleasure of being at that meeting, and should have hastened to Boston to attend the Convention of colored men that was to be held here on that day.

DR. KNOX—And of white men also.

MR. GARNET—Well, and of white men also—put a pin there! (*Laughter*). I emphasized the words "colored men" to show that we are in an age of progression. I remember when, a few years ago, to talk in New England of holding a Colored Men's Convention was to have the idea scouted. We had got so far ahead as to suppose we need not make any effort in the cause of liberty, especially as people of color. I knew they were wrong. I told them so. That spirit ran all over the free States; and bye and bye we swelled up to such dimensions that we despised to take the name of color; and then we said we must talk only about universal rights and universal liberty. I knew that the day would come when you would think that we, as colored people, had peculiar interests—feelings and interests that no other people had—and that we understood the cause better than any others, and that if we wanted the work done at all we must do it ourselves; and that when we had accomplished the object, we should lay aside all distinctive labors, and come together as men and women, members of the great American family. I looked, therefore, upon this fact as a matter of importance, that *colored men,* as it was stated in the call for the Convention, were to meet here. I wished the time might have been altered; that we of New York might have been here also. I thought it was to be a Convention to consider the interests of the colored people of this country, and do something to advance the great cause of human freedom.

I found, when the Convention was over, and I read the minutes, that there seemed to be two objects which that Convention had in view, and to which they most strictly and faithfully attended. The first was to attack the African Civilization Society generally, and its President in particular, to misrepresent my views on that subject, and on the great subject of humanity. That seemed to be the first object, and, mind you, it was a concerted plan to carry out this same measure in other parts of the country. In Poughkeepsie, Mr. Myers, of Albany, introduced a resolution, not among the regular resolutions brought forward by the Business Committee, but introduced by him on his own responsibility, and when the Secretary read it, a friend of mine and old co-worker in the cause of freedom, though not altogether agreeing with me, said:

"This is not the time and place for such action; you have sprung this on the Convention."

Mr. Myers said: *"O, yes, you must do it for it is to be done in Boston, and at all the other celebrations to-day."* So you see, while we knew nothing about it, it was a plan concerted, well arranged, among those ready to take that course.

Mr. Nell—Will you give way for a correction?

Mr. Garnet—Certainly.

Mr. Nell—I regret that you made that statement. I am authorized to deny it. It was not a part, at all, of the plan.

MR. GARNET—I expect the gentleman will get up many times before I am done. I intend to make some of your seats warm, to-night (*Laughter*). If it was not a concerted plan then what mean the resolutions brought forward on that subject by the Business Committee? I think my friend Nell was the Chairman. How do you get up resolutions unless by a concerted plan? Do you get up, and by instinct or intuition, frame and propose your resolutions? Were they not arranged in private before you came to that meeting? Yes, perhaps weeks before; and the officers knew exactly what kind of resolutions were to be passed, and come up armed to the teeth to battle them through; and you bagged them altogether, good and evil, so that the good could not be accepted without endorsing the bad, nor the bad rejected without rejecting the good.

The next object, which was far the best, and one of which I highly approve, was to give my old friend, George Downing, a bunch of flowers (*Great laughter*). Now, I approve of this courtesy on the part of Boston ladies, and I am sure it must have made my friend feel comfortable when he received those elegant flowers from the beauty and fashion of this Athens of America.

Now, then, as to my object in coming here to-night: Don't think I am come for the purpose of stirring up strife, of dealing in vituperation and misrepresentation, as some gentlemen did at that Convention. Let it be known that I come here simply to present my views on the subject in question, not to define my position. If twenty-five years of labor in the anti-slavery cause has not defined my position, certainly I shall not do it to-night. But I came to speak as a man to men, to tell what I believe on the subject, and to deny some things said by others.

I wrote to my friend, Rev. L. A. Grimes, of this city, a gentleman whom I respected for his amiable Christian character. I knew he was not with me and therefore I selected him and his church. I wanted the world to know I did nothing in a corner, but was willing to speak upon the house-tops. Brother Grimes wrote back, saying: "I am sorry to say that you cannot have my church for the purpose and at the time you request, and I must be excused from having anything whatever to do with the meeting." While I feel the wound, let me say to him come to New York, and, while I am the minister of Shiloh Church, if he wants to advocate any cause relating to humanity, to justice and truth, let him but ask the use of that church, and if it is in my power to give the pulpit to him, it shall be his, and if I cannot give it to him, I will pay for its use (*Applause*).

I wrote to my friend, Mr. Nell. In his usual manner, always courteous and kind, he told me very reasonably, that many of the people were out of town, and it was very difficult to get a meeting at this time of the year. He thought it was doubtful if there would be any to-night. I thought there would be, and my opinion seems to be sustained. I asked him to advertise the meeting in the "Liberator." Brother Nell did not do it—it was not done, though I wished the advertisement only to give publicity to the announcement. You are here, nevertheless.

I there referred to my friends on the platform [Messrs. Martin, Smith, and Pitts], and asked them if they would not see to it that a house should be open for me to speak upon this subject. They provided this house, and I extend to you my hearty and sincere thanks for your kindness on this occasion. But let me tell those brethren that, had there not been a church open for me in the city of Boston, I would have stood on the corners of your streets, or on Boston Common, and lifted up my voice (*Applause*). One word more. It is high time black men should stop imitating white men in deviltry (*Laughter*). They talk about humanity, and say, "Let justice be done though the heavens fall!" And if the heavens did fall, they would fall right upon them (*Renewed laughter*). We talk about white men closing the door upon us, and shutting out humanity—about ministers being afraid of their people, and allowing padlocks to be put upon their mouths. But may not white men say, "Physicians, heal yourselves"—"Go and take out the beam that is in your own eyes, and then shall ye see clearly to take out the mote that is in your brothers' eyes!" We have got to learn to tolerate free discussion. That is the first thing we want as colored people. Don't you know there are some colored men in Boston who, if they should, by circumstances, become slaveholders in the South, with their whips in their hands, would make the blood fly from their slaves till the very ground would be slippery with the crimson gore? (*"Yes!"* *"Yes!"*) They declaim against white men, and imitate them in their meanest and most devilish practices (*Applause*), to hold back the progress of the age, stifle free discussion, and lock the lips of those who would utter any sentiments not to their liking.

Ladies and gentlemen, the first matter I wished to speak of this evening is the charge that I am a Colonizationist. To my friend Mr. Downing—for I shall call him such still; nothing shall separate him from my heart, no matter how he esteems me— I still say to him, Go on; so far as you are right, God bless you! I sent a letter to him informing him that I should be here, and I asked him to be here also, and said I did not wish to say a word behind his back, as he has so freely talked behind mine, misrepresenting my feelings and views. Probably he is in the house tonight, and I shall be glad to see him and greet him. I am going to speak plainly and deliberately, so that it may be distinctly known what are my sentiments. It has been said that I am a Colonizationist. I am *not* a Colonizationist. Any man that says I am behind my back is an assassin and a coward; any man that says it to my face is a liar, and I stamp the infamous charge upon his forehead! I have hated the sentiments of the American Colonization Society from my childhood. I have learned to hold the same opinion in regard to the sentiments advocated by its slave-holding leaders up to the present time. I expect to do so until that Society shall change its sentiments, and let that change be known to the world. The American Colonization Society says this is not the home of the colored man. I say it *is* the home of the colored man, and it is my home (*Applause*). The American Colonization Society says the colored man cannot be elevated in this country. I believe nothing of the kind. There is no people in this world advancing faster in the cause of equal rights than the colored people. I believe the sky is brightening, and though I may not live to see it, the day is not distant when, from the Atlantic to the Pacific, from Maine to California, the shouts of redeemed millions shall be heard—when truth and peace shall fill the land, and songs of rejoicing shall go up to Heaven. The American Colonization Society says that nobody but black men are bound to evangelize and civilize Africa. I believe nothing of the kind. I believe that black men in general are bound by the laws of love and humanity, and the principles of the Gospel to do all they can for the land of our forefathers, and that the white people are bound in particular to do it, since they have robbed us of our lives, and become rich by our blood, and it is therefore for them to make sacrifices that Africa may be redeemed, and that they may bless it as they have so long cursed it.

These are my views in general. I will read them as I have written them down. These are my sentiments, and no others on the subject:

THE OBJECTS OF THE AFRICAN CIVILIZATION SOCIETY

1st. The immediate and unconditional abolition of slavery in the United States and in Africa, and the destruction of the African slave-trade both in this and that country.

If there is anyone who objects to that, please to rise and show me where the objection is. Silence gives consent. I knew there was common sense in Boston (*Applause*).

2. The destruction of prejudice against colored people in the United States, especially in the nominal free States of the North; and we propose to do this by urging upon the Abolitionists and the friends of humanity of every grade "the necessity of giving trades and employment to ourselves and to our children."

Do you object to that? If so, rise and speak.

A GENTLEMAN—Mr. Garnet, is that the Constitution of the Society you are reading there?

MR. GARNET—I am speaking my own sentiments, and those cherished by the men and women who act with me.

DR. KNOX—I would inquire if you are representing the Civilization Society in these sentiments?

MR. GARNET—I am representing what I proposed to represent —my own views and the objects of the African Civilization Society—nothing more or less.

3.   To assist in giving the Gospel to Africa, and thus render obedience unto the unrepealed command of our Lord Jesus Christ, to go into all the world and preach the Gospel to every creature.

4.   The civilization of Africa, by the introduction into that country of lawful trade and commerce; by the cultivation of cotton to supply the British and other cotton consuming markets, and delivering the civilized world from dependence on the cotton raised in the Southern States by slave labor, and by this means to strike the death-blow to American slavery.

Is this contrary to the laws of God, Christian love, or common sense? (*No! No!*)

Dr. Knox expressed his dissent, and offered to argue the question.

Mr. Garnet declined to discuss the subject, he having sufficient in the object which brought him to Boston to occupy the evening. Some people, he thought, would object to God Almighty sitting on His throne. (*Yes! Yes!*)

5.   To establish a grand centre of negro nationality, from which shall flow the streams of commercial, intellectual, and political power which shall make colored people respected everywhere.

Is there any objection to that?

DR. KNOX—Is this to be in the United States or Africa?

MR. GARNET—I hope in the United States, especially if they reopen the African slave trade. Then, if we do not establish a nationality in the South, I am mistaken in the spirit of my people. Let them bring in a hundred thousand a year! We do not say it is not a great crime, but we know that from the wickedness of man God brings forth good; and if they do it, before half a century shall pass over us we shall have a negro nationality in the United States. In Jamaica there are forty colored men to one white; Hayti is ours; Cuba will be ours soon, and we shall have every island in the Caribbean Sea (*Applause*).

I wish your attention to the next point, for it is something we do not understand—the proper management of money. We know how to make it, but not to keep it. We have gone to white men to borrow a dollar when we wanted one. If we are to stand on the right footing, we must act so that we can lend money instead of borrow.

6.   By the power of money and union of action in this country, to encourage our professional men of every occupation in arts and sciences of every grade, and thus keep the colored people here from the disrespect and contumely shown by others, and the despondency and despair felt by themselves under too many circumstances.

7.   All this to be done by the voluntary cooperation of the friends of universal freedom, irrespective of color, either by working with the Society here or assisting its objects in Africa.

Does anybody object to either of those sentiments?

These are our views. I have nothing more or less to say. Any man that has represented me as having other views, has made representations false and unkind. These are my views in public and in private.

. . .

Concluded from Last Week

I tell you, my friends, that we have been too long depending upon other people. Years have passed away and we have been looking to the Abolitionists to raise us. Abolitionists have done their part and done it well. I believe that God has a certain work for them to do, and that is to prepare the public mind for the full and free discussion of the subject, and the emancipation of the enslaved, and the enfranchisement of the nominally free colored people of this country; the rest of the work we have to do ourselves. White men cannot do it for us. I am not here to find fault with the friends who have labored long and endured much for us; but in many respects I fear they have not done all they might do. I fear, when they have laid down certain first principles, they have stopped there; and to-day, you know as well as I do, that if our children are brought forward to enter upon trades, or learn useful employments, if we go to Abolitionists, they do not seem much more ready to offer assistance than other men. In fact, without finding fault, I think I find, most generally, that the men who take our sons and daughters into their stores and work-shops, are not Abolitionists.

Abolitionists say it is not part of their work to do this. The subject is one on which we have to think. Our children are being educated. So far as Boston is concerned they are as well informed as white children. They are in the same schools and in the same classes. What prospect is before them when they go out into the world? You teach your daughters the refinements of elevated life. What next? When those girls are sent to look out for themselves, what is the hope and prospect before them? I am one of those men who say, here as elsewhere, that one employment before God and all honest, right-thinking men, is just as honorable as another. It is as honorable for me to take my saw and buck, or sweep the streets, if I do it as a man and a Christian, as to fill a senatorial chair. But you cannot get our children to think so; and if these are the occupations that your children are to be engaged in, if you wish to save them from destruction, my word for it, you had better not teach them quite so much, lest when they come up and take their positions in life, they become discouraged, as too many of our young people have been, and are lying all along the pathway of life, bruised, and mangled, and dying. Our fault is that we have not thought on the subject. We have not had the courage to think. We talk of staying here and "fighting it out." Our friend, Ezra R. Johnson, talked about fighting it out. And yet he went off to California and honorably made his fortune, and then went to New Bedford and sits there a high-minded gentleman and "fights it out" (*Laughter and applause*). If stand-still is your motto, see to it that you live up to it. Do not say one thing and do another.

Then, again, there is another objection. Some say I will not budge from this dear, sweet land. Why? Because white men say I shall go. I wouldn't go if Africa was strewn with gold and the shores were covered with silver. Why? Because white men say I must go. I will tell you what I think about it. *I* would go anywhere on this broad, green earth, if I could better my condition, and do good to society and preach the Gospel. I would go without caring whether a white man said go or stay. I believe that some people wouldn't go to Heaven if a white man should say they must go. They remind me of a crooked old deacon in New York, who always opposed everything that he did not himself originate. The spirit of God was about being poured out on the Church and the community, and it was resolved to have a protracted meeting. He arose, after several had spoken, and said, as usual, "Brethren, I cannot give my assent to that; I think it is not exactly the time; I don't think we'd better go at it now." Another good deacon got down on his knees and prayed to God after this manner: "Oh, Lord! here is this dear brother who has been bothering and pestering us for many years; we've tried to cure him, to convert him. We have failed; and now, Lord, if thou canst, convert him and sanctify his soul, and take him up into the kingdom of glory, and let him no more come out forever" (*Laughter*). The old deacon jumped up and said, "*I won't go!*" (*Great merriment*). Now, if I were on my way to Heaven, and some white man said to me, "Go up to Heaven," I would say, I will go, but I don't think your telling me to go would accelerate my journey forward. Let us be wise; let us rid ourselves of our folly and prejudice, and look at the subject as candid, independent, intelligent men (*Loud applause*).

Let me state a few facts for your consideration. On the coast of Africa there are now eight thousand white men engaged in commerce and trade. They are getting at the mouth of every river that runs out into the ocean; they are on either side of the rivers; they have gone up there, obtaining all the advantages of the market from the interior, all the ivory, gold, and palm oil, particularly, and valuable skins. They bring these to England and the United States, and they are becoming rich. They receive as profits from a single cargo from five to twenty thousand dollars. Go to these merchants and ask them about Africa, and they don't know anything about it. You cannot get a word out of them. There are eighty-three white men thus engaged in Lagos alone. We wrote, some time ago, to an English gentleman who has done a great deal for free cotton-growing in Africa. We asked for information and advice in regard to our prospect. He wrote back—"We are not in favor of colored people going there in small companies, for this reason: if they do *they will interrupt the trade already established between Africa and England.*" That opened our eyes. If that trade was of so much value that English manufacturers were anxious to preserve it to themselves, we thought that was the very reason we should go and take advantage of it. There is a gentleman at Staten Island, New York, who manufactures what we call sperm candles. They are made of bleached palm oil. This gentleman has, on Staten Island, a village of manufacturers. He has hundreds of men in his employment there. He sends out his ships to Africa, that come back laden with palm oil; and he then whitens it and makes it up into candles. He has accumulated a fortune of millions of dollars and lives in a princely palace in Fifth Avenue. And colored men, while they have suffered the white men to plunder the land of their forefathers of living souls, for three hundred years, now that the wonderful discoveries of Livingston, Barth, Bowen, and others, are opening the hitherto unknown wealth of that country, when God, and science, and unconquerable human energy, have turned the tide of fortune in our favor, we refuse to throw ourselves upon it simply because some white men have impudently said we shall go. He who tells me I shall leave my country is an impudent man, and he who says I shall not go, is a fool. I will do as I please, either to go or stay. The *common sense* of the world is in favor of this movement. We hold no other sentiments.

Now you can pass opposing resolutions in your New England Conventions, if you choose, but you can't stop such a man as Captain Roye bringing in his goods—importing the first sugar ever brought from Africa to the United States. You will not prevent him from putting his profits in his pocket and returning for more. You will not hinder such men as Joseph Turpin, Dr. Dunbar, and Mr. Johnson, from loading a vessel for Africa. You will not hinder any man that is disposed to do it. You might pass resolutions until they were stacked up as high as mountains, and they would laugh at them, and when they were ready would go, because their common sense is with them.

Again, I hold that the laws of trade and commerce are with

this movement. It cannot be otherwise. The resources of that country are opening, white men are daily equipping their vessels and filling their pockets, and laughing at us poor colored people quarreling among ourselves and destroying the character of every man who fails to agree with us. In California, after the white men have taken up the gold you will see my poor brother coming, all covered with dust, with his tongue lolling out (*great laughter*) to take what is left. Had they been advised to go there in early times, when they might have taken advantage of the opportunities which the country afforded, and they would have said, "I'm not going because I'm told to go there!" We can't please such people. It will be seen, after our more active, energetic Anglo-Saxon brethren have got rich by trade and commerce in Africa, then our people will be trotting there; then we will begin to talk about putting our funds together and buying vessels. *If there were a dozen ships sailing out of Boston harbor, keeping up a trade between these countries, that fact would do more for the overthrowing of slavery, in creating a respect for ourselves, and breaking down the walls of prejudice, than fifty thousand lectures of the most eloquent men of this land.* ("*True! true!*") I have gone along the docks in New York, and when I have seen those young men with their books in hand, taking account of the cargoes of the African vessels, I have asked Dr. Dunbar—"Doctor, do you receive anything like disrespect? Do you hear any unkind remarks?" Said he, "I receive nothing but the utmost respect." I saw white men who looked solemnly and respectfully on, and they came up and spoke to these young men, asked them the character of the cargo they were taking out, and wished them success, a safe voyage over, and happy and safe return. It is not, after all, our big talk that is going to break down prejudice; it is not your New England Conventions, your splendid speeches, and fiery denunciations; but if this adamantine wall is to fall, it will be when we shall come up and stand by the side of other men, and in every department of cultivated life show that we are their equals in every respect.

The spirit of the Gospel of Jesus is also with us, and I attach great importance to that, though some may not. I mean what I say—that unless the hand and power of God is in all this, we will never succeed; and had we clung to God with more fervor and faithfulness, I believe that before this time the chain of oppression would have been broken, and the oppressed gone free (*Applause*). I believe that God means to make us feel our dependence upon him in this great work, before he will crown it with success. Now, I hold that that commandment has never been repealed—"Go ye into all the world and preach the Gospel to every creature." *All* the world—not only America, not only down to Worcester, or down to Nahant, and get the bracing sea air and be refreshed, but to—

DR. KNOX—To South Carolina.

MR. GARNET—Yes Sir; why don't you go there? (*Laughter*).

Now let me tell you it is a withering shame to the colored Christians of the United States, that among all the religious people of color in Massachusetts, in all the New England States, among the hundreds of thousands in the Middle and Southern States, there is but barely one missionary sent to Hayti, Jamaica, Africa. That man was sent out last year by the Baptist Convention of colored ministers of this country—only one. It is a shame, let me say, that we have been so backward in this respect. If the churches would be blessed we must obey God.

There are some gentlemen, like this friend here, always throwing in our teeth: "Why don't you go down to South Carolina?" That is the old pro-slavery doctrine. They say that to all the anti-slavery ministers in the North. "Why don't you go to the South and preach your doctrine instead of standing here?" Let me ask the interrogator, why don't *you go* South and preach?

DR. KNOX—I am no preacher (*Laughter*).

MR. GARNET—But you are a hero and an Abolitionist, and certainly you would not laden other men with grievous burdens which you are unwilling to touch with one of your fingers. (*Good! good!*) It is very easy to say "Go thou"; but to say, "Let us go," is another thing.

One other thing and I must close. Wm. Wells Brown comes up and says: "I have no objections to the principles of the African Civilization Society but this one—I don't like its practice of *begging* around the country." About ten years before I went to England Mr. Brown commenced begging in the United States (*Laughter*). He begged from Maine to Georgia—no, he didn't go down there, but nothing but the line Mason and Dixon drew prevented him from going to Georgia (*Great laughter*). He begged with skill and effect. And when I went to England there was Mr. Brown, and, after one of his spirited lectures, and before he closed, he said he should have to crave a collection, to pay expenses. He begged in England, Scotland, Ireland, and Wales, "over the mountain and through the wildwood." And when I got here to Boston to see Mr. Brown, he is in the State of New York carrying on the same old trade (*Great merriment*).

A VOICE—That's his business.

MR. GARNET—Yes, and like most successful businessmen, he goes in for monopoly.

THEN MR. DOUGLASS SAYS: "O, I have no objection to civilizing Africa, and voluntary emigration. But I don't like this begging." It would be well for you if you, my friends, could succeed as well in begging as he has. He has labored hard and he has begged hard (*Laughter*). He has done well, and I wish him success. His fame belongs to our role, and his talents shed luster upon the land. But certainly he has learned by this time that all black public men approach *beggary,* as they ascend the scale of greatness. (*A voice—"That's so."*) So with all these lectures going through the country at ten dollars per week, and traveling expenses, and getting that from the people and then saying: "We are opposed to this begging." These brethren are like the fat ox, having got into clover themselves, they want to hook every body that comes in to get a bite (*Renewed merriment*). Every benevolent cause in this country is sustained by begging, as it is called—by the voluntary contribution of every one who chooses to give. Is there anything wrong in that? I tell you this talk about "begging" is perfect humbug, as great a one as the humbug of O'Connell's, who said there was a bug in Tipperary that could eat anything, he could eat iron and digest it as if it were a piece of bread.

We have got to put down these humbugs among our own

people. There are men who oppose everything they do not originate. They are the very men who cater to the prejudices of white men. (*"Hear! hear!"*) When called themselves to stand up they are as ready to bow down as the readiest. We must begin at Jerusalem. That is one of the objects of the Civilization Society. We have to civilize ourselves. I put my foot on that practice of those of my brethren who, if a black man comes in their shops, will not shave him. While you do that you have no right to talk about the white men turning you out of the cars and hotels (*Applause*).

In Saratoga I delivered a lecture in St. Nicholas Hall, to an overflowing concourse of people. The next night one of the proprietors of the great water-cure establishment there invited me to come to their parlor and repeat the lecture. Five of the slave-holders boarding there walked up to the clerk's office and said: "If you are going to have a negro speak here, give us our bills." "Take your bills; it is a free country." The other fifteen stayed. I gave my lecture. The parlor, one of the largest and finest of Saratoga, was crowded to overflowing. There is an example of a white man. Go to a hotel kept by some of the colored friends and they will look at you and begin to stutter, "Very sorry—but you know we have to—" (*Great merriment.* "*Who's that? Is it Downing?*") Well, I will not call any names. I will not say a word here in respect to my friend Downing. If he were here I would speak more plainly. I will tell you what some of you will do: you will abuse me for my course, and yourselves bow down to the prejudices of white men. But the truth it is, and it will bear its own weight. If these colored men say, "We can't entertain our people," and if they hold to that when they come to sit in high places, as your Presidents, tell them to go home and get civilized (*Applause*).

But when you see a man in humility, with no unkindness, telling the truth, don't you, ladies of Boston, go and rob your gardens of their flowers. I won't say anything more on that subject. But pray do nothing to roll back the tide of civilization among our people.

And now, but one more remark. It was said by a Boston friend, who has often taken me by the hand and sat by the same fire-side, and walked with me in the streets, and mused with me in sacred places: "I knew Garnet when he was poor and had not a cent in his pocket." I would say to him that if he knew me twenty-five years ago, when I was poor, he knows me to-day as the same poor man. And I expect to be a poor man till slavery is abolished. If slavery is not abolished before I die, I shall die a poor man. But in all my poverty my house has been open to the flying fugitive. (*"True!"* *"That's true!"*) One hundred and fifty, in a single year, have lodged under my roof; and I have never asked or received a penny for what I gave them, but divided with them my last crust.

I will now receive and answer any questions that may be put to me in respect to my views on the subject of African Civilization, or the Society of which I am President.

MR. WASHINGTON—I would merely ask whether this Civilization Society has any connection or anything to do with the Colonization Society?

MR. GARNET—Just about the same connection that the East has with the far West—no more connection or correspondence, written or implied.

Mr. Washington said he was not at the Convention; but his impression had been, from the similarity in some respects of the objects of the two Societies, that this was but the Colonization Society under a cloak.

MR. GARNET—Now it is my turn to ask you a question. Sir, do you believe that now?

MR. WASHINGTON—I have always believed Mr. Garnet to be a man of truth; and, as he says it is not true, of course I am satisfied.

MR. GARNET—I would further state that I know of some colonizationists who say they are determined to go to Heaven. There are some colored people in this house who are of the same determination. Are you going to stop on the road to Heaven because the colonizationists are going there?

A GENTLEMAN—What does your Society propose to do with the funds collected?

MR. GARNET—I do not see how any man who has been thinking and has kept his eyes open here can ask that question. I have already stated the objects of the Society.

Q. In what way are the funds to be applied in furthering the objects of the Society? You say the emigration is to be voluntary.

Mr. Garnet—They are to be used in aiding volunteers to carry out the objects of the Society.

Dr. Knox desired to offer some further remarks. He then claimed a right to discuss the subject treated by Mr. G., complained that free speech had been hewn down in his person, and denounced the meeting as pro-slavery.

Mr. Garnet—I thank you, my friends, for your kindness toward me and my cause. With a fair hearing and free discussion, the principles and objects of African Civilization will grow and take root in this land, until they shall fill the Christian world with their praise. There is not power enough in all the silent abodes of "Sleepy Hollow" to hold back the golden car of human progress. I care not a straw for the Scribes, Pharisees, and hypocrites; the common people will hear me. Those who will get on board will reach the goal in peace and triumph. Those who stand in the way will be crushed beneath its mighty wheels.

Mr. Garnet resumed his seat amid long and continued applause.

Rev. Mr. Martin then offered the following resolutions.

Whereas, the Rev. Henry Highland Garnet has stood prominently before the people of this country and Great Britain as the able representative and able advocate of the free colored people, and the slave; and

Whereas, He is universally respected by them as an honest man, a devoted Christian, and a staunch laborer in the cause of Abolitionism; and

Whereas, There has been the most commendable consistency of course, and the most zealous action on his part for the attainment of the great objects we have in view; therefore,

Resolved, That we, as colored people, have the utmost confidence in his integrity, feeling that his constant identity with us, and the sacrifices which he has made to the anti-slavery cause are worthy of our respect and entitled to our co-operation.

Resolved, That these resolutions be published in "Frederick Douglass' Paper" and "The Weekly Anglo-African" as the sense of this meeting.

The resolutions were opposed by Dr. Knox and five others, on the ground that they involved an endorsement of the African Civilization Society.

The resolutions were then carried by a very large majority, and the meeting adjourned.

The Weekly Anglo-African
September 19, 1859
Vol. 1, No. 9

7

THE POLITICAL DESTINY OF THE COLORED RACE
BY MARTIN R. DELANY

To the Colored Inhabitants of the United States:—

FELLOW-COUNTRYMEN: The duty assigned us is an important one, comprehending all that pertains to our destiny and that of our posterity, present and prospectively. And while it must be admitted that the subject is one of the greatest magnitude, requiring all that talents, prudence, and wisdom might adduce, and while it would be folly to pretend to give you the combined result of these three agencies, we shall satisfy ourselves with doing our duty to the best of our ability, and that in the plainest, most simple, and comprehensive manner.

Our object, then, shall be to place before you our true position in this country (the United States), the improbability of realizing our desires, and the sure, practicable, and infallible remedy for the evils we now endure.

We have not addressed you as *citizens*—a term desired and ever cherished by us—because such you have never been. We have not addressed you as *freemen*, because such privileges have never been enjoyed by any colored man in the United States. Why, then, should we flatter your credulity, by inducing you to believe that which neither has now, nor never before had, an existence? Our oppressors are ever gratified at our manifest satisfaction, especially when that satisfaction is founded upon false premises; an assumption on our part of the enjoyment of rights and privileges which never have been conceded, and which, according to the present system of the United States policy, we never can enjoy.

The *political policy* of this country was solely borrowed from, and shaped and modelled after, that of Rome. This was strikingly the case in the establishment of immunities, and the application of terms in their civil and legal regulations.

The term *citizen,* politically considered, is derived from the Roman definition, which was never applied in any other sense—*cives ingenui*; which meant, one exempt from restraint of any kind. (*Cives,* a citizen; one who might enjoy the highest honors in his own free town—the town in which he lived—and in the country or commonwealth; and *ingenui,* freeborn—of GOOD EXTRACTION.) All who were deprived of citizenship—that is, the right of enjoying positions of honor and trust—were termed *hostes* and *peregrini*; which are public and private enemies, and foreigners, or aliens to the country. (*Hostis,* a public, and sometimes private, enemy; and *peregrinus,* an alien, stranger, or foreigner.)

The Romans, from a national pride, to distinguish their inhabitants from those of other countries, termed them all "citizens," but, consequently, were under the necessity of specifying four classes of citizens: none but the *cives ingenui* being unrestricted in their privileges. There was one class, called the *jus quiritium,* or the wailing or *supplicating* citizen; that is, one who was continually *moaning, complaining,* or *crying for aid or succor.* This class might also include within themselves the *jus suffragii,* who had the privilege of *voting,* but no other privilege. They could vote for one of their superiors—the *cives ingenui*—but not for themselves.

Such, then, is the condition, precisely, of the black and colored inhabitants of the United States; in some of the states they answering to the latter class, having the privilege of *voting,* to elevate their superiors to positions to which they need never dare aspire or even hope to attain.

There has, of late years, been a false impression obtained, that the privilege of *voting* constitutes, or necessarily embodies, the *rights of citizenship.* A more radical error never obtained favor among an oppressed people. Suffrage is an ambiguous term, which admits of several definitions. But according to strict political construction, means simply "a vote, voice, approbation." Here, then, you have the whole import of the term *suffrage.* To have the "right of suffrage," as we rather proudly term it, is simply to have the *privilege*—there is no *right* about it—of giving our *approbation* to that which our *rulers may do,* without the privilege, on our part, of doing the same thing. Where such privileges are granted—privileges which are now exercised in but few of the states by colored men—we have but the privilege granted of saying, in common with others, who shall, for the time being, exercise *rights,* which, in him, are conceded to be *inherent* and *inviolate:* like the indented apprentice, who is summoned to give his approbation to an act which would be fully binding without his concurrence. Where there is no *acknowledged sovereignty,* there can be no binding power; hence, the suffrage of the black man, independently of the white, would be in this country unavailable.

Much might be adduced on this point to prove the insignificance of the black man, politically considered, in this country, but we deem it wholly unnecessary at present, and consequently proceed at once to consider another feature of this important subject.

Let it then be understood, as a great principle of political economy, that no people can be free who themselves do not constitute an essential part of the *ruling element* of the country in which they live. Whether this element be founded upon a true or false, a just or an unjust basis, this position in community is necessary to personal safety. The liberty of no man is secure who controls not his own political destiny. What is true of an individual is true of a family, and that which is true of a family is also true concerning a whole people. To suppose otherwise, is that delusion which at once induces its victim, through a period of long suffering, patiently to submit to every species of wrong; trusting against probability, and hoping against all reasonable grounds of expectation, for the granting of privileges and enjoyment of rights which never will be attained. This delusion reveals the true secret of the power which holds in peaceable subjection all the oppressed in every part of the world.

A people, to be free, must necessarily be *their own rulers;* that is, *each individual* must, in himself, embody the *essential ingredient*—so to speak—of the *sovereign principle* which composes the *true basis* of his liberty. This principle, when not exercised by himself, may, at his pleasure, be delegated to another—his true representative.

Said a great French writer, "A free agent, in a free government, should be his own governor"; that is, he must possess within himself the *acknowledged right to govern:* this constitutes him a *governor,* though he may delegate to another the power to govern himself.

No one, then, can delegate to another a power he never possessed; that is, he cannot *give an agency* in that which he never had a right. Consequently, the colored man in the United States, being deprived of the right of inherent sovereignty, cannot *confer* a franchise, because he possesses none to confer. Therefore, where there is no franchise, there can neither be *freedom* nor *safety* for the disfranchised. And it is a futile hope to suppose that the agent of another's concerns will take a proper interest in the affairs of those to whom he is under no obligations. Having no favors to ask or expect, he therefore has none to lose.

In other periods and parts of the world, as in Europe and Asia, the people being of one common, direct origin of race, though established on the presumption of difference by birth, or what was termed *blood,* yet the distinction between the superior classes and common people could only be marked by the difference in the dress and education of the two classes. To effect this, the interposition of government was necessary; consequently the costume and education of the people became a subject of legal restriction, guarding carefully against the privileges of the common people.

In Rome the patrician and plebeian were orders in the ranks of her people—all of whom were termed citizens *(cives)*—recognized by the laws of the country; their dress and education being determined by law, the better to fix the distinction. In different parts of Europe, at the present day, if not the same, the distinction among the people is similar, only on a modified, and in some kingdoms, probably more tolerant or deceptive policy.

In the United States our degradation being once—as it has in a hundred instances been done—legally determined, our color is sufficient, independently of costume, education, or other distinguishing marks, to keep up that distinction.

In Europe when an inferior is elevated to the rank of equality with the superior class, the law first comes to his aid, which, in its decrees, entirely destroys his identity as an inferior, leaving no trace of his former condition visible.

In the United States, among the whites, their color is made, by law and custom, the mark of distinction and superiority; while the color of the blacks is a badge of degradation, acknowledged by statute, organic law, and the common consent of the people.

With this view of the case—which we hold to be correct—to elevate to equality the degraded subject of law and custom, it can only be done, as in Europe, by an entire destruction of the identity of the former condition of the applicant. Even were this desirable, which we by no means admit, with the deep-seated prejudices engendered by oppression, with which we have to contend, ages incalculable might reasonably be expected to roll around before this could honorably be accomplished; otherwise, we should encourage, and at once commence, an indiscriminate concubinage and immoral commerce of our mothers, sisters, wives, and daughters, revolting to think of, and a physical curse to humanity.

If this state of things be to succeed, then, as in Egypt, under the dread of the inscrutable approach of the destroying angel, to appease the hatred of our oppressors, as a license to the passions of every white, let the lintel of each door of every black man be stained with the blood of virgin purity and unsullied matron fidelity. Let it be written along the cornice in capitals, "The *will* of the white man is the rule of my household." Remove the protection to our chambers and nurseries, that the places once sacred may henceforth become the unrestrained resort of the vagrant and rabble, always provided that the licensed commissioner of lust shall wear the indisputable impress of a *white* skin.

But we have fully discovered and comprehended the great political disease with which we are affected, the cause of its origin and continuance; and what is now left for us to do is to discover and apply a sovereign remedy, a healing balm to a sorely diseased body—a wrecked but not entirely shattered system. We propose for this disease a remedy. That remedy is emigration. This emigration should be well advised, and like remedies applied to remove the disease from the physical system of man, skilfully and carefully applied, within the proper time, directed to operate on that part of the system whose greatest tendency shall be to benefit the whole.

Several geographical localities have been named, among which rank the Canadas. These we do not object to as places of temporary relief, especially to the fleeing fugitive—which, like a palliative, soothes, for the time being, the misery—but cannot commend them as permanent places upon which to fix our destiny, and that of our children, who shall come after us. But in this connection we would most earnestly recommend to the colored people of the United States generally, to secure, by purchase, all of the land they possibly can while selling at low rates, under the British people and government; as that time may come, when, like the lands in the United States territories generally, if not as in Oregon and some other territories and states, they may be prevented entirely from settling or purchasing them—the preference being given to the white applicant.

And here we would not deceive you by disguising the facts that, according to political tendency, the Canadas, as all British America, at no very distant day, are destined to come into the United States.

And were this not the case, the odds are against us, because the ruling element there, as in the United States, is, and ever must be, white; the population now standing, in all British America, two and a half millions of whites to but forty thousand of the black race, or sixty-one and a fraction whites to one black!—the difference being eleven times greater than in the United States—so that colored people might never hope for anything more than to exist politically by mere sufferance; occupying a secondary position to the whites of the Canadas. The Yankees from this side of the lakes are fast settling in the Canadas, infusing, with industrious success, all the malignity and negro-hate inseparable from their very being, as Christian democrats and American advocates of equality.

Then, to be successful, our attention must be turned in a direction towards those places where the black and colored man comprise, by population, and constitute by necessity of numbers, the *ruling element* of the body politic; and where, when occasion shall require it, the issue can be made and maintained on this basis; where our political enclosure and national edifice can be reared, established, walled, and proudly defended on this great elementary principle of original identity. Upon this solid foundation rests the fabric of every substantial political structure in the world, which cannot exist without it; and so soon as a people or nation lose their original identity, just so soon must that nation or people become extinct. Powerful though they may have been, they must fall. Because the nucleus which heretofore held them together, becoming extinct, there being no longer a centre of attraction, or basis for a union of the parts, a dissolution must as naturally ensue as the result of the neutrality of the basis of adhesion among the particles of matter.

This is the secret of the eventful downfall of Egypt, Carthage, Rome, and the former Grecian states, once so powerful—a loss of original identity; and with it, a loss of interest in maintaining their fundamental principles of nationality.

This, also, is the great secret of the present strength of Great Britain, Russia, the United States, and Turkey; and the endurance of the French nation, whatever its strength and power, is attributable only to their identity as Frenchmen.

And doubtless the downfall of Hungary, brave and noble as may be her people, is mainly to be attributed to the want of identity of origin, and, consequently, a union of interests and purpose. This fact it might not have been expected would be admitted by the great Sclave in his thrilling pleas for the restoration of Hungary, when asking aid, both national and individual, to enable him to throw off the ponderous weight placed upon their shoulders by the House of Hapsburg.

Hungary consisted of three distinct "races"—as they called themselves—of people, all priding in, and claiming rights based on, their originality—the Magyars, Celts, and Sclaves. On the encroachment of Austria, each one of these races, declaring for nationality, rose up against the House of Hapsburg, claiming the right of self-government, premised on their origin. Between the three a compromise was effected; the Magyars, being the majority, claimed the precedence. They made an effort, but for the want of a unity of interests—an identity of origin—the noble Hungarians failed. All know the result.

Nor is this the only important consideration. Were we content to remain as we are, sparsely interspersed among our white fellow-countrymen, we never might be expected to equal them in any honorable or respectable competition for a livelihood. For the reason that, according to the customs and policy of the country, we for ages would be kept in a secondary position, every situation of respectability, honor, profit. or trust, either as mechanics, clerks, teachers, jurors, councilmen, or legislators, being filled by white men, consequently our energies must become paralyzed or enervated for the want of proper encouragement.

This example upon our children, and the colored people generally, is pernicious and degrading in the extreme. And how could it otherwise be, when they see every place of respectability filled and occupied by the whites, they pandering to their vanity, and existing among them merely as a thing of conveniency?

Our friends in this and other countries, anxious for our elevation, have for years been erroneously urging us to lose our identity as a distinct race, declaring that we were the same as other people; while at the very same time their own representative was traversing the world, and propagating the doctrine in favor of a *universal Anglo-Saxon predominance*. The "universal brotherhood," so ably and eloquently advocated by that Polyglot Christian Apostle[1] of this doctrine, had established as its basis a universal acknowledgment of the Anglo-Saxon rule.

The truth is, we are not identical with the Anglo-Saxon, or any other race of the Caucasian or pure white type of the human family, and the sooner we know and acknowledge this truth the better for ourselves and posterity.

The English, French, Irish, German, Italian, Turk, Persian, Greek, Jew, and all other races, have their native or inherent peculiarities, and why not our race? We are not willing, therefore, at all times and under all circumstances to be moulded into various shapes of eccentricity, to suit the caprices and conveniences of every kind of people. We are not more suitable to

[1] Elihu Burritt.

everybody than everybody is suitable to us; therefore, no more like other people than others are like us.

We have, then, inherent traits, attributes, so to speak, and native characteristics, peculiar to our race, whether pure or mixed blood; and all that is required of us is to cultivate these, and develop them in their purity, to make them desirable and emulated by the rest of the world.

That the colored races have the highest traits of civilization, will not be disputed. They are civil, peaceable, and religious to a fault. In mathematics, sculpture and architecture, as arts and sciences, commerce and internal improvements as enterprises, the white race may probably excel; but in languages, oratory, poetry, music, and painting, as arts and sciences, and in ethics, metaphysics, theology, and legal jurisprudence—in plain language, in the true principles of morals, correctness of thought, religion, and law or civil government, there is no doubt but the black race will yet instruct the world.

It would be duplicity longer to disguise the fact that the great issue, sooner or later, upon which must be disputed the world's destiny, will be a question of black and white, and every individual will be called upon for his identity with one or the other. The blacks and colored races are four-sixths of all the population of the world; and these people are fast tending to a common cause with each other. The white races are but one third of the population of the globe—or one of them to two of us—and it cannot much longer continue that two thirds will passively submit to the universal domination of this one third. And it is notorious that the only progress made in territorial domain, in the last three centuries, by the whites, has been a usurpation and encroachment on the rights and native soil of some of the colored races.

The East Indies, Java, Sumatra, the Azores, Madeira, Canary, and Cape Verde Islands; Socotra, Guardifui, and the Isle of France; Algiers, Tunis, Tripoli, Barca, and Egypt in the North, Sierra Leone in the West, and Cape Colony in the South of Africa; besides many other islands and possessions not herein named; Australia, the Ladrone Islands, together with many others of Oceanica; the seizure and appropriation of a great portion of the Western Continent, with all its islands, were so many encroachments of the whites upon the rights of the colored races. Nor are they yet content, but, intoxicated with the success of their career, the Sandwich Islands are now marked out as the next booty to be seized in the ravages of their exterminating crusade.

We regret the necessity of stating the fact, but duty compels us to the task, that, for more than two thousand years, the determined aim of the whites has been to crush the colored races wherever found. With a determined will they have sought and pursued them in every quarter of the globe. The Anglo-Saxon has taken the lead in this work of universal subjugation. But the Anglo-American stands preëminent for deeds of injustice and acts of oppression, unparalleled, perhaps, in the annals of modern history.

We admit the existence of great and good people in America, England, France, and the rest of Europe, who desire a unity of interests among the whole human family, of whatever origin or race.

But it is neither the moralist, Christian, nor philanthropist whom we now have to meet and combat, but the politician, the civil engineer, and skilful economist, who direct and control the machinery which moves forward, with mighty impulse, the nations and powers of the earth. We must, therefore, if possible, meet them on vantage ground, or, at least, with adequate means for the conflict.

Should we encounter an enemy with artillery, a prayer will not stay the cannon shot, neither will the kind words nor smiles of philanthropy shield his spear from piercing us through the heart. We must meet mankind, then, as they meet us—prepared for the worst, though we may hope for the best. Our submission does not gain for us an increase of friends nor respectability, as the white race will only respect those who oppose their usurpation, and acknowledge as equals those who will not submit to their oppression. This may be no new discovery in political economy, but it certainly is a subject worthy the consideration of the black race.

After a due consideration of these facts, as herein recounted, shall we stand still and continue inactive—the passive observers of the great events of the times and age in which we live; submitting indifferently to the usurpation by the white race of every right belonging to the blacks? Shall the last vestige of an opportunity, outside of the continent of Africa, for the national development of our race, be permitted, in consequence of our slothfulness, to elude our grasp, and fall into the possession of the whites? This, may Heaven forbid. May the sturdy, intelligent Africo-American sons of the Western Continent forbid.

Longer to remain inactive, it should be borne in mind, may be to give an opportunity to despoil us of every right and possession sacred to our existence, with which God has endowed us as a heritage on the earth. For let it not be forgotten that the white race—who numbers but *one* of them to *two* of us—originally located in Europe, besides possessing all of that continent, have now got hold of a large portion of Asia, Africa, all North America, a portion of South America, and all of the great islands of both hemispheres, except Paupau, or New Guinea, inhabited by negroes and Malays, in Oceanica; the Japanese Islands, peopled and ruled by the Japanese; Madagascar, peopled by negroes, near the coast of Africa; and the Island of Hayti, in the West Indies, peopled by as brave and noble descendants of Africa as they who laid the foundation of Thebias, or constructed the everlasting pyramids and catacombs of Egypt—a people who have freed themselves by the might of their own will, the force of their own power, the unfailing strength of their own right arms, and their unflinching determination to be free.

Let us, then, not survive the disgrace and ordeal of Almighty displeasure, of two to one, witnessing the universal possession and control by the whites of every habitable portion of the earth. For such must inevitably be the case, and that, too, at no distant day, if black men do not take advantage of the opportunity, by grasping hold of those places where chance is in their favor, and establishing the rights and power of the colored race.

We must make an issue, create an event, and establish for ourselves a position. This is essentially necessary for our effective elevation as a people, in shaping our national development, directing our destiny, and redeeming ourselves as a race.

If we but determine it shall be so, it *will* be so; and there is nothing under the sun can prevent it. We shall then be but in pursuit of our legitimate claims to inherent rights, bequeathed to us by the will of Heaven—the endowment of God, our common Parent. A distinguished economist has truly said, "God has implanted in man an infinite progression in the career of improvement. A soul capacitated for improvement ought not to be bounded by a tyrant's landmarks." This sentiment is just and true, the application of which to our case is adapted with singular fitness.

Having glanced hastily at our present political position in the world generally, and the United States in particular,—the fundamental disadvantages under which we exist, and the improbability of ever attaining citizenship and equality of rights in this country,—we call your attention next to the places of destination to which we shall direct emigration.

The West Indies, Central and South America, are the countries of our choice, the advantages of which shall be made apparent to your entire satisfaction. Though we have designated them as countries, they are, in fact, but one country, relatively considered, a part of this, the Western Continent. As now politically divided, they consist of the following classification, each group or division placed under its proper national head:—

The French Islands

	Square miles	Population in 1840
Guadeloupe	675	124,000
Martinico	260	119,000
St. Martin, N. part	15	6,000
Mariegalente	90	11,500
Deseada	25	1,500

Danish Islands

Santa Cruz	80	34,000
St. Thomas	50	15,000
St. John	70	3,000

SWEDISH

	Square miles	Population in 1840
St. Bartholomew	25	8,000

DUTCH

St. Eustatia	10	20,000
Curacao	375	12,000
St. Martin, S. part	10	5,000
Saba	20	9,000

VENEZUELA

Margarita	00	16,000

SPANISH

Cuba	43,500	725,000
Porto Rico	4,000	325,000

BRITISH

Jamaica	5,520	375,000
Barbadoes	164	102,000
Trinidad	1,970	45,000
Antigua	108	36,000
Grenada and the Granadines	120	29,000
St. Vincent	121	36,000
St. Kitts	68	24,000
Dominica	275	20,000
St. Lucia	275	18,000
Tobago	120	14,000
Nevis	20	12,000
Montserrat	47	8,000
Tortola	20	7,000
Barbuda	72	0,000
Anguilla	90	3,000
Bahamas	4,440	18,000
Bermudas	20	10,000

HAYTIEN NATION

	Square miles	Population in 1840
Hayti	000	800,000

In addition to these there are a number of smaller islands, belonging to the Little Antilles, the area and population of which are not known, many of them being unpopulated.

These islands, in the aggregate, form an area—allowing 40,000 square miles to Hayti and her adjunct islands, and something for those the statistics of which are unknown—of about 103,000, or equal in extent to Rhode Island, New York, New Jersey, and Pennsylvania, and little less than the United Kingdom of England, Scotland, Ireland, and the principality of Wales.

The population being, on the above date, 1840, 3,115,000 (three millions one hundred and fifteen thousand), and allowing an increase of *ten per cent.* in ten years, on the entire population, there are now 3,250,000 (three millions two hundred and fifty thousand) inhabitants, who comprise the people of these islands.

CENTRAL AMERICA

	Population in 1840
Guatemala	800,000
San Salvador	350,000
Honduras	250,000
Costa Rica	150,000
Nicaragua	250,000

These consist of five states, as shown in the above statistics, the united population of which, in 1840, amounted to 1,800,000 (one million eight hundred thousand) inhabitants. The number at present being estimated at 2,500,000 (two and a half millions), shows in thirteen years, 700,000 (seven hundred thousand), being one third and one eighteenth of an increase in population.

SOUTH AMERICA

	Square miles	Population in 1840
New Grenada	450,000	1,687,000
Venezuela	420,000	900,000
Ecuador	280,000	600,000
Guiana	160,000	182,000
Brazil	3,390,000	5,000,000
North Peru	300,000	700,000
South Peru	130,000	800,000
Bolivia	450,000	1,716,000
Buenos Ayres	750,000	700,000
Paraguay	88,000	150,000
Uruguay	92,000	75,000
Chili	170,000	1,500,000
Patagonia	370,000	30,000

The total area of these states is 7,050,000 (seven millions and fifty thousand) square miles; but comparatively little (450,000 square miles) less than the whole area of North America, in which we live.

But one state in South America, Brazil, is an abject slave-holding state; and even here all free men are socially and politically equal, negroes and colored men partly of African descent holding offices of honor, trust, and rank, without restriction. In the other states slavery is not known, all the inhabitants enjoying political equality, restrictions on account of color being entirely unknown, unless, indeed, necessity induces it, when, in all such cases, the preference is given to the colored man, to put a check to European assumption and insufferable Yankee intrusion and impudence.

The aggregate population was 14,040,000 (fourteen millions and forty thousand) in 1840. Allowing for thirteen years the same ratio of increase as that of the Central American states— being one third (4,680,000)—and this gives at present a population of 18,720,000 in South America.

Add to this the population of the Antilles and Guatemala,

and this gives a population in the West Indies, Central and South America, of 24,470,000 (twenty-four millions four hundred and seventy thousand) inhabitants.

But one seventh of this population, 3,495,714 (three millions four hundred and ninety-five thousand seven hundred and fourteen) being white, or of pure European extraction, there is a population throughout this vast area of 20,974,286 (twenty millions nine hundred and seventy-four thousand two hundred and eighty-six) colored persons, who constitute, from the immense preponderance of their numbers, the *ruling element*, as they ever must be, of those countries.

There are no influences that could be brought to bear to change this most fortunate and Heaven-designed state and condition of things. Nature here has done her own work, which the art of knaves nor the schemes of deep-designing political impostors can ever reach. This is a fixed fact in the zodiac of the political heavens, that the blacks and colored people are the stars which must ever most conspicuously twinkle in the firmament of this division of the Western Hemisphere.

We next invite your attention to a few facts, upon which we predicate the claims of the black race, not only to the tropical regions and *south temperate zone* of this hemisphere, but to the whole continent, North as well as South. And here we desire it distinctly to be understood, that, in the selection of our places of destination, we do not advocate the *southern* scheme as a concession, nor yet at the will nor desire of our North American oppressors; but as a policy by which we must be the greatest political gainers, without the risk or possibility of loss to ourselves. A gain by which the lever of political elevation and machinery of national progress must ever be held and directed by our own hands and heads, to our own will and purposes, in defiance of the obstructions which might be attempted on the part of a dangerous and deep-designing oppressor.

From the year 1492, the discovery of Hispaniola—the first land discovered by Columbus in the New World—to 1502, the short space of ten years, such was the mortality among the natives, that the Spaniards, then holding rule there, "began to employ a few" Africans in the mines of the island. The experiment was effective—a successful one. The Indian and the African were enslaved together, when the Indian sunk, and the African stood.

It was not until June the 24th, of the year 1498, that the continent was discovered by John Cabot, a Venetian, who sailed in August of the previous year, 1497, from Bristol, under the patronage of Henry VII, King of England.

In 1517, the short space of but fifteen years from the date of their introduction, Carolus V, King of Spain, by right of a patent, granted permission to a number of persons annually to supply the islands of Hispaniola (St. Domingo), Cuba, Jamaica, and Porto Rico with natives of Africa, to the number of four thousand annually. John Hawkins, a mercenary Englishman, was the first person known to engage in this general system of debasing our race, and his royal mistress, Queen Elizabeth, was engaged with him in interest, and shared the general profits.

The Africans, on their advent into a foreign country, soon experienced the want of their accustomed food, and habits, and manner of living.

The aborigines subsisted mainly by game and fish, with a few patches of maize, or Indian corn, near their wigwams, which were generally attended by the women, while the men were absent engaged in the chase, or at war with a hostile tribe. The vegetables, grains, and fruits, such as in their native country they had been accustomed to, were not to be obtained among the aborigines, which first induced the African laborer to cultivate "patches" of ground in the neighborhood of the mining operations, for the purpose of raising food for his own sustenance.

This trait in their character was observed and regarded with considerable interest; after which the Spaniards and other colonists, on contracting with the English slave dealers—Captain Hawkins and others—for new supplies of slaves, were careful to request that an adequate quantity of seeds and plants of various kinds, indigenous to the continent of Africa, especially those composing the staple products of the natives, be selected and brought out with the slaves to the New World. Many of these were cultivated to a considerable extent, while those indigenous to America were cultivated with great success.

Shortly after the commencement of the slave trade under Elizabeth and Hawkins, the queen granted a license to Sir Walter Raleigh to search for uninhabited lands, and seize upon all unoccupied by Christians. Sir Walter discovered the coast of North Carolina and Virginia, assigning the name "Virginia" to the whole coast now comprising the old Thirteen States.

A feeble colony was here settled, which did not avail much, and it was not until the month of April, 1607, that the first permanent settlement was made in Virginia, under the patronage of letters patent from James I, King of England, to Thomas Gates and associates. This was the first settlement of North America, and thirteen years anterior to the landing of the Pilgrims on Plymouth Rock.

And we shall now introduce to you, from acknowledged authority, a number of historical extracts, to prove that previous to the introduction of the black race upon this continent but little enterprise of any kind was successfully carried on. The African or negro was the first *available contributor* to the country, and consequently is by priority of right, and politically should be, entitled to the highest claims of an eligible citizen.

> No permanent settlement was effected in what is now called the United States, till the reign of James the First.—*Ramsay's Hist. U. S.*, vol. i. p. 38.
>
> The month of April, 1607, is the epoch of the first permanent settlement on the coast of Virginia, the name then given to all that extent of country which forms thirteen states.—*Ib.* p. 39.

The whole coast of the country was at this time explored, not for the purpose of trade and agriculture—because there were then no such enterprises in the country, the natives not producing sufficient of the necessaries of life to supply present wants, there being consequently nothing to trade for—but, like their Spanish and Portuguese predecessors, who occupied the islands and different parts of South America, in search of gold and other precious metals.

Trade and the cultivation of the soil, on coming to the New World, were foreign to their intention or designs, consequently, when failing of success in that enterprise, they were sadly disappointed.

At a time when the precious metals were conceived to be the peculiar and only valuable productions of the New World, when every mountain was supposed to contain a treasure and every rivulet was searched for its golden sands, this appearance was fondly considered as an infallible indication of the mine. Every hand was eager to dig. . . .

"There was now," says Smith, "no talk, no hope, no work; but dig gold, wash gold, refine gold. With this imaginary wealth the first vessel returning to England was loaded, while the *culture of the land* and every useful occupation was *totally neglected.*

The colonists thus left were in miserable circumstances for want of provisions. The remainder of what they had brought with them was so small in quantity as to be soon expended, and so damaged in course of a long voyage as to be a source of disease.

. . . In their expectation of getting gold, the people were disappointed, the glittering substance they had sent to England proving to be a valueless mineral. Smith, on his return to Jamestown, found the colony reduced to thirty-eight persons, who, in despair, were preparing to abandon the country. He employed caresses, threats, and even violence in order to prevent them from executing this fatal resolution.—*Ramsay's Hist. U. S.*, pp. 45, 46.

The Pilgrims or Puritans, in November, 1620, after having organized with solemn vows to the defence of each other, and the maintenance of their civil liberty, made the harbor of Cape Cod, landing safely on "Plymouth Rock" December 20th, about one month subsequently. They were one hundred and one in number, and from the toils and hardships consequent to a severe season, in a strange country, in less than six months after their arrival, "forty persons, nearly one half of their original number," had died.

> In 1618, in the reign of James I, the British government established a regular trade on the coast of Africa. In the year 1620 negro slaves began to be imported into Virginia, a Dutch ship bringing twenty of them for sale.—*Sampson's Historical Dictionary*, p. 348.

It will be seen by these historical reminiscences, that the Dutch ship landed her cargo at New Bedford, Massachusetts—the whole coast, now comprising the old original states, then went by the name of Virginia, being so named by Sir Walter Raleigh, in honor of his royal mistress and patron, Elizabeth, the Virgin Queen of England, under whom he received the patent of his royal commission, to seize all the lands unoccupied by Christians.

Beginning their preparations in the slave trade in 1618, just two years previous—allowing time against the landing of the first emigrants for successfully carrying out the project—the African captives and Puritan emigrants, singularly enough, landed upon the same section of the continent at the same time (1620), the Pilgrims at Plymouth, and the captive slaves at New Bedford, but a few miles, comparatively, south.

> The country at this period was one vast wilderness. The continent of North America was then one continued forest. . . . There were no horses, cattle, sheep, hogs, or tame beasts of any kind. . . . There were no domestic poultry. . . . There were no gardens, orchards, public roads, meadows, or cultivated fields. . . . They often burned the woods that they could advantageously plant their corn. . . . They had neither spice, salt, bread, butter, cheese, nor milk. They had no set meals, but eat when they were hungry, or could find anything to satisfy the cravings of nature. Very little of their food was derived from the earth, except what it spontaneously produced. . . . The ground was both their seat and table. . . . Their best bed was a skin. . . . They had neither iron, steel, nor any metallic instruments.—*Ramsay's Hist.*, pp. 39, 40.

We adduce not these extracts to disparage or detract from the real worth of our brother Indian—for we are identical as the subjects of American wrongs, outrages, and oppression, and therefore one in interest—far be it from our designs. Whatever opinion he may entertain of our race—in accordance with the impressions made by the contumely heaped upon us by our mutual oppressor, the American nation—we admire his, for the many deeds of heroic and noble daring with which the brief history of his liberty-loving people is replete. We sympathize with him, because our brethren are the successors of his in the degradation of American bondage; and we adduce them in evidence against the many aspersions heaped upon the African race, avowing that their inferiority to the other races, and unfitness for a high civil and social position, caused them to be reduced to servitude.

For the purpose of proving their availability and eminent fitness alone—not to say superiority, and not inferiority—first suggested to Europeans the substitution of African for that of Indian labor in the mines; that their superior adaptation to the difficulties consequent to a new country and different climate made them preferable to Europeans themselves; and their superior skill, industry, and general thriftiness in all that they did, first suggested to the colonists the propriety of turning their attention to agricultural and other industrial pursuits than those of mining operations.

It is evident, from what has herein been adduced—the settlement of Captain John Smith being in the course of a few months reduced to thirty-eight, and that of the Pilgrims at Plymouth from one hundred and one to fifty-seven in six months—that the whites nor aborigines were equal to the hard, and to them insurmountable, difficulties which then stood wide-spread before them.

An endless forest, the impenetrable earth—the one to be removed, and the other to be excavated; towns and cities to be built, and farms to be cultivated—all presented difficulties too arduous for the European then here, and entirely unknown to the native of the continent.

At a period such as this, when the natives themselves had fallen victims to the tasks imposed upon them by the usurpers, and the Europeans also were fast sinking beneath the influence and weight of climate and hardships; when food could not be obtained, nor the common conveniences of life procured; when arduous duties of life were to be performed, and none capable of doing them, save those who had previously, by their labors, not only in their own country, but in the new, so proven themselves capable, it is very evident, as the most natural consequence, the Africans were resorted to for the performance of every duty common to domestic life.

There were no laborers known to the colonists, from Cape Cod to Cape Lookout, than those of the African race. They entered at once into the mines, extracting therefrom the rich treasures which for a thousand ages lay hidden in the earth; when, plunging into the depths of the rivers, they culled from their sandy bottoms, to the astonishment of the natives and surprise of the Europeans, minerals and precious stones, which added to the pride and aggrandizement of every throne in Europe.

And from their knowledge of cultivation—an art acquired in their native Africa—the farming interests in the North and planting in the South were commenced with a prospect never dreamed of before the introduction on the continent of this most interesting, unexampled, hardy race of men. A race capable of the endurance of more toil, fatigue, and hunger than any other branch of the human family.

Though pagans for the most part in their own country, they required not to be taught to work, and how to do it; but it was only necessary to bid them work, and they at once knew what to do, and how it should be done.

Even up to the present day, it is notorious that in the planting states the blacks themselves are the only skilful cultivators of the soil, the proprietors or planters, as they are termed, knowing little or nothing of the art, save that which they learn from the African husbandman; while the ignorant white overseer, whose duty is to see that the work is attended to, knows still less.

Hemp, cotton, tobacco, corn, rice, sugar, and many other important staple products, are all the result of African skill and labor in the southern states of this country. The greater number of the mechanics of the South are also black men.

Nor was their skill as herdsmen inferior to their other proficiencies, they being among the most accomplished trainers of horses in the world.

Indeed, to this class of men may be indebted the entire country for the improvement South in the breed of horses. And those who have travelled in the southern states could not have failed to observe that the principal trainers, jockeys, riders, and judges of horses were men of African descent.

These facts alone are sufficient to establish our claim to this country, as legitimate as that of those who fill the highest stations by the suffrage of the people.

In no period since the existence of the ancient enlightened nations of Africa have the prospects of the black race been brighter than now; and at no time during the Christian era have there been greater advantages presented for the advancement of any people than at present those which offer to the black race, both in the eastern and western hemispheres; our election being in the western.

Despite the efforts to the contrary, in the strenuous endeavors for a supremacy of race, the sympathies of the world, in their upward tendency, are in favor of the African and black races of the earth. To be available, *we* must take advantage of these favorable feelings, and strike out for ourselves a bold and manly course of *independent action* and *position;* otherwise, this pure and uncorrupted sympathy will be reduced to pity and contempt.

Of the countries of our choice, we have stated that one province and two islands were slaveholding places. These, as before named, are Brazil in South America, and Cuba and Porto Rico in the West Indies. There are a few other little islands of minor consideration: the Danish three, Swedish one, and Dutch four.

But in the eight last referred to, slavery is of such a mild type, that, however objectionable as such, it is merely nominal.

In South America and the Antilles, in its worst form, slavery is a blessing almost, compared with the miserable degradation of the slaves under our upstart, assumed superiors, the slaveholders of the United States.

In Brazil color is no badge of condition, and every freeman, whatever his color, is socially and politically equal, there being black gentlemen, of pure African descent, filling the highest positions in state under the emperor. There is, also, an established law by the Congress of Brazil, making the crime punishable with death for the commander of any vessel to bring into the country any human being as a slave.

The following law has passed one branch of the General Legislative Assembly of Brazil, but little doubt being entertained that it will find a like favor in the other branch of that august general legislative body:—

1. All children born after the date of this law shall be free.

2. All those shall be considered free who are born in other countries, and come to Brazil after this date.

3. Every one who serves from birth to seven years of age, any of those included in article one, or who has to serve so many years, at the end of fourteen years shall be emancipated, and live as he chooses.

4. Every slave paying for his liberty a sum equal to what he cost his master, or who shall gain it by honorable gratuitous title, the master shall be obliged to give him a free paper, under the penalty of article one hundred and seventy-nine of the criminal code.

5. Where there is no stipulated price or fixed value of the slave, it shall be determined by arbitrators, one of which shall be the public *promoter* of the town.

6. The government is authorized to give precise regulations for the execution of this law, and also to form establishments necessary for taking care of those who, born after this date, may be abandoned by the owners of slaves.

7. Opposing laws and regulations are repealed.

Concerning Cuba, there is an old established law, giving any slave the right of a certain *legal tender*, which, if refused by the slaveholder, he, by going to the residence of any parish priest, and making known the facts, shall immediately be declared a freeman, the priest or bishop of the parish or diocese giving him his "freedom papers." The legal tender, or sum fixed by law, we think does not exceed two hundred and fifty Spanish dollars. It may be more.

Until the Americans intruded themselves into Cuba, contaminating society wherever they located, black and colored gentlemen and ladies of rank mingled indiscriminately in society. But since the advent of these negro-haters, the colored people of Cuba have been reduced nearly, if not quite, to the level of the miserable, degraded position of the colored people of the United States, who almost consider it a compliment and favor to receive the notice or smiles of a white.

Can we be satisfied, in this enlightened age of the world, amid the advantages which now present themselves to us, with the degradation and servility inherited from our fathers in this country? God forbid. And we think the universal reply will be, We will not!

Half a century brings about a mighty change in the reality of existing things and events of the world's history. Fifty years ago our fathers lived. For the most part they were sorely oppressed, debased, ignorant, and incapable of comprehending the political relations of mankind—the great machinery and motive-power by which the enlightened nations of the earth were impelled forward. They knew but little, and ventured to do nothing to enhance their own interests beyond that which their oppressors taught them. They lived amidst a continual cloud of moral obscurity; a fog of bewilderment and delusion, by which they were of necessity compelled to confine themselves to a limited space—a *known* locality—lest by one step beyond this they might have stumbled over a precipice, ruining themselves beyond recovery in the fall.

We are their sons, but not the same individuals; neither do we live in the same period with them. That which suited them, does not suit us; and that with which they may have been contented, will not satisfy us.

Without education, they were ignorant of the world, and fearful of adventure. With education, we are conversant with its geography, history, and nations, and delight in its enterprises and responsibilities. They once were held as slaves; to such a condition we never could be reduced. They were content with privileges; we will be satisfied with nothing less than rights. They felt themselves happy to be permitted to beg for rights; we demand them as an innate inheritance. They considered themselves favored to live by sufferance; we reject it as a degradation. A subordinate position was all they asked for; we claim entire equality or nothing. The relation of master and slave was innocently acknowledged by them; we deny the right as such, and pronounce the relation as the basest injustice that ever scourged the earth and cursed the human family. They admitted themselves to be inferiors; we barely acknowledge the whites as equals, perhaps not in every particular. They lamented their irrecoverable fate, and incapacity to redeem themselves and their race. We rejoice that, as their sons, it is our happy lot and high mission to accomplish that which they desired, and would have done, but failed for the want of ability to do.

Let no intelligent man or woman, then, among us be found at the present day, exulting in the degradation that our enslaved parents would gladly have rid themselves had they had the intelligence and qualifications to accomplish their designs. Let none be found to shield themselves behind the plea of our brother bondmen in ignorance, that we know not *what* to do, nor *where* to go. We are no longer slaves, as were our fathers, but freemen; fully qualified to meet our oppressors in every relation which belongs to the elevation of man, the establishment, sustenance, and perpetuity of a nation. And such a position, by the help of God our common Father, we are determined to take and maintain.

There is but one question presents itself for our serious consideration, upon which we *must* give a decisive reply: Will we transmit, as an inheritance to our children, the blessings of unrestricted civil liberty, or shall we entail upon them, as our only political legacy, the degradation and oppression left us by our fathers?

Shall we be persuaded that we can live and prosper nowhere but under the authority and power of our North American white oppressors? that this (the United States) is the country most, if not the only one, favorable to our improvement and progress? Are we willing to admit that we are incapable of self-government, establishing for ourselves such political privileges, and making such internal improvements as we delight to enjoy, after American white men have made them for themselves?

No! Neither is it true that the United States is the country best adapted to *our* improvement. But that country is the best in which our manhood—morally, mentally, and physically—can be *best developed;* in which we have an untrammelled right to the enjoyment of civil and religious liberty; and the West Indies, Central and South America, present now such advantages, superiorly preferable to all other countries.

That the continent of America was designed by Providence as a reserved asylum for the various oppressed people of the earth, of all races, to us seems very apparent.

From the earliest period after the discovery, various nations sent a representative here, either as adventurers and speculators, or employed laborers, seamen, or soldiers, hired to work for their employers. And among the earliest and most numerous class who found their way to the New World were those of the African race. And it has been ascertained to our minds, beyond a doubt, that when the continent was discovered, there were found in the West Indies and Central America tribes of the black race, fine looking people, having the usual characteristics of color and hair, identifying them as being originally of the African race; no doubt, being a remnant of the Africans who, with the Carthaginian expedition, were adventitiously cast upon this continent, in their memorable adventure to the "Great Island," after sailing many miles distant to the west of the "Pillars of Hercules"—the present Straits of Gibraltar.

We would not be thought to be superstitious, when we say, that in all this we can "see the finger of God." Is it not worthy of a notice here, that while the ingress of foreign whites to this continent has been voluntary and constant, and that of the blacks involuntary and but occasional, yet the whites in the southern part have *decreased* in numbers, *degenerated* in character, and become mentally and physically *enervated* and imbecile; while the blacks and colored people have studiously *increased* in numbers, *regenerated* in character, and have grown mentally and physically vigorous and active, developing every function of their manhood, and are now, in their elementary character, decidedly superior to the white race? So, then, the white race could never successfully occupy the southern portion of the continent; they must, of necessity, every generation, be repeopled from another quarter of the globe. The fatal error committed by the Spaniards, under Pizarro, was the attempt to exterminate the Incas and Peruvians, and fill their places by European whites. The Peruvian Indians, a hale, hardy, vigorous, intellectual race of people, were succeeded by those who soon became idle, vicious, degenerated, and imbecile. But Peru, like all the other South American states, is regaining her former potency, just in proportion as the European race decreases among them. All the labor of the country is performed by the aboriginal natives and the blacks, the few Europeans there being the merest excrescences on the body politic—consuming drones in the social hive.

Had we no other claims than those set forth in a foregoing part of this address, they are sufficient to induce every black and colored person to remain on this continent, unshaken and unmoved.

But the West Indians, Central and South Americans, are a noble race of people; generous, sociable, and tractable—just the people with whom we desire to unite; who are susceptible of progress, improvement, and reform of every kind. They now desire all the improvements of North America, but being justly jealous of their rights, they have no confidence in the whites of the United States, and consequently peremptorily refuse to permit an indiscriminate settlement among them of this class of people; but placing every confidence in the black and colored people of North America.

The example of the unjust invasion and forcible seizure of a large portion of the territory of Mexico is still fresh in their memory; and the oppressive disfranchisement of a large number of native Mexicans, by the Americans—because of the color and race of the natives—will continue to rankle in the bosom of the people of those countries, and prove a sufficient barrier henceforth against the inroads of North American whites among them.

Upon the American continent, then, we are determined to remain, despite every opposition that may be urged against us.

You will doubtless be asked—and that, too, with an air of seriousness—why, if desirable to remain on this continent, not be content to remain *in* the United States. The objections to this—and potent reasons, too, in our estimation—have already been clearly shown.

But notwithstanding all this, were there still any rational, nay, even the most futile grounds for hope, we still might be stupid enough to be content to remain, and yet through another period of unexampled patience and suffering, continue meekly to drag the galling yoke and clank the chain of servility and degradation. But whether or not in this God is to be thanked and Heaven blessed, we are not permitted, despite our willingness and stupidity, to indulge even the most distant glimmer of a hope of attaining to the level of a well-protected slave.

For years we have been studiously and jealously observing the course of political events and policy on the part of this country, both in a national and individual state capacity, as pursued towards the colored people. And he who, in the midst of them, can live without observation, is either excusably ignorant, or reprehensibly deceptious and untrustworthy.

We deem it entirely unnecessary to tax you with anything like the history of even one chapter of the unequalled infamies perpetrated on the part of the various states, and national decrees, by legislation, against us. But we shall call your particular attention to the more recent acts of the United States; because, whatever privileges we may enjoy in any individual state, will avail nothing when not recognized as such by the United States.

When the condition of the inhabitants of any country is fixed by legal grades of distinction, this condition can never be changed except by express legislation. And it is the height of folly to expect such express legislation, except by the inevitable force of some irresistible internal political pressure. The force necessary to this imperative demand on our part we never can obtain, because of our numerical feebleness.

Were the interests of the common people identical with ours, we, in this, might succeed, because we, as a class, would then be numerically the superior. But this is not a question of the rich against the poor, nor the common people against the higher classes, but a question of white against black—every white person, by legal right, being held superior to a black or colored person.

In Russia, the common people might obtain an equality with

the aristocracy, because, of the sixty-five millions of her population, forty-five millions are serfs or peasants; leaving but twenty millions of the higher classes—royalty, nobility, and all included.

The rights of no oppressed people have ever yet been obtained by a voluntary act of justice on the part of the oppressors. Christians, philanthropists, and moralists may preach, argue, and philosophize as they may to the contrary: facts are against them. Voluntary acts, it is true, which are in themselves just, may sometimes take place on the part of the oppressor; but these are always actuated by the force of some outward circumstances of self-interest equal to a compulsion.

The boasted liberties of the American people were established by a constitution, borrowed from and modelled after the British *magna charta*. And this great charter of British liberty, so much boasted of and vaunted as a model bill of rights, was obtained only by force and compulsion.

The barons, an order of noblemen, under the reign of King John, becoming dissatisfied at the terms submitted to by their sovereign, which necessarily brought degradation upon themselves—terms prescribed by the insolent Pope Innocent III, the haughty sovereign Pontiff of Rome—summoned his majesty to meet them on the plains of the memorable meadow of Runnymede, where, presenting to him their own Bill of Rights—a bill dictated by themselves, and drawn up by their own hands—at the unsheathed points of a thousand glittering swords, they commanded him, against his will, to sign the extraordinary document. There was no alternative: he must either do or die. With a puerile timidity, he leaned forward his rather commanding but imbecile person, and with a trembling hand and single dash of the pen, the name KING JOHN stood forth in bold relief, sending more terror throughout the world than the mystic handwriting of Heaven throughout the dominions of Nebuchadnezzar, blazing on the walls of Babylon. A consternation, not because of the *name* of the king, but because of the rights of *others*, which that name acknowledged.

The king, however, soon became dissatisfied, and determining on a revocation of the act—an act done entirely contrary to his will—at the head of a formidable army spread fire and sword throughout the kingdom.

But the barons, though compelled to leave their castles, their houses and homes, and fly for their lives, could not be induced to undo that which they had so nobly done—the achievement of their rights and privileges. Hence the act has stood throughout all succeeding time, because never annulled by those who *willed* it.

It will be seen that the first great modern Bill of Rights was obtained only by a force of arms: a resistance of the people against the injustice and intolerance of their rulers. We say the people—because that which the barons demanded for themselves, was afterwards extended to the common people. Their only hope was based on their *superiority of numbers.*

But can we, in this country, hope for as much? Certainly not. Our case is a hopeless one. There was but *one* John, with his few sprigs of adhering royalty; and but *one* heart, at which the threatening points of their swords were directed by a thousand barons; while in our case, there is but a handful of the oppressed, without a sword to point, and *twenty millions* of Johns or Jonathans—as you please—with as many hearts, tenfold more relentless than that of Prince John Lackland, and as deceptious and hypocritical as the Italian heart of Innocent III.

Where, then, is our hope of success in this country? Upon what is it based? Upon what principle of political policy and sagacious discernment do our political leaders and acknowledged great men—colored men we mean—justify themselves by telling us, and insisting that we shall believe them, and submit to what they say—to be patient, remain where we are; that there is a "bright prospect and glorious future" before us in this country! May Heaven open our eyes from their Bartimean obscurity.

But we call your attention to another point of our political degradation—the acts of state and general governments.

In a few of the states, as in New York, the colored inhabitants have a partial privilege of voting a white man into office. This privilege is based on a property qualification of two hundred and fifty dollars worth of real estate. In others, as in Ohio, in the absence of organic provision, the privilege is granted by judicial decision, based on a ratio of blood, of an admixture of more than one half white; while in many of the states there is no privilege allowed, either partial or unrestricted.

The policy of the above-named states will be seen and detected at a glance, which, while seeming to extend immunities, is intended especially for the object of degradation.

In the State of New York, for instance, there is a constitutional distinction created among colored men—almost necessarily compelling one part to feel superior to the other—while among the whites no such distinctions dare be known. Also, in Ohio, there is a legal distinction set up by an upstart judiciary, creating among the colored people a privileged class by birth! All this must necessarily sever the cords of union among us, creating almost insurmountable prejudices of the most stupid and fatal kind, paralyzing the last bracing nerve which promised to give us strength.

It is upon this same principle, and for the self-same object, that the general government has long been endeavoring, and is at present knowingly designing to effect a recognition of the independence of the Dominican Republic, while disparagingly refusing to recognize the independence of the Haytien nation—a people four fold greater in numbers, wealth, and power. The Haytiens, it is pretended, are refused because they are *negroes;* while the Dominicans, as is well known to all who are familiar with the geography, history, and political relations of that people, are identical—except in language, they speaking the Spanish tongue—with those of the Haytiens; being composed of negroes and a mixed race. The government may shield itself by the plea that it is not familiar with the origin of those people. To this we have but to reply, that if the government is thus ignorant of the relations of its near neighbors, it is the height of presumption, and no small degree of assurance, for it to set up itself as capable of prescribing terms to the one, or conditions to the other.

Should they accomplish their object, they then will have succeeded in forever establishing a barrier of impassable separation, by the creation of a political distinction between those peoples, of superiority and inferiority of origin or national existence. Here, then, is another stratagem of this most determined and untiring enemy of our race—the government of the United States.

We come now to the crowning act of infamy on the part of the general government towards the colored inhabitants of the United States—an act so vile in its nature, that rebellion against its demands should be promptly made in every attempt to enforce its infernal provisions.

In the history of national existence, there is not to be found a parallel to the tantalizing insult and aggravating despotism of the provisions of Millard Fillmore's Fugitive Slave Bill, passed by the Thirty-third Congress of the United States, with the approbation of a majority of the American people, in the year of the Gospel of Jesus Christ eighteen hundred and fifty.

This bill had but one object in its provisions, which was fully accomplished in its passage, that is, the reduction of every colored person in the United States—save those who carry free papers of emancipation, or bills of sale from former claimants or owners—to a state of relative *slavery;* placing each and every one of us at the *disposal of any and every white* who might choose to *claim* us, and the caprice of any and every upstart knave bearing the title of "commissioner."

Did any of you, fellow-countrymen, reside in a country, the provisions of whose laws were such that any person of a certain class, who, whenever he, she, or they pleased, might come forward, lay a claim to, make oath before (it might be) some stupid and heartless person, authorized to decide in such cases, and take, at their option, your horse, cow, sheep, house and lot, or any other property, bought and paid for by your own earnings—the result of your personal toil and labor—would you be willing, or could you be induced by any reasoning, however great the source from which it came, to remain in that country? We pause, fellow-countrymen, for a reply.

If there be not one yea, of how much more importance, then, is your *own personal safety* than that of property? Of how much more concern is the safety of a wife or husband, than that of a cow or horse; a child, than a sheep; the destiny of your family, to that of a house and lot?

And yet this is precisely our condition. Any one of us, at any moment, is liable to be *claimed, seized,* and *taken* into custody by any white, as his or her property—to be *enslaved for life*—and there is no remedy, because it is the *law of the land!* And we dare predict, and take this favorable opportunity to fore-warn you, fellow-countrymen, that the time is not far distant, when there will be carried on by the white men of this nation an extensive commerce in the persons of what now compose the free colored people of the North. We forewarn you, that the general enslavement of the whole of this class of people is now being contemplated by the whites.

At present, we are liable to enslavement at any moment, pro-vided we are taken *away* from our homes. But we dare venture further to forewarn you, that the scheme is in mature contem-plation, and has even been mooted in high places, of har-monizing the two discordant political divisions in the country by again reducing the free to slave states.

The completion of this atrocious scheme only becomes neces-sary for each and every one of us to find an owner and master at our own doors. Let the general government but pass such a law, and the states will comply as an act of harmony. Let the South but *demand* it, and the North will comply as a *duty* of compromise.

If Pennsylvania, New York, and Massachusetts can be found arming their sons as watch-dogs for Southern slave hunters; if the United States may, with impunity, garrison with troops the court-house of the freest city in America; blockade the streets; station armed ruffians of dragoons, and spiked artillery in hos-tile awe of the people; if free, white, high-born and bred gen-tlemen of Boston and New York are smitten down to the earth,[2] refused an entrance on professional business into the court-

[2] John Jay, Esq., of New York, son of the late distinguished jurist, Hon. William Jay, was, in 1852, as the counsel of a fugitive slave, brutally assaulted and struck in the face by the slave-catching agent and counsel, Busteed.

houses, until inspected by a slave hunter and his counsel, all to put down the liberty of the black man, then, indeed, is there no hope for us in this country!

It is, fellow-countrymen, a fixed fact, as indelible as the covenant of God in the heavens, that the colored people of these United States are the slaves of any white person who may choose to claim them!

What safety or guarantee have we for ourselves or families? Let us, for a moment, examine this point.

Supposing some hired spy of the slave power residing in Illinois, whom, for illustration, we shall call Stephen A., Counsellor B., a mercenary hireling of New York, and Commissioner C., a slave catcher of Pennsylvania, should take umbrage at the acts or doings of any colored person or persons in a free state; they may, with impunity, send or go on their knight errantry to the South (as did a hireling of the slave power in New York—a lawyer by profession), give a description of such person or persons, and an agent with warrants may be immediately despatched to swear them into slavery forever.

We tell you, fellow-countrymen, any one of you here assembled—your humble committee who report to you this paper—may, by the laws of this land, be seized, whatever the circumstances of his birth, whether he descends from free or slave parents—whether born north or south of Mason and Dixon's line—and ere the setting of another sun, be speeding his way to that living sepulchre and death-chamber of our race—the curse and scourge of this country—the southern part of the United States. This is not idle speculation, but living, naked, undisguised truth.

A member of your committee has received a letter from a

Also, Mr. Dana, an honorable gentleman, counsel for the fugitive Burns, one of the first literary men of Boston, was arrested on his entrance into the court-house, and not permitted to pass the guard of slave-catchers, till the slave agent and counsel, Loring, together with the overseer, Suttle, *inspected* him, and ordered that he might be *allowed* to pass in! After which, in passing along the street, Mr. Dana was ruffianly assaulted and murderously felled to the earth by the minions of the dastardly Southern overseer.

gentleman of respectability and standing in the South, who writes to the following effect. We copy his own words:—

> There are, at this moment, as I was to-day informed by Colonel W., one of our first magistrates in this city, a gang of from twenty-five to thirty vagabonds of poor white men, who, for twenty-five dollars a head, clear of all expenses, are ready and willing to go to the North, make acquaintance with the blacks in various places, send their descriptions to unprincipled slaveholders here,—for there are many of this kind to be found among the poorer class of masters,—and swear them into bondage. So the free blacks, as well as fugitive slaves, will have to keep a sharp watch over themselves to get clear of this scheme to enslave them.

Here, then, you have but a paragraph in the great volume of this political crusade and legislative pirating by the American people over the rights and privileges of the colored inhabitants of the country. If this be but a paragraph—for such it is in truth—what must be the contents when the whole history is divulged! Never will the contents of this dreadful record of crime, corruption, and oppression be fully revealed, until the trump of God shall proclaim the universal summons to judgment. Then, and then alone, shall the whole truth be acknowledged, when the doom of the criminal shall be forever sealed.

We desire not to be sentimental, but rather would be political; and therefore call your attention to another point—a point already referred to.

In giving the statistics of various countries, and preferences to many places herein mentioned, as points of destination in emigration, we have said little or nothing concerning the present governments, the various state departments, nor the condition of society among the people.

This is not the province of your committee, but the legitimate office of a Board of Foreign Commissioners, whom there is no doubt will be created by the convention, with provisions and instructions to report thereon, in due season, of their mission.

With a few additional remarks on the subject of the British Provinces of North America, we shall have done our duty, and completed, for the time being, the arduous, important, and momentous task assigned to us.

The British Provinces of North America, especially Canada West—formerly called Upper Canada—in climate, soil, productions, and the usual prospects for internal improvements, are equal, if not superior, to any northern part of the continent. And for these very reasons, aside from their contiguity to the northern part of the United States—and consequent facility for the escape of the slaves from the South—we certainly should prefer them as a place of destination. We love the Canadas, and admire their laws, because, as British Provinces, there is no difference known among the people—no distinction of race. And we deem it a duty to recommend, that for the present, as a temporary asylum, it is certainly advisable for every colored person, who, desiring to emigrate, and is not prepared for any other destination, to locate in Canada West.

Every advantage on our part should be now taken of the opportunity of *obtaining* LANDS, while they are to be had cheap, and on the most easy conditions, from the government.

Even those who never contemplate a removal from this country of chains, it will be their best interest and greatest advantage to procure lands in the Canadian Provinces. It will be an easy, profitable, and safe investment, even should they never occupy nor yet see them. We shall then be but doing what the whites in the United States have for years been engaged in—securing unsettled lands in the territories, previous to their enhancement in value, by the force of settlement and progressive neighboring improvements. There are also at present great openings for colored people to enter into the various industrial departments of business operations: laborers, mechanics, teachers, merchants, and shop-keepers, and professional men of every kind. These places are now open, as much to the colored as the white man, in Canada, with little or no opposition to his progress; at least in the character of prejudicial preferences on account of race. And all of these, without any hesitancy, do we most cheerfully recommend to the colored inhabitants of the United States.

But our preference to other places over the Canadas has been cursorily stated in the foregoing part of this paper; and since the writing of that part, it would seem that the predictions or apprehensions concerning the Provinces are about to be verified by the British Parliament and Home Government themselves. They have virtually conceded, and openly expressed it —Lord Brougham in the lead—that the British Provinces of North America must, ere long, cease to be a part of the British domain, and become annexed to the United States.

It is needless—however much we may regret the necessity of its acknowledgment—for us to stop our ears, shut our eyes, and stultify our senses against the truth in this matter; since, by so doing, it does not alter the case. Every political movement, both in England and the United States, favors such an issue, and the sooner we acknowledge it, the better it will be for our cause, ourselves individually, and the destiny of our people in this country.

These Provinces have long been burdensome to the British nation, and her statesmen have long since discovered and decided as an indisputable predicate in political economy, that any province as an independent state, is more profitable in a commercial consideration to a country than when depending as one of its colonies. As a child to the parent, or an apprentice to his master, so is a colony to a state. And as the man who enters into business is to the manufacturer and importer, so is the colony which becomes an independent state to the country from which it recedes.

Great Britain is decidedly a commercial and money-making nation, and counts closely on her commercial relations with any country. That nation or people which puts the largest amount of money into her coffers, are the people who may expect to obtain her greatest favors. This the Americans do; consequently —and we candidly ask you to mark the prediction—the British will interpose little or no obstructions to the Canadas, Cuba, or any other province or colony contiguous to this country, falling into the American Union; except only in such cases where there would be a compromise of her honor. And in the event of a seizure of any of these, there would be no necessity for such a sacrifice; it could readily be avoided by diplomacy.

Then there is little hope for us on this continent, short of those places where, by reason of their numbers, there is the greatest combination of strength and interests on the part of the colored race.

We have ventured to predict a reduction of the now nominally free into slave states. Already has this "reign of terror" and dreadful work of destruction commenced. We give you the quotation from a Mississippi paper, which will readily be admitted as authority in this case:—

> Two years ago a law was passed by the California legislature, granting *one year* to the owners of slaves carried into the territory previous to the adoption of the constitution, to remove them beyond the limits of the state. Last year the provision of this law *was extended twelve months longer.* We learn by the late California papers that a bill has just passed the Assembly, by a vote of 33 to 21, *continuing the same law in force until* 1855. The provisions of this bill embraces *slaves who have been carried to California since the adoption of her constitution,* as well as those who were there previously. The large majority by which it passed, and the opinions advanced during the discussion, *indicates a more favorable state of sentiment in regard to the rights of slaveholders in California than we supposed existed.—Mississippian.*

No one who is a general and intelligent observer of the politics of this country, will after reading this, doubt for a moment the final result.

At present there is a proposition under consideration in California to authorize the holding of a convention to amend the constitution of that state, which doubtless will be carried into effect; when there is no doubt that a clause will be inserted, granting the right to *hold slaves at discretion* in the state. This being done, it will meet with general favor throughout the country by the American people, and the *policy be adopted on the state's rights principle.* This alone is necessary, in addition to the insufferable Fugitive Slave Law, and the recent nefarious Nebraska Bill—which is based upon this very boasted American policy of the state's rights principle—to reduce the free to slave states, without a murmur from the people. And did not the

Nebraska Bill disrespect the feelings and infringe upon the political rights of Northern *white* people, its adoption would be hailed with loud shouts of approbation, from Portland, Maine, to San Francisco.

That, then, which is left for us to do, is to *secure* our liberty; a position which shall fully *warrant* us *against* the *liability* of such monstrous political crusades and riotous invasions of our rights. Nothing less than a national indemnity, indelibly fixed by virtue of our own sovereign potency, will satisfy us as a redress of grievances for the unparalleled wrongs, undisguised impositions, and unmitigated oppression which we have suffered at the hands of this American people.

And what wise politician would otherwise conclude and determine? None, we dare say. And a people who are incapable of this discernment and precaution are incapable of self-government, and incompetent to direct their own political destiny. For our own part, we spurn to treat for liberty on any other terms or conditions.

It may not be inapplicable, in this particular place, to quote, from high authority, language which has fallen under our notice since this report has been under our consideration. The quotation is worth nothing, except to show that the position assumed by us is a natural one, which constitutes the essential basis of self-protection.

Said Earl Aberdeen recently, in the British House of Lords, when referring to the great question which is now agitating Europe, "One thing alone is certain, that the only way to obtain a sure and honorable peace, is to *acquire a position* which may *command* it; and to gain such a position, *every nerve and sinew* of the empire should be strained. The pickpocket who robs us is not to be let off because he offers to restore our purse"; and his lordship might have justly added, "should never thereafter be intrusted or confided in."

The plea, doubtless, will be, as it already frequently has been raised, that to remove from the United States, our slave brethren would be left without a hope. They already find their way in large companies to the Canadas, and they have only to be made sensible that there is as much freedom for them South as there is North; as much protection in Mexico as in Canada; and the fugitive slave will find it a much pleasanter journey and more easy of access, to wend his way from Louisiana and Arkansas to Mexico, than thousands of miles through the slave-holders of the South and slave-catchers of the North to Canada. Once into Mexico, and his farther exit to Central and South America and the West Indies would be certain. There would be no obstructions whatever. No miserable, half-starved, servile Northern slave-catchers by the way, waiting, cap in hand, ready and willing to do the bidding of their contemptible Southern masters.

No prisons nor court-houses, as slave-pens and garrisons, to secure the fugitive and rendezvous the mercenary gangs, who are bought as military on such occasions. No perjured marshals, bribed commissioners, nor hireling counsel, who, spaniel-like, crouch at the feet of Southern slaveholders, and cringingly tremble at the crack of their whip. No, not as may be encountered throughout his northern flight, there are none of these to be found or met with in his travels from the Bravo del Norte to the dashing Orinoco—from the borders of Texas to the boundaries of Peru.

Should anything occur to prevent a successful emigration to the south—Central, South America, and the West Indies—we have no hesitancy, rather than remain in the United States, the merest subordinates and serviles of the whites, should the Canadas still continue separate in their political relations from this country, to recommend to the great body of our people to remove to Canada West, where, being politically equal to the whites, physically united with each other by a concentration of strength; when worse comes to worse, we may be found, not as a scattered, weak, and impotent people, as we now are separated from each other throughout the Union, but a united and powerful body of freemen, mighty in politics, and terrible in any conflict which might ensue, in the event of an attempt at the disturbance of our political relations, domestic repose, and peaceful firesides.

Now, fellow-countrymen, we have done. Into your ears have we recounted your own sorrows; before your own eyes have we exhibited your wrongs; into your own hands have we committed your own cause. If these should prove inadequate to remedy this dreadful evil, to assuage this terrible curse which has come upon us, the fault will be yours and not ours; since we have offered you a healing balm for every sorely aggravated wound.

MARTIN R. DELANY, Pa.
WILLIAM WEBB, Pa.
AUGUSTUS R. GREEN, Ohio
EDWARD BUTLER, Mo.
H. S. DOUGLAS, La.
A. DUDLEY, Wis.
CONAWAY BARBOUR, Ky.
WM. J. FULLER, R. I.
WM. LAMBERT, Mich.
J. THEODORE HOLLY, N. Y.
T. A. WHITE, Ind.
JOHN A. WARREN, Canada

APPENDIX I

FROM THE MINUTES OF THE ALBANY
CONVENTION OF COLORED CITIZENS, 1840

AN ABSTRACT of the proceedings of the Convention appeared in this paper soon after the Convention was held. We now give our readers every thing in the proceedings of that important body, which has not already appeared, excepting rules of order, and some other incidental matter, &c.—The whole would have appeared sooner, but as it was intended to publish the minutes in pamphlet form, it was thought best to wait until they had so appeared, and the pamphlets nearly disposed of. Those of our readers who have not done themselves the great favor by purchasing the pamphlet, will here be put in possession of the proceedings.—*Ed., Col. Am.*

After the President had taken his seat, and declared the Convention open for regular business, it was, on motion of Charles B. Ray.

Resolved, That all persons favorable to the call for this Convention, and who have come under that call to deliberate in the doings of these meetings, be requested to hand in their names to the standing committee, as delegates to this Convention.

Resolved, That a committee of two, consisting of Charles L. Reason, of New York, and Rev. Eli N. Hall, of Albany, be appointed to draft rules for the government of this Convention.

Resolved, That a committee of ten be appointed, to suggest, in a becoming form, business for this Convention. Adopted.

The following gentlemen were appointed as a business committee:

CHARLES B. RAY, of New York, *Chairman*
    James W. Duffin, Geneva
    Charles S. Morton, Albany

Elimus P. Rodgers, Whitesboro
John Wendell, Schenectady
Armstrong Archer, Williamsburgh
Theodore S. Wright, New York
Patrick H. Reason, New York
Frederick Olney, New York
George Baltimore, Troy
Abner H. Francis, Buffalo

After adopting these preliminary arrangements, at 12 o'clock the Convention adjourned, to meet at 2 o'clock P.M.

Tuesday Afternoon—The business committee reported, by their chairman, the following preamble and resolutions:

Whereas, We have assembled together here in convention, to devise means, and deliberately to act, and to call upon all who are willing, to assist us in acting, that we may remove that proscriptive clause in our State Constitution, contained in these words: "No man of color, unless he shall have been for three years a citizen of this State, and for one year next preceding any election, shall be seized and possessed of a freehold estate of the value of two hundred and fifty dollars, over and above all debts and incumbrances charged thereon, and shall have been actually rated and paid a tax thereon, shall be entitled to vote at any such election"—we think it our place here to declare, that we hold all distinctions between native-born citizens growing out of complexion, as unjust—not because it restricts us socially, with respect to the rest of the community, but because it unwarrantably withholds rights inherent to us as men, and farther guaranteed by the noble charter of our country's liberty; it therefore becomes us, as the objects of this proscription, directly to state the ground of our grievances, to protest against the unrighteous discrimination, and to appeal to the reason, and nobler sentiments of the power holding majority, for its peaceable but thorough overthrow:—therefore be it.

Resolved, That all laws established for human government, and all systems, of whatever kind founded in the spirit of complexional cast, are in violation of the fundamental principles of

Divine law, evil in their tendencies, and should therefore be effectually destroyed.

Resolved, That the toleration of complexional difference in the State of New York, is a stain upon its Constitution, and attaches it to the great system of oppression in the land, so vital to our national character—since it is upheld, not only in direct opposition to the common rights of humanity, but also runs counter to those very political principles asserted by the framers of our republican government.

Resolved, That the Act of the Convention of 1821, which amended the State Constitution so as to extend the right of suffrage to one portion of the citizens of the State, unrestricted, and demand for its exercise a property qualification of another portion, was a violation of every principle of justice, anti-republican, and repugnant to the assertion of man's equality, upon which our government is founded.

Resolved, That the discrimination introduced by the adoption of the above mentioned article was a violation of justice, because it deprived us of those rights which should have been enjoyed in common by all native-born citizens, because it guaranteed to foreigners naturalized, advantages over denizens of the soil; because it oppressed those who fought and bled for their country's freedom, and thereby were entitled to the unrestricted enjoyment of its political institutions.

Resolved, That we look upon it as anti-republican, and repugnant to the assertion of man's equality, upon which our government is founded; first because 45,000 of the inhabitants of this State are excluded from the basis of representation; and secondly, because the proscription, merely on account of color, denies the declaration, that "all men are created free and equal," results in the limitation of our liberties, and consequently in the curtailment of our means of "pursuing happiness."

Resolved, That the exclusion of colored men from a free exercise of the elective franchise, gave a falsity to the high ground which the State had taken on the subject of slavery, tore down the principles of its own profession, and was an evidence to slaveholders of their triumph, degrading to a State calling itself free, and holding liberal principles.

Resolved, That we hold the elective franchise as a mighty lever for elevating in the scale of society any people, and feel sensible, that without it, WE are but nominally free, the vital means of our improvement being paralyzed; we do therefore, believe it obligatory upon us, and do hereby pledge ourselves to each other, to use all just means in our power, by devoting a portion of our time, talent, and substance, to agitate this question, until we obtain a restoration of this inestimable boon.

Resolved, That a committee of three be appointed to draw up an address to our people, setting forth our duties in relation to the foregoing resolution, and to the cause of human rights in general.

Resolved, That the committee consist of Henry H. Garnet, Charles B. Ray, and Theodore S. Wright.

Resolved, That the government of our country having made provision for those aggrieved, to petition for a redress of grievances; and we, the people of color in this State, being sorely aggrieved by that clause of the Constitution, heretofore cited, which deprives us of the right of suffrage upon a property qualification; we do, therefore, call upon our people throughout the State, extensively to petition the Legislature on this subject.

Resolved, That a committee of three be appointed to report on the above resolution.

Alexander Crummell, J. W. Duffin, and Rev. J. N. Marrs, were the committee. On motion,

Resolved, That a committee of three be appointed to collect from the delegates statistics of our people.

Resolved, That Abner H. Francis, Michael Dougee, and Uriah Boston, be said committee.

Resolved, That a committee of three be appointed on incidental expenditures. Rev. Thomas James, Rev. John Chester, and Henry R. Crummell were appointed.

Resolved, That a committee of three be appointed on printing. It was made up of P. H. Reason, C. B. Ray, and A. Crummell.

Resolved, That H. H. Garnet, E. P. Rodgers, and Rev. Eli N. Hall, be a Committee to draft resolutions and appoint public speakers for a meeting this evening. Adjourned.

Wednesday Morning, Aug. 19. On motion,

Resolved, That the Convention go into a committee of the whole, this afternoon, immediately upon organizing, to hear statistical statements from the delegates.

Resolved, That a committee of six be appointed to draw up an address to the people of the State of New York, upon the political condition of our people. Adopted.

A. Crummell, Rev. J. Sharp, T. S. Wright, P. H. Reason, C. B. Ray, and C. L. Reason, were appointed that committee.

On motion,

Resolved, That a committee of two be appointed to draft a form of petition, praying to the next legislature for the right of suffrage; the said petition to be signed by the President, Vice Presidents and Secretaries, as well as the entire delegation assembled here in behalf of the colored people in this State.

Resolved, That P. H. Reason, and A. Crummell be the committee.

The following resolution was then submitted:

Resolved, That inasmuch as the possession of a freehold estate, to the amount of $250 secures to us the elective franchise, we do, therefore, strongly recommend to our people throughout the State to become possessors of the soil, inasmuch as that not only elevates them to the rights of freemen, but increases the political power in the State, in favor of our political and social elevation.

A very spirited debate arose on this resolution, owing to the exception taken to that part of it which asserted that the attainment of a certain amount of property, *"elevates us to the rights of freeman."* The resolution was supported in the affirmative by C. B. Ray, T. S. Wright, E. P. Rodgers, chiefly, and opposed by H. H. Garnet, U. Boston, A. Crummell, and others. The discussion on the resolution continued till near the close of the session, when Mr. Ray introduced an amendment, which was as strongly opposed, owing to its containing, as was contended the same objectionable features as the original resolution. While yet the question was pending, the Convention adjourned at half past 12 o'clock.

Wednesday Afternoon. The minutes were read and approved.
The Convention went into a committee of the whole, to receive statistical statements; Austin Stewart in the chair. A number of very important facts respecting the real and personal
estate owned in the represented places and their vicinities—the
state of schools, churches, &c., were made known—statistics of
many places removed from the seats of representation, were
communicated by delegates who had made it their duty to
procure such general information. The committee sat in very
pleasant meeting, for one hour and forty-five minutes, when it
rose and reported progress, the facts obtained being handed
over to the committee on statistics, to be kept by them for the
further use of the committee on the address.

Mr. Ray's amendment, which was under consideration at the
close of the morning session, was called up, and after some
further discussion, was laid indefinitely upon the table.

On motion,

Resolved, That a committee of eight, one from each senatorial
district, be appointed by the house, to form plans and sugges-
tions, by which we can effectually and harmoniously proceed
in our future efforts to obtain the right of suffrage.

Resolved, That P. H. Reason, U. Boston, Wm. Topp, E. P.
Rodgers, A. H. Francis, A. Dunbar, J. Sharp, and James W.
Duffin, be that committee.

The committee appointed on Wednesday morning to report
a form of petition for the special signatures of the Convention,
reported through P. H. Reason, chairman, the following, which
was adopted.

FORM OF PETITION

The State Convention of colored citizens assembled at Albany, on the 18th, 19th and 20th, to consider their political
condition, in behalf of their brethren throughout the State,
would respectfully represent;

That although by the nature of the government we are taught,
that an equality, not of property or favor, but of rights, is the
firmest foundation of liberty, and that on which democracy is

founded—yet, by Art. II. Sec. 1. State Constitution, a distinction is made with regard to them of the most serious nature—which, while it acknowledges them as citizens, denies them the rights which all others possess attached to that honorable appellation.

They would submit it to your honorable body, whether it can be for the benefit of the community, that a part should be depressed and degraded; whether humanity and policy do not alike suggest the propriety of elevating the character of the humblest members of the State, by not debarring them from the most efficient instrument of their elevation, simply on account of complexional difference.

In view, therefore, of the injustice and levelling policy of this act, they would respectfully ask, that by an amendment, the enjoyment of equal political rights and privileges, may be extended to them as to foreigners. In time, they would respectfully pray for the abolition of that part of the State Constitution which imposes upon them unequally a property qualification for the use of the franchise.

Signed, &c.

The committee appointed on Wednesday morning to draw up certain instructions or recommendations to the people on petitioning, in behalf of the convention, submitted through the chairman, Alexander Crummell, the following:

The committee on the resolution which has reference to petitioning, would beg leave most respectfully to

REPORT

Prayer is one of the earliest and most spontaneous of all human exercises. Man is a creature of wants, which are ever presented in continuous succession. From his imperfect and dependent nature, petitionary addresses are ever attendant upon him, from the dawn of existence to the last slow lingering descent and appearance of life.

In this feature of human character, man meets with sympathy and instruction in entire universal being. In proportion to the extent of want, and the intenseness of desire, so is the depth and fervor of the petition, the earnestness of its tone, and the frequency of its presentation.

The colored people of this State are, from the non-possession of the right of suffrage, the proscribed class. This proscription is the fountain Marah, from whence proceed those bitter waters that run through all the various ramifications of society, connecting themselves with all our relations, tainting and embittering the fresh streams of existence in their pure and healthy flow. The consciousness of want in this matter is deep, strong, and universal—and so should the expression of it be.

The mode of giving an adequate and natural development of the sense of wrong and want, is for the aggrieved class, in a community where rights have been wrested from them, to appeal to the better principles, the fundamental sentiments of our common humanity, and make a continual and earnest entreaty for their restoration.

In making such appeals and entreaties, we have much to expect. Oppression, prejudice, and injustice, although they have made sad and dire work with man's better nature; although they have withered many of the best affections and noble sentiments of the human heart, and impaired much of the clearness of man's mental vision and the moral beauty of his spiritual nature; yet reason is not wholly destroyed: the image of God is not yet entirely effaced from the nature of man. There are yet remaining to him, high sentiments and gentle sympathies, and deep laid principles, which create a fellow feeling between man and man—which constitute a bond connecting and binding together the heart of universal humanity The principle of rectitude is as universal among men as the light of the sun. Conscience, well described as

> "God's most intimate presence in the soul,
> And his most perfect image in the world,"

still remains, exerting her power over the thoughts, and words, and actions of men.

To these sentiments we can yet appeal. From our own human consciousness can we make our most earnest and effectual entreaties to our fellowmen in power. Such an appeal cannot but be heard. It will receive deference from its very nature. It will bring forth sympathy by reason of the source from whence it proceeds. It will meet with favor, from being in accordance with the spirit of the age. It will command respect, from its consonance with universal justice. It will secure its success and triumph, from the light of reason, the principles of Christianity, and the dictates of living and eternal right. The committee would therefore recommend the following resolutions:

Resolved, That it is a solemn duty of the free colored people, in city, town, village, and hamlet, continually and earnestly TO PETITION the Legislature for an equal and impartial exercise of the elective franchise, until they effect a consummation of their desires.

Resolved, That the petition which has been used in various places in the State, and copies of which we have at hand, be recommended to our people for the purpose of petitioning.

Respectfully submitted,
ALEX. CRUMMELL, Ch'n.

James W. Duffin,   *Committee*
Rev. J. N. Mars.

The business committee reported the following resolution:
On motion,
Resolved, That the report of the Committee be accepted and adopted.

On motion,
Resolved, That we recommend to our people to become possessors of the soil within the limits of this State, if possible, as a means to their becoming more permanent residents, happier in their circumstances, and elevated in their condition.

Resolved, That in recommending our people to possess themselves of the soil, we no less protest against that clause in the Constitution of the State, which requires a property qualification of us, in order to exercise the elective franchise—considering it wrong in principle, sapping the foundation of self government, and contrary to all notions of natural justice.

Resolved, That each delegate be assessed in the sum of 25 cents, to defray in part the expense of publishing the proceedings of this convention, and that a committee of three be appointed to attend to this business forthwith.

Henry R. Crummell, U. Boston, and J. W. Loguen, were appointed the committee, who occupied the rest of the session in performing the duty assigned, bringing in a report before adjournment of $27.47 cts. collected.

The convention adjourned at a quarter past 5 o'clock.

Thursday Morning, Aug. 20. The business committee reported the following resolutions:

Resolved, That the idea contained in the Declaration of Independence, that men should inherit rights aside from accidental circumstances or factitious arrangements, it is a sentiment set forth, not merely in that document, but one that is also consonant universally with reason and revelation.

Resolved, That the framers of the State Constitution, in practically embodying the principles contained in the above resolution, formed the government of the State fundamentally republican.

Resolved, That one of the distinctive and peculiar features of republicanism, is, that rights are to be guaranteed and extended, without arbitrary or unnatural distinctions.

Resolved, That whenever, in the administration of such a government, a portion of its citizens are deprived (from any such invidious), of an equal participation of the privileges and prerogatives of citizenship, the principles of republicanism are manifestly violated.

Resolved, That to the non-possession of the elective franchise may be traced most of the degradation to which we, as a people, have been for years subjected, and is the fruitful source of unnumbered and unmitigated civil, literary, and religious wrongs.

Resolved, That in proportion as we are treated with disrespect, contumely, and neglect, in our political, literary, and ecclesiastical relations, from the want of the elective franchise

—so would we command respect and influence in these different relations by the possession of it.

Resolved, That there is great hope for the politically oppressed in their own exertions, relying upon the favor of heaven, and appealing to the just sentiments of those in political power.

Resolved, That the way to obtain rights that have been wrested from a depressed people, is, by the continual presentation of the first principles of political freedom, truth, and justice, accompanied by corresponding efforts on the part of the proscribed.

The following report was handed in by Patrick H. Reason, chairman of the committee:

REPORT

The committee of eight, one from each senatorial district, appointed to suggest a plan by which we can effectually and harmoniously proceed in our future efforts for the right of suffrage, respectfully report the following resolutions:

1. Resolved, That a committee of seven be appointed, consisting of four members from Albany and three from Troy, whose duty it shall be to procure signatures to petitions, and to correspond with other committees throughout the State, appointed for the same purpose.

2. Resolved, That a committee of five from each county in the State, except New York, where there shall be a committee of ten, be appointed in accordance with the last clause of the above resolution—said committees to be termed "county committees."

3. Resolved, That it shall be the duty of the county committees to forward their petitions, when prepared, to the central committee, postage paid, and at as early a date as possible; and the chairman of the central committee to present the same in person to some member or committee of the legislature.

The committee would recommend the house to go immediately into a committee of the whole, to appoint the several county committees.

Respectfully submitted,

Patrick H. Reason,
Uriah Boston,
William H. Topp,
Elimus P. Rodgers,   *Committee*
Abner H. Francis,
Ambrose Dunbar,
James Sharp,
James W. Duffin.

On motion,

Resolved, That the report of the committee be accepted.

Resolved, That the first resolution of the committee be adopted.

Resolved, That the central committee of seven consist of the following members: H. H. Garnet, Troy; chairman C. S. Morton, M. Dougee, John P. Anthony, S. Myers, Albany; G. H. Baltimore, and Daniel Jones, of Troy.

Resolved, That we go immediately into a committee of the whole, to appoint county committees.

The convention went into committee of the whole, R. P. G. Wright in the chair.

On motion,

Resolved, That the third resolution of the committee be adopted.

Resolved, That the committee be discharged with thanks.

Mr. Henry H. Garnet, as chairman of the committee on the address to the colored people, submitted. On motion,

Resolved, That the report of the committee on the address be adopted.

Mr. Alexander Crummell, from the committee on the address, reported an address.

On motion of Charles L. Reason,

Resolved, That the report of the committee on the address to the people of the State, be accepted and adopted; the committee continued, and empowered to embody facts and statistics, as furnished by the appropriate committee; and that it be published with the signatures of the President and secretaries, after having received the careful revision and sanction of this same committee in New York.

Adjourned at half past twelve o'clock.

Thursday Afternoon. The committee on expenditures reported as follows, and were discharged.

REPORT

The committee on expenditures beg leave to report:

For lights for public meetings,	$1.50
Sexton's services, 3 days at $1,	3.00
Quills and paper,	00.37½
Total,	$4.87½

Moved, That William H. Topp pay the above bills.

The business committee reported the following resolutions: On motion,

Resolved, That while we deem it our imperious duty to co-operate with our friends in all lawful measures for the promotion of every great work, and especially for the cause of human rights, we maintain it to be important, also, in view of our peculiar circumstances, and of the importance to our cause of embodying the unbiassed sentiments of our people, that we assemble together, as occasion may require, in public conventions.

On motion,

Resolved, That a National Convention of our people is a movement of great magnitude, inasmuch as it imports to embody the representatives of 500,000 of the people scattered throughout our extended country; a movement, therefore, to be entered upon, not hastily, but only after mature, extensive, and harmonious deliberation by the whole people; therefore, we disapprove of the national moral reform convention, to be held by call in New Haven, on the 10th September, because [it is] entered upon too hastily—too limited and indefinite in its objects—and located by no means to accommodate the majority of our spreading people.

On motion,

Resolved, That this convention exceedingly deprecate any system of general emigration offered to our people, as calculated to throw us into a state of restlessness, to break up all those settled habits which would otherwise attach us to the soil, and to furnish our enemies with arguments to urge our removal from the land of our birth.

The above resolution gave rise to somewhat of a debate, owing to the opposition of Messrs. Charles L. Reason and Alexander Crummell, who contended that it was introduced in opposition to the object of the convention, as set forth in its call.—They were overruled, however, and the resolution adopted. On motion,

Resolved, That the signal success which has attended the noble cause of human rights in Europe and in our own country, is encouraging to our hearts, and is cause of devout gratitude to the God of the oppressed.

This resolution also met with opposition by the same gentlemen for a like reason, but was finally adopted. On motion,

Resolved, That this country is our country; its liberties and privileges were purchased by the exertions and blood of our fathers, as much as by the exertions and blood of other men; the language of the people is our language; their education our education; the free institutions they love, we love; the soil to which they are wedded, we are wedded; their hopes are our hopes; their God is our God; we were born among them; our lot is to live among them, and be of them; where they die, we will die; and where they are buried, there will we be buried also.

On motion,

Resolved, That a publishing committee of four, of the city of New York, be appointed to publish the proceedings of this convention in the most convenient manner, and at the earliest possible day.

Mr. Wm. H. Topp, from the committee on expenditures, reported a balance of $27.00, expenses deducted, now in his hands, which was, by motion, placed in the hands of Mr. Charles B. Ray, as chairman of the publishing committee.

Mr. Alexander Crummell having made some becoming remarks on the unanimity of feeling that had pervaded the meetings, which he in a great measure attributed to the calm judgment and dignity of the presiding officer—moved, that the thanks of the convention be presented to our worthy President, Mr. Austin Stewart, for the patient and dignified manner in which he has presided over the deliberations of this convention, and that the members rise as they respond to the motion.

The motion was affirmed unanimously, the whole house standing.

The President made a reply, the members again rising, in which he said that he was really thankful that it was his happiness to take part in the doings of a body which had assembled for so great an object; he was pleased to see the earnest and willing spirit that had brought each individual brother here, kept up in so friendly a manner; he reciprocated the patient manner in which they had yielded to his frequent opposing decisions, and hoped and trusted that the work which they had accomplished, would tell for much good on our whole people.

On motion of Uriah Boston, it was

Resolved, That the thanks of the convention be tendered to the secretaries, for the willing manner in which they have performed their duties.

The Vice President, Rev. John T. Raymond, here presented to the President, and through him to the delegates generally, sentiments expressive of the cordial feeling of the people of Albany toward them, in whose behalf he spoke, and expressed their entire approval of the measures and spirit adopted by the convention, and their thanks in anticipation of the probably good influence that would follow from the views that from day to day had been thrown out in the meetings.

A short reply was again made by the President.

A hymn was sung, and the closing prayer made by the Rev. Theodore S. Wright. Adjourned.[1]

[1] From *The Colored American,* January 2, 1841.

APPENDIX II

OPPOSITION TO BLACK SEPARATISM:

THREE LETTERS BY WILLIAM WHIPPER

No. I

FRIEND RAY:—It is with a high sense of the goodness of Almighty God, in sparing and protecting us from many of the afflictions that have scourged the "human race," and swept from existence a portion of the distinguished advocates of human rights during the past year, that I take up my pen to return your congratulations on the advent of "the new year," with the prospect and success that must attend an ardent, zealous, and untiring advocacy of the principles of our common cause.

Through the kindness of a friend I have just received for perusal, a copy of the "Minutes of the Albany Convention of Colored Citizens." It is a rich and valuable pamphlet. As I am opposed to the *manner* of its organization, I cannot, therefore, subscribe to the proceedings, as a whole, but I find in many of the reports and resolutions, principles and sentiments that are eternal and immutable. Principles that must and will dethrone slavery, and obliterate prejudice. I hope that all our friends and enemies throughout the land will endeavor to procure a copy of the proceedings of the convention, as they ought to be read by every family, and be placed in every library.

And now, my dear sir, I congratulate you as chairman of the business committee, and also every individual member of that body—the cause of liberty, justice, and equality, on the righteous, noble, and invulnerable stand you have taken in the report and resolutions you have taken on the 11th page. The first resolution will be admired by the friends of liberty and equality in all future generations, viz.:

Resolved, That ALL LAWS established for human government, and ALL SYSTEMS, of *whatever* KIND, founded in the

SPIRIT OF COMPLEXIONAL CAST, are in *violation of the fundamental principles of* DIVINE LAW, *evil in their tendencies,* and should, therefore, be EFFECTUALLY DESTROYED.

Now, my dear sir, I believe the doctrines contained in the above resolution, have emanated from the pure fountain of heaven-born truth, and that all those that quench their thirst by partaking of that living stream will be governed by the principles it dictates. With the advocates of such principles, I delight to labor. The principles of this resolution are not only applicable to the "Church and government under which we live," but they reach to every organization for human improvement throughout the various ramifications of society. It seeks the entire destruction of all those invidious complexional distinctions, whether in institutions or "systems" that exclude by constitutional landmarks, any member of the human family from the common rights and privileges of membership, on account of complexional variations. I regard the resolution, as a two-edged sword, that will divide asunder those distinctive features in the various "systems" and constitutions throughout our country, that have been fostered by a spirit of hatred and selfishness, no matter by whom, or what complexion they were formed. The fiat of the convention has gone forth, and proclaimed their condemnation as being contrary to the spirit of the "Divine law, and the political principles of the framers of our republican government."

I hope your active and combined exertions may not only prove instrumental in giving New York a free constitution, but that the same genial influence may effect the much desired reformation in both our federal and state governments. But we should not stop here, civil tyranny is not more odious than religious despotism. Look at the incorporated feature of complexional distinction in our churches, schools, beneficial, and literary societies. Are these to be extended, tolerated, and supported in their present shape? Can we hope to be successful in reforming others before we procure a reformation among ourselves? Experience answers, no! while the resolution asserts that such institutions *ought to be destroyed.* The resolution saps the very foundation principle on which nearly all the institutions in our country are based. It is not confined to written constitutions, but utters forth its condemnation on "all systems," hence all those churches whose written constitutions are not defaced by the insertion of the terms, "white, colored or African," but whose practice, by the influence of a detestable prejudice, is such as to exclude persons of a certain complexion from a participation in the rights, privileges, and enjoyments of the same, are alike guilty of an infringement of the "divine law." Nor is this all, the very paper you edit bears upon its title the very distinctive feature, which is the object of the resolution to obliterate? I do, therefore, humbly hope that the principles of the resolution will fall on its distinctive title and grind it to powder. The convention, in passing this resolution, not only aided in bringing odium on the title of your paper, but it occupied a still higher ground, they ushered forth a withering condemnation on the form of their own organization. For it is an indisputable fact, that the convention was formed by a system of representation, based on complexional cast, and, therefore, in the language of the resolution, "was in violation of the principles of divine law, evil in its tendency and should therefore have been effectually destroyed." I trust that all future conventions may guard against the errors of the past, and be governed by the spirit of this resolution, so that a consistency in principle, as well as unity of action, may be the legitimate means by which we shall be enabled to carry our cause onward to its final consummation.

I remain yours in the cause of liberty and equality.[1]

WM. WHIPPER
Philadelphia, January 3, 1841

No. II

DEAR SIR:—I regard the action of the "Albany Convention" as calculated to produce a new era in our cause. It matters but little whether we contemplate the object which called the delegates together, or the distinctive feature of their organization,

[1] From *The Colored American,* January 30, 1841, Vol. I, No. 48.

the effect of their proceedings must produce important results. I am therefore constrained by a sense of duty to solicit for them the consideration their importance demands. In the execution of this task I crave your indulgence.

In my letter of the 3d inst., I endeavored to notice the operation of the general principles involved in the first resolution, as well as its practical bearing on the whole people in their various forms of government.

I must now proceed to the 2d resolution which is marked by a boundary line, but is equally strong in principle over the space it is intended to operate. It reads as follows:

"Resolved, That the toleration of complexional difference in the State of New York is a stain upon its constitution, and attaches it to the great system of oppression in the land, so vital to our national character, since it is upheld, not only in direct opposition to the common rights of humanity, but also runs counter to those very political principles asserted by the framers of our republican government." Now, sir, it is to be expected, that state action by the colored people of New York as a means of attaining their rights as Americans, will be followed by a state action, among the same class in other states. I do therefore appeal to them in behalf of their down-trodden situation—their love of republican principles—of civil and religious liberty to strictly examine the principles on which the "Albany Convention" was based, in order that they may discover whether its *model* claims their admiration, as the most righteous and successful method for the government of their future operations. Now I aver that the above resolution is either true or false. If it be true that the "toleration of complexional distinction in the state of New York, is a stain upon its constitution, and attaches it to the great system of oppression in the land, and in direct opposition to the rights of humanity," it is equally true of every other state constitution where that distinction exists, as well as the constitution of the United States. But the principle of the resolution does not stop here. It protests against the "toleration of complexional distinction in the State of New York." I cannot but regard this protest as an implicit appeal to the Legislature of New York to repeal all the "complexionally" distinctive charters within the state, in order that such institutions and associations may not only be regarded as odious, but unlawful. If this be the true meaning of the resolution, it meets my cordial approbation. It is peculiarly appropriate for any people that have long been trodden under foot by the "iron heel" of any peculiar despotism that when they appeal to the rectitude of just principles in behalf of their deliverance, that they should first exhibit to the world, that they were not only prepared to act upon those principles themselves, but that they had hurled that principle of despotism from their own borders. It speaks well for the purity of principle that must have existed in the convention to have passed such a resolution, yet it appears passing strange that such a body convened under a complexionally distinct call should so far transgress the principle of their own organization as virtually to declare it in direct opposition to the "rights of humanity." Now, sir, I respectfully ask if the amended constitution of the State of New York is "in opposition to the rights of humanity" on account of complexional difference, are not the "Colored Churches," schools, benevolent and beneficial societies, formed and sustained in equal violation of the great fundamental principles of human rights? What evidence will the colored people as a body be able to exhibit to the legislators, of your great commonwealth, that you are in principle opposed to that obnoxious feature in your State Constitution, while you use no endeavors to abolish it from those institutions within your control? They will very naturally conclude that interest alone animates you in your arduous labors to obtain a full and complete enfranchisement. I do not however anticipate that any thing that I have written will have a tendency to change the position of our brethren in your state, but I hope they may pursue such a course of action, as will render them consistent in the eyes of those on whom they wish to operate, by commencing a warfare against the complexionally distinctive feature in every institution whether formed by white or colored people.

The spirit of the resolution truly contemplates such a method of action.

What I have said respecting the Albany Convention and what I regard as their very inconsistent course as equally applicable to our people in this state. We too protested against the insertion of the term "white" in our State Constitution while we were nurturing and sustaining in our midst near one hundred institutions with "colored and African" charters, and the result was as might have been expected, I might *almost* say as we deserved.

There is no people on earth justly entitled to the commiseration of mankind on account of their peculiar situation until they are equally ready and willing to render the same justice to others.

As a people we are deeply afflicted with "colorophobia" (and notwithstanding there may have been causes sufficient to implant it into our minds), it is arrayed against the spirit of Christianity, republican freedom, and our common happiness, and ought once now and forever to be abolished. It is an evil that must be met, and we *must meet it now.* The holy cause of human freedom, the success and happiness of future generations depend upon it. We must throw off the distinctive features in the charters of our churches, and other institutions. We have refused to hear ministers preach from the pulpit, because they would not preach against slavery. We must pursue the same course respecting prejudice against complexion. I verily believe that no man ought to be employed as a pastor of any Christian Church, that would consent to preach to a congregation where the "negro pew" exists; and I also believe it to be a violation of Christian principles for any man to accept the pastoral charge of a Church under a charter based on complexional distinction. You now see my friend, that I am willing to accept the resolution in its catholic spirit. I trust that it will not be asking too much of you, and those that voted for it, to aid in promoting its faithful application to all existing institutions within your control.

I remain yours in the cause of liberty and equality.[2]

WM. WHIPPER
Columbia, January 12, 1841

[2] From *The Colored American,* February 6, 1841, Vol. I, No. 49.

No. III

FRIEND RAY—SIR:—Your papers of the 9th and 16th insts., have not come to hand, and I have no means of ascertaining whether my letters of the 3d and 12th insts., have reached you. I will, therefore, continue my remarks on the report of the committee. My former communications referred to the first two resolutions in the report, and those that follow are but general *definitions* of those great first principles on which the report is based. I cannot but regard them as dignified in tone—pure in principle —and patriotic in sentiment, and (with the exception of a single word in the 7th resolution), worthy to have emanated from the purest and most intellectual body of men, ever associated to promote the holy cause of human freedom.

My object in writing to you is not to oppose the doings, objects, or principles incorporated in the proceedings of the convention. My desire is to receive light on another subject that I conceive has an important bearing on our common cause, and should regulate and govern our future action. I therefore hope you will hear me for the cause I advocate. It is this. I wish to know, through the medium of the Colored American, from the friends of complexionally distinctive organizations, why those noble resolutions, that are based on the eternal principles of right and justice to "all men," could not have emanated, with equal force, power, and consistency, from a body of men, associated under a *call* made in strict conformity with the spirit of the resolutions? 2ndly, I respectfully ask any member of the Albany Convention to point out the resolution in the minutes of the same, where the white man's voice, or vote of equal talent, would not have been equivalent to his own? 3dly. If talents, zeal, wisdom, a love for the cause of equal liberty and justice, were necessary materials for carrying out the spirit, object, and principles of the convention, was it either wisdom, justice, or good policy, to exclude any man on account of his complexion? Or rather, was it not bad policy not to have embraced all friendly to a universal extension of the elective franchise, and the friends of holy and impartial freedom in the State of New York, in the *call* for such a *convention?*

These are a few of the interrogatories, that I hope may be satisfactorily answered, through the medium of your paper for the especial benefit of our brethren in other states. I admonish you in time, not to base your reply on the tyrant's plea— "*necessity.*" We have already suffered too much from "*necessity.*" We have been enslaved by "*necessity*"—we are disfranchised by "*necessity*"—we are excluded from the places for divine worship—from schools—from honorable, useful, and profitable employment—from the halls of literature and science—and from the pursuit of knowledge, by a "*fatal necessity.*" We are excluded from the common privileges of human beings, in steamboats, railroads, and hotels, by this same "*necessity.*" In short we are a ruined people, and our whole situation is owing to this degrading—this tyrannical "plea of *necessity.*" Nor would I have you vindicate your position by any appeal to the VIRTUE *of our complexion.* In this we shall be equally wanting. The white man will be equally able to establish the dignity of his Anglo-Saxon blood, and the *virtue* of his complexion. The effect of such an argument would be to establish, on the ground of principle, the present separate existence of the two distinct complexions. It will prove equally unavailing to place the argument on the ground that it is expedient for the time being, because we are pleading for an equal enrolment in the order of humanity, and it would be inconsistent in us to stand opposed to the most limited exertions, to achieve its practical accomplishment. If the position the convention occupied can be defended at all, I hope it will be on the ground of principle, so that we may all be able to see the intrinsic beauty of the principle, and thus be led to adopt it as our future guide. It may be thought by some, that I am uncharitable, in placing you on the ground of defence respecting the *call of the convention.* But I trust that you will not regard the task of great magnitude, since you so freely embrace those principles. It ought to be a settled maxim, that those who mark out leading principles for the advancement of any people, that they should at all times be ready to defend them. I have another, and a very important reason for requesting you to assume the position. It is this. It being already known to you, that among those of our people who are willing to labor for moral, social, intellectual, and civil advancement, a difference of opinion on this subject exists that prevents them from laboring in the same department together. The A.M.R. Society, which sprang from the "Convention of free people of color," adopted principles, the exact antipode of those of the call of the convention in Albany, and yet it would have been in strict accordance with the Society's principles, to have adopted every resolution passed by that body. Now sir, we see plainly that there is no difference of opinion with respect to the principles that ought to be maintained, it is only as to the *method of organization*. Your paper, while it has been styled the "only legitimate organ of the colored people," has opposed the course pursued by the Society, both by its former editor, as well as under your own administration.

Now I maintain, that "whatever is morally right for a white man to do," is "morally right for a colored man to do," and vice versa. If this position be correct (and I presume you will not gainsay it), then, if it were right for white men to form the A.S.S. on the broad platform principle, it naturally follows, that it was right for colored men to form the A.M.R.S. on the same basis, and maintain it by the same principles. It appears to me, then, that if the basis of these two societies, agreeable to your own arguments, be correct, the position occupied by the Albany Convention must be wrong. As you have advocated the correctness of them both, I leave you standing on the horns of the dilemma to explain.

I remain yours, in the cause of liberty and equality.[3]

WM. WHIPPER
Columbia, January 17, 1841

[3] From *The Colored American*, February 20, 1841, Vol. I, No. 51.

INDEX